British History and He on the Web

A Directory

STUART A. RAYMOND

Published by
The Federation of Family History Societies (Publications) Ltd.
Units 15-16, Chesham Industrial Estate
Oram Street, Bury
Lancashire, BL9 6EN, U.K.

in association with:
S.A. & M.J. Raymond
P.O. Box 35
Exeter
EX1 3YZ
Phone: 01392 252193
Email: samjraymond@btopenworld.com
Http: www.samjraymond.btinternet.co.uk/igb.htm

ISBNs:
Federation of Family History Societies: 1 86006 184 2
S.A. & M.J. Raymond: 1 899668 39 X

First published 2004

Printed and Bound by the Alden Group, Osney Mead, Oxford OX2 0EF

Contents

Introduction

Interest in the study of British history and heritage has grown enormously in recent decades. Academics and amateur enthusiasts, archaeological researchers and metal detectorists, re-enactors and architectural historians, all share a passion for the past. The past decade has seen the rise of an entirely new medium through which this interest can be developed - the internet. And developed it has been - there are now many thousand sites available to the student of our past. The aim of this book is to identify some of the more useful sites, and to provide a properly classified listing of them so that they can be easily located. The sad fact is that finding sites on the internet is a very hit and miss activity. And although there are a number of 'gateways' (listed in chapter 1, and at the beginning of other chapters) none of them provide both adequate subject indexing and quality control. It has been my objective to provide both.

This listing is far from being comprehensive; it is based on my own researches on the web, and includes only what I consider important or useful sites. Some of these are intended for use in schools, and I have tried to note this where appropriate. There are a number of deliberate exclusions. Genealogical sites are already covered in the other volumes in the F.F.H.S. Web Directories series (listed on the back cover). With the exception of nationally important institutions, libraries and archives have been excluded (many have already been listed in my *Family history on the web*. 3rd. ed. F.F.H.S., 2004.)

It is planned to issue a separate volume to list sites likely to be of interest to tourists and visitors, and these have been excluded. Literature and the arts have not been covered here; they also deserve a separate volume.

The internet changes at speed, and it is likely that some of the URLs listed here will be out of date by the time you consult this book. In order to locate the sites in question, you should search the title of the site, or perhaps the last section of the URL, on a search engine such as:

- Google
  www.google.com

Alternatively, there is now a site which specialises in storing web pages which are no longer current; the page you are unable to find is likely to be at:

- Internet Archive Wayback Machine
  web.archive.org/web/web.php

This book has been typed by Cynthia Hanson, and seen through the press by Bob Boyd. My thanks go to them, and also to the officers of the Federation of Family History Societies and my family for their support.

Stuart A. Raymond

1. General Gateways, Bibliographies, *etc.*

A useful introduction to the web for historians is provided by:
* Internet for Historians / Francis Condron and Grazyna Cooper
  www.vts.rdn.ac.uk/tutorial/history

Gateways
There are many general gateways, some listing thousands of sites, but none really adequate to the task they seek to perform. Those covering particular topics are listed in the relevant chapter below. General sites include:
* Best of History Websites
  www.besthistorysites.net/
* The British Academy Portal
  www.britac.ac.uk/portal/index.html
* British History Links
  www.britannia.com/history/hlinks.html
* British History Online
  www.british-history.ac.uk
  Includes text of many publications, mostly listed here separately.
* History: American and British
  www.libraries.rutgers.edu/rul/rr__gateway/research__guides/history/
                                                        history.shtml
* History Guide
  www.historyguide.de
  Gateway; click on 'Great Britain and Ireland' under 'regions'.
* History On-Line
  www.history.ac.uk/search/
  International in scope, with many British sites listed. Includes the on-line version of *Theses completed* and *Theses in progress* from 1995.
* History.uk.com
  www.history.uk.com
  Encyclopaedic directory of resources.
* Humbul Humanities Hub: History
  www.humbul.ac.uk/history/
  Gateway, international in scope.

* Internet Resources for Historians
  www.humbul.ac.uk/vts/history
* Luminarium
  www.luminarium.org/lumina.htm
  Anthology of, and gateway to, English literature, medieval-17th c., but also of wider historical interest.
* Netserf: the Internet Connection for Medieval Resources
  www.netserf.org/
* WWWVL: The World Wide Web Virtual Library: History: Central Catalogue
  www.ukans.edu/history/VL/
  Gateway to world history with much of British relevance.
* Yahoo Directory: History: United Kingdom
  dir.yahoo.com/Arts/Humanitites/History/By__Region/Countries/
                                                    United__Kingdom/
* WWW-VL: History of the United Kingdom
  www.ukans.edu/history/VL/europe//uk.html
* World Wide Virtual Library: History: Medieval England
  www.ukans.edu/kansas/uk-med/index.html
* British History
  h.webring.com/hub?ring=britishhistory
  Webring.
* British and Irish Authors on the Web
  lang.nagoya-u.ac.jp/~matsuoka/UK-authors.html
* Internet Modern History Sourcebook
  www.fordham.edu/halsall/mod/modsbook.html
  Many original sources, some of them listed here separately.

Bibliographies
* Royal Historical Society Bibliography
  www.rhs.ac.uk/bibwel.asp
  The major listing of British historical publications.
* Historical Abstracts
  sb1.abc-clio.com:81/
  Subscription service
* What Every Medievalist Should Know / James Marchand
  www.the-orb.net/wemsk/wemskmenu.html
  Basic bibliography.
* Research Bibliographies on the Political and Social History of Western Europe, 800-1200 / Thomas Head
  urban.hunter.cuny.edu/~thead/biblios.htm
  Includes some British material.

- Early Modern Britain: a bibliography / Sears McGee Fall
  www.h-net.msu.edu/%7Ealbion/bibs/bib-tudor-stuart.html
  Written in 1994, but still useful.
- The Urban Past: an international urban history bibliography
  www.uoguelph.ca/history/urban/citybib.html
  International in scope, but with many British citations.
- BOPCRIS: unlocking key British government publications
  www.bopcris.ac.uk/bop1688/browse/browtop.html
  Abstracts of government publications 1688-1995, with some full texts.
- Unlocking Key British Government Information 1688-1995
  www.bopcris.ac.uk/
  Government publications online.
- Index to Theses: a comprehensive listing of theses with abstracts
  accepted for higher degrees by universities in Great Britain and Ireland
  www.theses.com
  Includes many on British history. Subscription service.
- Reviews in History
  www.history.ac.uk/reviews/index.html
  Reviews of recent historical works.
- Texts and calendars since 1982: a survey
  www.hmc.gov.uk/socs/list.htm
  Online update of MULLINS, E.L.C. *Texts and calendars: an analytical guide to serial publications*. Royal Historical Society, 1978. Supplement, 1983. This lists the innumerable editions and indexes of original sources published by record societies, and is indispensible for the serious historian.

Full Text Sites

A number of sites offer the full text of classic and other texts for downloading. These are listed here. Some of the specific works they offer are individually listed in appropriate chapters below. It should be noted that many of these works are available on several different sites, which have not necessarily all been identified here.

- Electronic Text Collections
  history.hanover.edu/etexts.html
  Gateway to free text sites.
- The Online Books Page
  digital.library.upenn.edu/books/
  Gateway to full text sites.
- Alex Catalogue of Electronic Texts
  www.informations.com/alex/
  Includes many full-text works by authors such as Burke, Bunyan, Hobbs, Locke, Mill, Paine, *etc.*
- Early English Books Online
  eebo.chadwyck.com/home
  Over 125,000 books published 1475-1700; subscription service.
- Bartleby.com: Great Books Online
  www.bartleby.com
  Full-text of many classics, some listed here separately.
- Electronic Texts and Documents
  tudorhistory.org/files/texts.html
  Mainly texts of original sources.
- The History of Economic Thought Website
  cepa.newschool.edu/het/
  Includes brief biographies, and some of the works, of most major economists, 16-20th c.
- McMaster University Archive for the History of Economic Thought
  socserv2.socsci.mcmaster.ca/~econ/ugcm/3ll3/
  Many classic texts, some of which are listed separately here.
- The Oxford Text Archive
  ota.ahds.ac.uk
  Full text of many historical works.
- Project Gutenburg
  www.promo.net/pg/history.html
  Includes numerous books on-line.
- Questia: the online library: British History
  www.questia.com/popular Searches/british_history.jsp
  Thousands of online books; a few listed below individually.
- Renascence Editions: an online repository of works published in English between the years 1477 and 1799.
  darkwing.uoregon.edu/~rbear/ren.htm
  Many full-text works, some listed here.
- Schoenberg Center for Electronic Text & Image
  dewey.library.upenn.edu/sceti/
- AHDS History
  ahds.ac.uk/history/index.htm
  Major collection of digitised historical resources.

2. Support for Historical and Heritage Projects

Financial aid and other support for historical and heritage projects and research is available from a wide range of organisations. The web pages of a few of these are listed here, as is a diary of events page.

- The Architectural Heritage Fund
  www.ahfund.org.uk/
- Awards For All
  www.awardsforall.org.uk/
  Offers small grants for heritage and other purposes.
- Commanet
  www.commanet.org/
  Charity promoting community archives of still and video images, text and oral narratives *etc.*
- Past Forward
  www.pastforward.co.uk/
  Organisation dedicated to creating heritage-based projects.
- Cultural Heritage Learning Network
  www.chnto.co.uk/general/welcome.html
  Training for employment in the heritage sector.
- Local Heritage Initiative
  www.lhi.org.uk
  Grant-making body; details of numerous projects.
- Conferences and Exhibitions
  www.history.ac.uk/conferences/index.html
  Forthcoming historical events.
- IHR Awards: Awards & Prizes
  www.history.ac.uk/awards/prizes.html
  For academic research.
- Army Museums Ogilby Trust
  www.armymuseums.co.uk
  Trust to encourage regimental museums.

3. Institutions, Libraries and Archives

British history and heritage is the concern of a wide range of institutions - libraries, record offices, museums, universities, societies, etc. The major national institutions have extensive web sites, and these will be listed here. Many universities have centres devoted to the study of specific topics; these too are listed here. The websites of local studies libraries and record offices have already been listed in the present author's *Family history on the web: a directory for England and Wales* and its companion volumes for Scotland and Ireland. A listing of museum web sites will be provided in a forthcoming volume (although a handful of the more important sites are listed below). For societies, see chapter 4; institutions for Ireland, Scotland and Wales are listed in chapters 22-4. I have not listed university departments of history (although archaeological departments are listed). There are too many, and in any case their interests are usually much wider than just British history.

This listing is not to be taken as definitive; it simply tries to identify some of the more important sites, and doubtless there are omissions.

Libraries
There are a number of gateways to libraries. These include:
- OPACS in Britain and Ireland: a directory of library catalogues and services in Britain and Ireland
  **www.hero.ac.uk/reference__resources/
  opacs__in__britain__and__ireland__3795.cfm**
  i.e. Online Public Access Catalogues

- BUBL UK: Libraries
  bubl.ac.uk
  Lists UK national, public, and university libraries, including university library catalogues on-line.
- COPAC
  www.copac.ac.uk
  Union catalogue of 26 major national and university libraries.
- Libdex
  www.libdex.com/
  Lists thousands of library catalogues world-wide.
- The UK Public Libraries Page
  dspace.dial.pipex.com/town/square/ac940/ukpublib.html

Record Offices

Most record offices also have a web presence; their pages typically include details of location, opening hours, services and collections. Some provide on-line catalogues of their resources, and sometimes extensive information relating to the subject they cover. There are a number of gateway and online listings:

- ARCHON
  www.nationalarchives.gov.uk/archon/
  Directory of record offices, and portal to archive web-sites.
- County Record Offices in England and Wales
  genealogy.8k.com/main3.html
  Postal addresses only; no links.
- English Record Offices and Archives on the Web
  www.oz.net/~markhow/englishros.htm
- Archivesinfo-UK Archival Repositories on the Internet
  www.archivesinfo.net/uksites.html

A number of union listings of archive holdings *etc.* are also available:

- National Register of Archives
  www.nra.nationalarchives.gov.uk/nra/
  Index to archives in many repositories.
- A2A: Access to Archives
  www.a2a.org.uk
  Index to some of the collections of 335 record offices throughout the UK.
- Archives Hub
  www.archiveshub.ac.uk
  Archives in UK universities and colleges.

- BARLEY, M.W., et al. *A guide to British topographical collections.* CBA occasional paper. 1974.
  ads.ahds.ac.uk/catalogue/library/cba/op6.cfm
- National Union Catalog of Manuscript Collections
  lcweb.loc.gov/coll/nucmc/
  Union catalog of manuscripts held in the U.S.A., including much British material.

Accessions to repositories are listed in:
- Accessions to Repositories
  www.nationalarchives.gov.uk/accessions/
  Annual survey

For London repositories, see:
- AIM25: Archives in London and the M25 area
  www.aim25.ac.uk/

British Library

- British Library
  www.bl.uk
  Houses what is arguably the largest collection of books on British history; also newspapers, manuscripts, *etc.* A few of its important pages are listed below, but there are many others.
- British Library Book Catalogue
  blpc.bl.uk
- British Library: Manuscripts Catalogue
  molcat.bl.uk
- British Library Newspaper Library
  www.bl.uk/catalogues/newspapers.html
- British Library Sound Archive: Oral History: National Life Story Collection
  www.bl.uk/collections/sound-archive/nlsc.html
- Collect Britain
  www.collectbritain.co.uk/collections/pip/
  Images from the British Library's collection.
- The British Library: Asia, Pacific & Africa Collections
  www.bl.uk/collections/orientalandindian.html
  Includes pages on the India Office Records.

National Archives

- National Archives
  www.nationalarchives.gov.uk
  The major British archive repository, holding the records of British national government. Access to catalogue of over 8,000,000 documents. Formerly known as the Public Record Office.
- An Overview of the Public Record Office Website
  www.genuki.org.uk/indexes/PROContents.html
  Unofficial guide from a family historian's perspective.
- National Archives Research Guides
  www.catalogue.nationalarchives.gov.uk/researchguidesindex.asp
  Invaluable guides to a wide variety of sources.
- Documents Online
  www.documentsonline.nationalarchives.gov.uk/
  Digitised records from the National Archives.

Miscellaneous Institutions

- English Heritage
  www.english-heritage.org.uk/
  Includes many pages on historic houses, archaeology, conservation, *etc.*
- National Monuments Record
  www.english-heritage.org.uk/
  Click on 'public archive'. Holdings include aerial photographs, data on archaeological sites, listed buildings, descriptions, *etc.*

Museum websites are listed at:
- Museums around the UK on the Web
  icom.museum/vlmp/uk.html

For a database of museum collections, see:
- Cornucopia: Discovering UK Collections
  www.cornucopia.org.uk/

University sites are gatewayed at:
- UK Universities & University Colleges
  www.webmaster.bham.ac.uk/ukuwww.html

Individual historians are listed at:
- Teachers of History in the United Kingdom
  www.history.ac.uk/ihr/Resources/Teachers/index.html

Specialist university centres and other institutions include:
- AHRB Centre for North-East England History
  www.dur.ac.uk/neehi.history/homepage.htm
  At the University of Durham.
- The AHRB Research Centre for Environmental History
  www.cehp.stir.ac.uk/
- The Bedford Centre for the History of Women
  www.rhul.ac.uk/Bedford-Centre/
  At Royal Holloway University of London.
- CELL: Centre for Editing Lives and Letters
  www.livesandletters.ac.uk
  At Queen Mary College and Birkbeck University of London.
- Centre for Contemporary British History
  icbh.ac.uk/welcome.html
- University of Leicester Centre for English Local History
  www.le.ac.uk/elh/
- Centre for Manx Studies
  dbweb.liv.ac.uk/manninagh/
  In the University of Liverpool.
- Centre for Metropolitan History
  www.history.ac.uk/cmh/cmh.main.html
  Includes list of projects, seminars, research in progress, *etc.*
- Centre for North West Regional Studies
  www.lancs.ac.uk/users/cnwrs/
- The Centre for Research into Freemasonry
  www.shef.ac.uk/hri/freemasons.htm
  At Sheffield University.
- Centre for the History of Medicine
  www2.warwick.ac.uk/fac/arts/history/chm/
  At the University of Warwick.
- Centre for the History of Science Technology and Medicine
  www.imperial.ac.uk/historyofscience/
  At Imperial College, London.
- CHSTM: Centre for the History of Science Technology and Medicine, & Wellcome Unit for the History of Medicine
  www.chstm.ac.uk/
  At the University of Manchester.

- Centre for the History of Women's Education
  www.wkac.ac.uk/education/hwe.htm
  At King Alfred's, Winchester
- The Centre for the History of the Book
  www.arts.ed.ac.uk/chb/index.html
  At Edinburgh University.
- Centre for the Study of the History of Medicine
  medweb.bham.ac.uk/histmed/
  At the University of Birmingham.
- Centre for Urban History, University of Leicester
  www.le.ac.uk/urbanhist/
- Centre of East Anglian Studies
  www.uea.ac.uk/his/ceas/
  At the University of East Anglia
- Churchill Archives Centre
  www.chu.cam.ac.uk/archives/home.shtml
  Houses Churchill's paper, plus over 570 collections of 20th c. personal
  papers.
- The Churchill Centre
  www.winstonchurchill.org/
  In Washington, D.C.
- Commonwealth War Graves Commission
  www.cwgc.org/
- East Midlands Oral History Archive
  www.le.ac.uk/emoha/
  Covering Leicestershire and Rutland.
- Folger Shakespeare Library
  www.folger.edu/Home__02b.html
  Independent research library in Washington D.C., with extensive
  British collections.
- Friends House Library
  www.quaker.org.uk
  For Quaker history.
- Hall-Carpenter Archives
  www.lse.ac.uk/library/archive/gutoho/hall__carpenter__archives.htm
  Gay archives post 1958.
- University of Essex Department of History. Historical Censuses and
  Social Surveys Research Group
  www.essex.ac.uk/history/hcssrg/index.htm

- History of Advertising Trust Archive
  www.hatads.org.uk/
- History of Dentistry Research Group
  www.rcpsglasg.ac.uk/hdrg/
  At the University of Glasgow.
- House of Lords Record Office
  www.parliament.uk
- Huguenot Library: University College, London
  www.ucl.ac.uk/Library/huguenot.htm
- Huntington Library, Art Collections, and Botanical Gardens
  www.huntington.org
  Independent research library in California with extensive collections of
  British history, including manuscripts.
- Imperial War Museum
  www.iwm.org.uk
- University of Leeds Institute for Medieval Studies
  www.leeds.ac.uk/cms/
  Incorporates the Centre for Medieval Studies, the *International
  medieval bibliography,* and the International Medieval Congress.
- Institute for Name Studies
  www.nottingham.ac.uk/english/research/CENS/about.html
- University of Exeter: Institute of Cornish Studies
  www.ex.ac.uk/ics/ics/
- Institute of Historic Building Conservation
  www.ihbc.org.uk/
- History: the Website / Institute of Historical Research
  www.history.ac.uk
  Includes a number of major web-pages listed separately here.
- Janus Home Page
  janus.lib.cam.ac.uk/
  Union catalogue of archives and manuscripts in Cambridge.
- Labour History Archive and Study Centre
  www.nmlhweb.org/archive.htm
  In Manchester.
- King's College, London: Liddell Hart Centre for Military Archives
  www.kcl.ac.uk/lhcma/top.htm
- Lambeth Palace Library
  www.lambethpalacelibrary.org

- Manchester Centre for Regional History
  www.mcrh.org.uk/
  At Manchester Metropolitan University.
- Mass Observation Archive
  www.sussex.ac.uk/library/massobs/index.html
  The archive holds reports of social surveys *etc.,* of the mid-20th century.
- Methodist Archives and Research Centre
  rylibweb.man.ac.uk/data1/dg/text/method.html
- Modern Records Centre
  modernrecords.warwick.ac.uk/
- National Army Museum
  www.nmm.ac.uk/
- The National Fairground Archive
  www.shef.ac.uk/nfa/
  Library collection at the University of Sheffield.
- The Newberry Library
  www.newberry.org/
  Independent research library in Chicago with extensive British collections.
- Oxford Radiocarbon Accelerator Unit
  www.rlaha.ox.ac.uk/orau/
- Quaker Archives Database
  www.leeds.ac.uk/library/spcoll/quaker/quakint1.htm
  Index to documents held by Leeds University Library, 17-20th c.
- The Regional History Centre at the University of the West of England
  humanities.uwe.ac.uk/regionhistory/
- Richard Rawlinson Center for Anglo-Saxon Studies & Manuscript Research
  www.wmich.edu/medieval/research/rawl/
- United Kingdom Centre for the History of Nursing
  www.qmuc.ac.uk/hn/history/
  Partnership of the Royal College of Nursing and the Queen Margaret University College, Edinburgh.
- UK National Inventory of War Memorials
  www.iwm.org.uk/collections/niwm/index.htm
- Wellcome Library: the Wellcome Library for the History and Understanding of Medicine
  library.wellcome.ac.uk/
- Dr. Williams Library
  www1.rhbnc.ac.uk/hellenic-institute/DrWilliam's.html
  Nonconformist collection.
- The Women's Library
  www.thewomenslibrary.ac.uk/
- WCML: the Working Class Movement Library
  www.wcml.org.uk/
  Based in Salford.
- The Yale Centre for Parliamentary History
  www.yale.edu/ycph/

4. Societies

There are numerous historical societies with web presences. Some of them have very wide historical interests, e.g. the Royal Historical Society; others are very specialist, e.g. the Milestone Society. The listing here is in four sections, i.e. historical societies, archaeological societies, re-enactment societies, and county / local societies. The numerous family history societies are not listed here, since they have already been listed in the present author's *Family history on the web: a directory for England and Wales,* and in its Irish and Scottish companion volumes. Record societies are also not listed.

A. Historical Societies

- Arms and Armour Society
  www.armsandarmour.net
- Association for Heritage Interpretation
  www.heritageinterpretation.org.uk/
- The Bibliographical Society
  www.bibsoc.org.uk/
  Includes table of contents of *The Library*.
- Book History Postgraduate Network
  www.bhpn.bham.ac.uk/
- Brewery History Society
  breweryhistory.com/
  Includes contents list of *Brewery history*.
- British Agricultural History Society
  www.bahs.org.uk/
  Includes contents listing of the *Agricultural history review*.
- British Association for Victorian Studies
  www.qub.ac.uk/en/socs/bavs/bavs.htm
- British Association of Numismatic Societies
  www.coinclubsfreeserve.co.uk/
- British Association of Paper Historians
  www.baph.freeserve.co.uk/

- The British Brick Society
  www.britishbricksoc.free-online.co.uk/index.htm
- British Numismatic Society
  www-cm.fitzmuseum.cam.ac.uk/coins/britnumsoc/
- British Records Association
  www.hmc.gov.uk/bra/
- British Society for the History of Pharmacy
  www.bshp.org/
- British Society for the History of Science
  www.bshs.org.uk
  Includes guide to history of science courses.
- Captain Cook Society
  www.captaincooksociety.com/
- Catholic Archive Society
  www.catholic-history.org.uk/catharch/
- Catholic History
  www.catholic-history.org.uk/
  Umbrella site for various national and local catholic history societies.
- The Chapels Society
  www.britarch.ac.uk/chapelsoc/
  Historic nonconformist architecture.
- The Church Monuments Society
  freespace.virgin.net/john.bromilow/CMS/index.html
- The Cromwell Association: Oliver Cromwell
  www.olivercromwell.org
- Ða Engliscan Gesiþas
  www.kami.demon.co.uk/gesithas/index.html
  Anglo-Saxon language and literature society.
- Early English Text Society
  www.eets.org.uk/
- The Ecclesiastical History Society
  www.ehsoc.org.uk/
- Churches: Site of the Ecclesiological Society
  www.ecclsoc.org/
  Many links to sites relating to ecclesiastical architecture.
- Economic History Society
  www.ehs.org.uk/
- The English Civil War Society
  www.english-civil-war-society.org/public__html/

- The English Civil War Society of America
  www.ecwsa.org/
- English Place Name Society
  www.nottingham.ac.uk/english/research/EPNS/index.html
- The Garden History Society
  www.gardenhistorysociety.org/
- Gunpowder Plot Society
  www.gunpowder-plot.org/
- The Harleian Society
  harleian.co.uk
  Publishers of heraldic visitation returns.
- The Haskins Society for Anglo-Saxon, Viking, Anglo-Norman and Angevin History
  www.haskins.cornell.edu/
- The Historical Association
  193.43.140.245/home.htm
- History of Education Society (U.K.)
  www.historyofeducation.org.uk/
- The International John Bunyan Society
  www.ualberta.ca/~dgay/Bunyan.htm
- The John Dee Society
  www.johndee.org
- The John Hampden Society
  www.johnhampden.org/
- Library and Information History Group
  www.cilip.org.uk/groups/lhg/welcome.html
  Includes part contents listing of *Library history.*
- Local Studies Group
  www.cilip.org.uk/groups/lsg/index.html
  Of the Chartered Institute of Library and Information Professionals.
- The Lollard Society
  home.att.net/~lollard/home.html
- Medieval Dress & Textile Society
  www.medats.org.uk/
- Midland Catholic History Society
  www.catholic-history.org.uk/midland/
  Covers Herefordshire, Oxfordshire, Shropshire, Staffordshire, Warwickshire and Worcestershire; includes indexes / contents listings of journals.
- Milestones Online
  www.milestonesonline.co.uk/
  Milestone Society.
- NAMHO: National Association of Mining History Organizations
  www.namho.org/
- National Piers Society
  www.piers.co.uk/
- The Newcomen Society: for the Study of the History of Science and Technology
  www.newcomen.com/
- North American Conference on British Studies
  www.nacbs.org/
- Oral History Society
  www.oralhistory.org.uk/
- Oxford Bibliographical Society
  www.oxbibsoc.org.uk/
- Palmerston Forts Society
  users.argonet.co.uk/education/dmoore/
- Pub History Society
  www.pubhistorysociety.co.uk
- The Railway & Canal Historical Society
  www.bodley.ox.ac.uk/external/rchs/
  Includes recent contents listing of the society's *journal.*
- The Research Society for Victorian Periodicals
  aztec.asu.edu/rsvp/
- The Richard III Society
  www.richardiii.net/
- Richard III Society: American Branch
  www.r3.org/
- The Richard Baxter Society
  members.tripod.com/~oboofcom/index-3.html
- Royal Historical Society
  www.rhs.ac.uk
- The Royal Numismatic Society
  www.users.dircon.co.uk/~rns/index.html
- Selden Society
  www.selden-society.qmw.ac.uk/
  Record society for legal history.
- Selden Society
  www.law.harvard.edu/programs/selden__society/main.html
  U.S. site.
- Society for Clay Pipe Research
  www.scpr.fsnet.co.uk/

- Society for the History of Astronomy
  www.shastro.org.uk/
- Society for the Social History of Medicine
  www.sshm.org/
- Society of Architectural Historians of Great Britain
  www.sahgb.org.uk/
- Society of Archivists
  www.archives.org.uk/
- Society of Genealogists
  www.sog.org.uk/
- The South West Maritime History Society
  www.swmaritime.org.uk/
- The Strict Baptist Historical Society
  www.strictbaptisthistory.org.uk/
- Time Team
  www.channel4.com/history/timeteam/
- The Tyndale Society
  www.tyndale.org/
  16th c. Bible translator.
- U.K.F.C.: United Kingdom Fortifications Club
  www.ukfortsclub.org.uk/
  Includes database of sites.
- Unlocking the Archives
  www.unlockingthearchives.rgs.org/
  Of the Royal Geographical Society.
- Save Britain's Heritage: campaigning for threatened historic buildings
  www.savebritainsheritage.org/main.htm
- The U.K. Association of Preservation Trusts
  www.heritage.co.uk/apt
  Includes links to the websites of many preservations trusts, not otherwise mentioned here.
- The Victorian Society
  www.victorian-society.org.uk/
  For the study and protection of Victorian architecture and art.
- The Waterways Trust
  www.thewaterwaystrust.com/
  Includes details of museums and archives of British Waterways.
- Wesley Historical Society
  www.wesleyhistoricalsociety.org.uk/

- The West of England & South Wales Women's History Network
  humanities.uwe.ac.uk/swhisnet/swhisnet.htm
  Based at the University of the West of England.
- Womens History Network
  www.womenshistorynetwork.org/index.htm

B. Archaeological Societies
A gateway to archaeological societies is provided by:
- CBA Guide to U.K. Archaeology Online
  www.britarch.ac.uk/info/socs.html

County and local archaeological societies are listed in section D below.
Sites of national organisations include:
- A.A.R.G.: Aerial Archaeology Research Group
  aarg.univie.ac.at/
- Ancient Metallurgy Research Group
  www.brad.ac.uk/acad/archsci/depart/resgrp/amrg/amrginfo.htm
  At the University of Bradford.
- Archaeological Ceramic Building Materials Group
  www.tegula.freeserve.co.uk/acbmg.html
- Association for Environmental Archaeology
  www.envarch.net/aea/aea.html
- Associaton for Industrial Archaeology
  www.industrial-archaeology.org.uk/
- Association for Roman Archaeology
  www.zyworld.com/zarriba/ara.htm
- Association for the History of Glass
  www.historyofglass.org.uk/
- ASPROM: Association for the Study and Preservation of Roman Mosaics
  www.asprom.org
- Association of Archaeological Illustrators and Surveyors
  www.aais.org.uk/
- Association of Local Government Archaeological Officers
  www.algao.org.uk/
- The British Archaeological Association
  www.britarch.ac.uk/baa/
- Ceramic Petrology Group
  www.ceramicpetrology.uklinux/index.html
- The Finds Research Group
  www.frg700-1700.org.uk/

14

- Historical Metallurgy Society
  hist-met.org/
- Institute of Field Archaeologists
  www.archaeologists.net/
  Professional body for archaeologists.
- The Lithic Studies Society
  www.britarch.ac.uk/lithics/index.html
- Medieval Pottery Research Group
  www.medievalpottery.org.uk
  Includes contents list of the group's journal, *Medieval ceramics.*
- Medieval Settlement Research Group
  www.britarch.ac.uk/msrg/index.html
- Midland Archaeological Research Society
  mars-fieldsurveys.co.uk/4517.html
  Society for identifying metalwork.
- Mining History Network
  www.exeter.ac.uk/~RBurt/MinHistNet/
  Includes bibliographies, discussion forum, list of mining historians, *etc.*
- The Nautical Archaeology Society
  www.nasportsmouth.org.uk/
- Neolithic Studies Group
  csweb.bournemouth.ac.uk/consci/text/nsghome.htm
- Northern Mine Research Society
  www.nmrs.co.uk/
- The Prehistoric Society
  www.ucl.ac.uk/prehistoric/
- Rescue: the British Archaeological Trust
  www.rescue-archaeology.freeserve.co.uk/
- Roman Finds Group
  www.romanfindsgroup.org.uk/
- Royal Archaeological Institute
  www.royalarchaeolinst.org/
- The Shotton Project: a Midlands Palaeolithic Network
  www.arch-ant.bham.ac.uk/shottonproject/
- Society for Church Archaeology
  www.britarch.ac.uk/socchurcharchaeol/
- The Society for Landscape Studies
  www.landscapestudies.com/
  Includes abstracts of the society's journal, *Landscape history.*

- The Society for Medieval Archaeology
  www.socmedarch.org/
- The Society for Post-Medieval Archaeology
  www.spma.org.uk/
- Society for the Promotion of Roman Studies
  www.sas.ac.uk/icls/Roman/
- S.P.A.B.: the Society for the Protection of Ancient Buildings
  www.spab.org.uk/
- Study Group for Roman Pottery
  www.sgrp.org/
- Young Archaeologists Club
  www.britarch.ac.uk/yac/

C. Re-Enactment Societies
- Angelcynn: Anglo-Saxon Living History 400-900 A.D.
  www.angelcynn.org.uk
- The Arthurian Society
  www.durolitum.co.uk/
  Re-enactment group.
- Brigantia: Celtic Re-enactment
  www.ironage.demon.co.uk/brigantia/
- Clann Tartan: Colonel Gaffrey's Regiment
  www.clanntartan.org/
- The Colchester Roman Society
  www.romanauxilia.com/crswebsite/INDEX.htm
  Re-enactment group.
- Conquest: Society of Anglo-Norman Living History
  www.conquest.pwp.blueyonder.co.uk/
- Dark Ages Society
  www.netcomuk.co.uk/~kpollock/das/
- The Fairfax Battalia
  www.fairfax.org.uk/
- The History Re-enactment Workshop
  www.historyreenactment.org.uk/
- London Riot Re-Enactment Society
  c8.com/anathematician/lrrs.htm
- Lord Thomas Burgh K.G.'s Retinue
  www.lord-burgh.com/
  Wars of the Roses re-enactment group.

- Plantagenet Medieval Archery & Combat Society
  www.the-plantagenets.freeserve.co.uk/
- The Red Wyvern Society
  www.red-wyverns.org.uk/
  Wars of the Roses re-enactment.
- Regia Anglorum: Anglo-Saxon, Viking, Norman and British Living
  History
  www.regia__org/
  Re-enactment society.
- Rosa Mundi Medieval Re-enactment Society
  www.dur.ac.uk/b.m.hodgson/rosamundi/
  15th c.
- Sceaftesige Garrison Web Site
  ourworld.compuserve.com/homepages/DaveTelford/
  Anglo-Saxon and Viking re-enactment society.
- The Sealed Knot: English Civil War Re-enactment
  www.sealedknot.org/index.asp
  Includes many articles on civil war history.
- The Siege Group
  www.siegegroup.co.uk
  Re-enactment group.
- Sir John Owen's Companye of Foote
  www.englishcivilwar.com/
  Re-enactment group.
- Wars of the Roses Federation
  war.of.the.roses.fed.freehosting.net/fedindex.htm
  Re-enactment groups.
- The White Company (1450-1485): living history during the Wars of the
  Roses
  white-co1450-1485.8k.com/

D. County and Local Historical and Archaeological Societies

Despite the title, a gateway to numerous local history societies is
provided by:
- English Genealogy Resources with Web Sites
  www.geocities.com/Heartland/Canyon/6387/england.html

In the following listing, where there is a links page for a county, the
societies listed on it have not necessarily all been separately listed here.

Bedfordshire
- Local History in Bedfordshire
  www.museums.bedfordshire.gov.uk/localgroups/
  Links page for local societies.
- Bedfordshire Archaeological Council
  www.museums.bedfordshire.gov.uk/localgroups/bac.html
  Includes list of contents of *Bedfordshire Archaeological Journal*.
- Ampthill & District Archaeological & Local History Society
  www.museums.bedfordshire.gov.uk/localgroups.ampthill2.html
- Bedford Archaeological and Local History Society
  www.bedfordshire.gov.uk/localgroups/bedford.html
- Manshead Archaeological Society of Dunstable
  www.museums.bedfordshire.gov.uk/localgroups/manshead.html

Berkshire
- Berkshire Archaeological Society
  www.berksarch.co.uk/
- Berkshire Local History Association
  www.blha.org.uk/
  Includes links to 'societies and associations' in Berkshire.
- Abingdon Area Archaeological and Historical Society
  www.aaahs.org.uk/

Buckinghamshire
- Buckinghamshire Archaeological Society
  www.buckscc.gov.uk/museum/services/bas.stm
- North Bucks Archaeological Society
  www.nbas.org.uk/
- Harslope & District Historical Society
  www.mkheritage.co.uk/hdhs/index.html
- Marlow Archaeological Society
  www.marlowarchaeology.org/

Cambridgeshire
- Cambridgeshire Local History Society
  www.cambridgeshirehistory.com/Societies/clhs/
  Includes index to the society's journals, 1950-1999.

- Cambridge Antiquarian Society
  www.arch.cam.ac.uk/cas/
- Cambridge Archaeology Field Group
  www.cambridge-archaeology.org.uk

Cheshire *see also* Lancashire
- Cheshire Local History Association
  www.cheshirehistory.org.uk/
- Cheshire Local History Association
  www.cheshirehistory.org.uk/
  Includes list of c.30 member societies, mostly not otherwise listed here.
- Chester Archaeological Society
  www.chesterarchaeolsoc.org.uk/
  Includes list of journal contents since 1887.
- Tameside Archaeology Society
  www.tas-archaeology.org.uk/
- Wirral and North Wales Field Archaeology
  www.field-archaeology.net/

Cornwall
- Cornwall Archaeological Society
  www.cornisharchaeology.org.uk/
  Includes list of journal contents.
- Trevithick Society
  www.zawn.freeserve.co.uk/
  Industrial archaeology in Cornwall.
- Caradon Archaeology Group
  freespace.virgin.net/m.peacock/
- St. Keverne Local History Society
  www.st-keverne.com/History/

Cumberland
- Cumberland & Westmorland Antiquarian & Archaeological Society
  www.cwaas.org.uk/
  Includes contents listing of the society's *transactions* since 1975.
- Cumbria Industrial History Society
  www.cumbria-industries.org.uk/cihs.htm

Derbyshire
- Derbyshire Archaeological Society
  www.nottingham.ac.uk/~aczsjm/das/
  www.ccc.nottingham.ac.uk/~aczsjm/das/
  Includes subject index to the society's *journal.*

- Peak District Mines Historical Society
  www.tidza.demon.co.uk/
  Includes 'A list of British mines in 1896'.
- Whitwell Local History Group
  www.wlhg.freeuk.com/

Devon
- Devon Archaeological Society
  www.ex.ac.uk/das/
- Devon History Society
  www.devonhistorysociety.org.uk/
  Includes directory of Devon local societies.
- The Lustleigh Society
  www.lustleighsociety.org/
- Old Plymouth Society
  www.oldplymouthsociety.org/
- Widecombe & District Local History Group
  www.widecombe-in-the-moor.com/history/projects.htm

Dorset
- Dorset Natural History and Archaeological Society
  home.clara.net/dorset/museum/page22.html
- East Dorset Antiquarian Society
  www.edas-archaeology.org.uk/
- Langton Matravers
  www.langtonia.org.uk/
  Site of Langton Matravers Local History and Preservation Society.

Durham
- Architectural and Archaeological Society of Durham and Northumberland
  www.communigate.co.uk/ne/aasdn/
- Durham County Local History Society
  www.durhamweb.org.uk/dclhs/
- Cleveland & Teesside Local History Society
  www.ctlhs.org.uk/
- Tow Law, Deerness & District History Society
  www.historysociety.org.uk/

Essex
- Essex History.net
  www.essexhistory.net/
  Hosts 6 society web pages.
- Essex Archaeological and Historical Congress
  www.essexhistory.net/EssexCongress.htm
  Includes list of member societies, with some web pages not otherwise mentioned here.
- Essex Society for Archaeology and History
  www.essex.ac.uk/history/esah/DEFAULT.HTM
- Essex Historic Buildings Group
  www.hadfelda.demon.co.uk/ehbghome.htm
- Clacton and District Local History Society
  www.clactonhistory.com/
- Maldon Archaeological and Historical Group
  www.mahgmaldon.fsnet.co.uk
- Newham History Society
  www.essexhistory.net/newhamhistory.htm
- Sutton Hoo Society
  www.suttonhoo.org/
- Wanstead Historical Society
  www.essexhistory.net/wansteadhistorical.htm
- Woodford Historial Society
  www.essexhistory.net/woodfordhistorical.htm

Gloucestershire & Bristol
- The Beehive: Clubs and Societies
  beehive.thisisgloucestershire.co.uk/
  default__asp?WCI=HomePage&C=29&SiteFirstLetter=A
  Gateway to Gloucestershire societies, including many concerned with history and archaeology.
- Bristol and Gloucestershire Archaeological Society
  home.freeuk.net/bgas/
- Gloucestershire Local History Committee
  home.freeuk.com/gloshistory/
  Links to many local history and archaeology societies.
- Industrial Archaeology in Gloucestershire
  home.freeuk.com/ray.wilson/gsia/
  Site of Gloucestershire Society for Industrial Archaeology; includes contents listing of its journal and newsletter.

- B.A.A.S.: Bristol and Avon Archaeological Society
  www.digitalbristol.org/members/baas/index.htm
- Bristol Past: Website of the Fishponds Local History Society
  www.fishponds.free.uk.com/
  Includes articles on Bristol history.
- Bristol Threatened History Society
  www.digitalbristol.org/members/bths/
- Cirencester Archaeological & Historical Society
  beehive.thisisgloucestershire.co.uk/default.asp?WCI=SiteHome&ID=8172
- Downend Local History Society
  myweb.tiscali.co.uk/jfathompsoon/dlhs/society.htm
- Forest of Dean Local History Society
  homepages.which.net/~keith.walker3/NEWLHSopening.htm
- Dean Archaeological Group
  www.deanarchaeology.org.uk/
- Gloucester and District Archaeological Research Group
  www.gadarg.org.uk
- Leckhampton Local History Society
  www.geocities.com/llhsgl53/
- Tewkesbury Historical Society
  www.ths.freeuk.com/
- Tewkesbury Battlefield Society
  www.tewkesbury.org.uk/battlefield/
  1471 battle

Hampshire
- Hampshire Field Club & Archaeological Society
  www.fieldclub.hants.org.uk/
  Includes recent contents list of *Hampshire studies*.
- Hampshire Industrial Archaeology Society
  www.hants.gov.uk/suiag/
- N.E.H.H.S.: North East Hampshire Historical & Archaeological Society
  www.hants.gov.uk/nehhas/
- N.W.S.A.D. History Society
  www.dutton.force9.co.uk/nwsadhs/
  Covers the Hampshire villages of North Waltham, Steventon, Ashe, and Dean.
- Bitterne Local History Society
  www.bitterne.net/

- Titchfield History Society
  www.communigate.co.uk/hants/ths/

Herefordshire
- Bromyard & District Local History Society
  www.bromyardhistory.org.uk/

Hertfordshire
- Herts Direct: Local Historical Societies
  www.hertsdirect.org/infoadvice/leisure/activities/hthist3y/
  ?view=Heritage
  Directory of societies.
- Abbots Langley Local History Society
  www.allhs.btinternet.co.uk
- Royston and District Local History Society
  www.royston.clara.net/localhistory/

Huntingdonshire
- Huntingdonshire Local History Society
  www.huntslocalhistory.org.uk/

Kent
- Council for Kentish Archaeology
  www.the-cka.fsnet.co.uk/
- Kent Archaeological Society
  www.kentarchaeology.org.uk/
  The society's journal, *Archaeologia Cantiana,* is to be published online. A few articles are already available, as are full contents listings.
- Cantiaci Time Team Forum Friends
  www.ttforumfriends.com/cantiaci.htm
- Beckenham Historical Association
  dspace.dial.pipex.com/town/plaza/aj93/
  Branch of the Historical Association.
- Bexley Archaeological Group
  www.bag.org.uk/
- Bromley Borough Local History Society
  mysite.freeserve.com/BBLHS1/

- Greenwich Industrial History Society
  gihs.gold.ac.uk/
  Includes abstracts of articles from the society's *newsletters.*
- Orpington and District Archaeological Society
  www.odas.org.uk/

Lancashire
- Lancashire Local History Federation
  myweb.tiscali.co.uk/localhistory/
  Includes links to websites of member societies.
- The Historic Society of Lancashire and Cheshire
  www.hslc.org.uk/
  Includes index to journal.
- The Lancashire and Cheshire Antiquarian Society
  www.cheshirehistory.org.uk/Members/LCAS.htm
- Northern Mill Engine Society
  www.nmes.org/
  At Bolton, Lancs.
- Brindle Historical Society
  www.brindlehistoricalsociety.org.uk/
- Chadderton Historical Society
  www.chadderton-hs.freeuk.com
- Chorley and District Historical and Archaeological Society
  www.boyd.harris.btinternet.co.uk/hist/
- Darwen Archaeology Society
  www.communigate.co.uk/lancs/darwenarchaeologysociety2/
- Lancaster Archaeological and Historical Society
  www.ednet.lancs.ac.uk/LAHS/
- Leyland Historical Society
  www.houghton59.fsnet.co.uk/Home%20Page.htm
- Manchester Bibliographical Society
  www.netcomuk.co.uk/~scragg/page4.html
- Mere Brow Local History Society
  www.merebrow.com/historysociety.html
- Merseyside Archaeological Society
  www.liv.ac.uk/sacos/events/mas.htm
- Prestwich Heritage Society
  www.prestwich-heritage.com/
- Warrington Archaeological & Historical Society
  www.warrington-past-present.cwc.net/wahs.htm

- Wigan Archaeological Society
  www.wiganarchsoc.co.uk/

Leicestershire
- Leicestershire Archaeological and Historical Society
  www.le.ac.uk/archaeology/lahs/lahs.html
  Includes index to the society's *transactions*.
- Leicestershire Industrial History Society
  www.rod.sladen.org.uk/LIHS.htm
- Vaughan Archaeological and Historical Society
  www.le.ac.uk/elh/vahs/
  Covers Leicestershire and Rutland.
- Market Harborough Historical Society
  www.btinternet.com/~graham.stretton/
- Swannington Heritage Trust
  www.swannington-heritage.co.uk

Lincolnshire
- The Society for Lincolnshire History and Archaeology
  www.lincolnshirepast.org.uk/
  Includes recent contents listing of *Lincolnshire past and present*.
- North East Lincolnshire Archaeology & Local History Society
  www.nelalhs.org.uk/

London & Middlesex
- City of London Archaeological Society
  www.colas.org.uk/
- G.L.I.A.S.: the Greater London Industrial Archaeology Society
  www.glias.org.uk/
  Includes database of sites.
- London and Middlesex Archaeological Society
  www.owlpost.plus.com/lamas/
- The London Topographical Society
  www.topsoc.org/
- Society of Antiquaries of London
  www.sal.org.uk
- S.C.O.L.A.: the Standing Conference on London Archaeology
  ds.dial.pipex.com/town/parade/np03/scola/
- Camden History Society
  www.camdennet.org.uk/groups/chs/

- The East London History Society
  www.eastlondonhistory.fsnet.co.uk/
  Covers Tower Hamlets, Hackney, and Newham. Includes index to the *East London record*, and the society's *newsletter*.
- Enfield Archaeological Society
  www.enfarchsoc.org/
- Fulham and Hammersmith Local History Society
  homepage.ntlworld.com/bathos/fhhs/index.htm
- Hayes & Harlington Local History Society
  hayes.middx.net/framehistory.htm
- H.A.D.A.S.: the Hendon and District Archaeological Society
  www.hadas.org.uk/
- Hornsey Historical Society
  www.hornseyhistorical.org.uk/
- The Island History Trust
  www.islandhistory.org.uk
  Isle of Dogs.
- Islington Archaeology & History Society
  www.libraries.islington.gov.uk/inform/published/1522/1612.html
- Ruislip, Northwood and Eastcote Local History Society
  www.melhs.flyer.co.uk/
- Willesdon Local History Society
  www.london-northwest.com/sites/wlhs/

Norfolk
- Federation of Norfolk Historical and Archaeological Societies
  www.poppyland.co.uk/federation/
  Includes directory of member societies.
- Norfolk Historic Buildings Group
  www.nhbg.fsnet.co.uk/
- Great Yarmouth & District Archaeological Society
  www.gydas.fsnet.co.uk/
  Includes index of articles in the *Yarmouth archaeologist*.
- Markyate Local History Society
  www.hoggie.demon.co.uk/markyate/

Northamptonshire
- Northamptonshire Association for Local History
  www.northants-history.org.uk/
  Includes a 'resource register' of studies of particular places.

- Northamptonshire Archaeological Society
  www.jwaller.co.uk/nas/
- Northamptonshire Industrial Archaeology Group
  www.niag.org.uk/
- Gretton Local History Society
  www.grettonvillage.org.uk/history/
- Ise Archaeological Research Society
  www.ise.archaeology.ukgateway.net/
- Rushden & District Local History Society
  freepages.virgin.net/bob.safford/rdhs/
- Upper Nene Archaeological Society
  members.aol.com/unarchsoc/unashome.htm

Northumberland
- North West Labour History Group
  www.wcml.org.uk/nwlhg/home.html
  Includes journal contents list since 2001, and a few articles.
- The Society of Antiquaries of Newcastle upon Tyne
  www.newcastle-antiquaries.org.uk/
- Rothbury & Coquetdale History Society
  www.rothbury.com/village/orgs/historysoc.htm

Nottinghamshire
- The Nottinghamshire Local History Association
  www.local-history.com/nlha/
  Includes directory of 'local history societies in Nottinghamshire' (most without a web presence); also contents listing of *the Nottinghamshire historian.*
- The Thoroton Society of Nottingham
  www.thorotonsociety.org.uk/
- Nottinghamshire Industrial Archaeology Society
  www.rod.sladen.org.uk/NIAS.htm
- Farndon Archaeological Research Institute
  www.fari.org/
- Keyworth & District Local History Society
  www.keyworth-history.org.uk/
- Lenton Times: the magazine of Lenton Local History Society
  www.lentontimes.co.uk/
  Includes articles.
- The Old Mansfield Society
  www.old-mansfield.org.uk/

- Warsop Vale Local History Society
  www.warsopvale.com/

Oxfordshire
- Oxfordshire County Council: Community Groups: History
  www.oxfordshire.gov.uk/index/living/commgroupsintro/
  community__groups.htm?subsid=781162405
  Directory of Oxfordshire local history societies.
- O.A.H.S.: Oxfordshire Architectural and Historical Society
  www.oahs.org.uk/
- Iffley Local History Society
  www.iffleyhistory.org.uk/
- Kidlington & District Historical Society
  www.communigate.co.uk/oxford/kidhist/

Rutland
- Rutland Local History & Record Society
  www.rutnet.co.uk/rlhrs/
  Includes contents list of *Rutland record.*

Shropshire
- Broseley Local History Society
  www.broseley.org.uk/
- Madeley Local Studies Group
  www.localhistory.madeley.org.uk/
- Wrekin Local Studies Forum
  uk.geocities.com/wlsfuk/
  Includes pages for participating societies.

Somerset
- Celebrating Somerset: Archaeology/Local History Societies
  www.somerset.gov.uk/celebratingsomerset/residents/pages/
  historysocieties.htm
  Directory.
- S.A.N.H.S.: Somerset Archaeological & Natural History Society
  www.sanhs.org/
  Includes directory of associated societies.
- The Severn Estuary Levels Research Committee
  www.selrc.dial.pipex.com/
- Bath & Camerton Archaeological Society
  www.quest-net.org/w__view.asp?websiteid=26
  www.al40k.supanet.com/

- Chard History Group
  www.users.globalnet.co.uk/%7Ecarterw/
- Clevedon Civic Society: Local History
  www.clevedon-civic-society.org.uk/history.htm
- Yeovil Archaeological & Local History Society
  www-users.york.ac.uk/~jfg101/yalhs.htm

Staffordshire
- Staffordshire History: Societies & Organizations
  www.staffshistory.org.uk/societies.htm
  Directory.
- Staffordshire Archaeological and Historical Society
  www.britishlibrary.net/sahs/
  Includes contents listing of *transactions*.
- Staffordshire Industrial Archaeology Society
  www.staffsia.org.uk/
  Includes list of journal contents.
- Betley Local History Society
  blhs.co.uk/
- Black Country Society
  www.blackcountrysociety.co.uk/default.asp
  Includes many articles.
- Smethwick Local History Society
  www.dumbleton-williams.fsnet.co.uk/
  www.smethwicklocalhistorysociety.co.uk/
- Potteries Pub Preservation Group
  www.pppg.supanet.com/
- Uttoxeter Archaeology Society
  www.uttoxeter-archaeology.org/
- Willenhall History Society
  www.shercliff.demon.co.uk/WHS/
- Wolverhampton Archaeology Group
  www.tlaloc.demon.co.uk/
- Wolverhampton History and Heritage Society
  www.localhistory.scit.wlv.ac.uk/home.htm
  Includes many articles.

Suffolk
- Suffolk Institute of History and Archaeology
  www.suffolkarch.org.uk/

- Suffolk Local History Council
  www.suffolklocalhistorycouncil.org.uk/
  Includes list of member organizations.
- The Foxearth and District Local History Society
  www.foxearth.org.uk/
- Kettlebaston Memorial Project
  www.kettlebaston.suffolk.gov.uk/
- Newmarket Local History Society
  www.wood-ditton.org.uk/newmarketlhs.htm

Surrey
- Surrey Archaeological Society
  www.surreyarchaeology.org.uk/
  Includes abstracts from recent issues of *Surrey archaeological collections*.
- Wealden Iron Research Group
  users.argonaut.co.uk/users/tonysing/WIRG/
- The Bourne Society
  www.bournesociety.org.uk/
- The Brookwood Cemetery Society
  www.tbcs.org.uk/
- Croydon Natural History and Scientific Society
  www.greig51.freeserve.co.uk/cnhss/
  Includes recent contents list of the society's *bulletin*, with full text of some articles.
- Dorking Local History Group
  www.merivale.u-net.com/
- Ewhurst History Society
  www.ewhurst.history.ukgateway.net/
- Felbridge & District History Group
  www.jeremy-clarke.freeserve.co.uk/
- Horley Local History Society
  www.horleyhistory.org.uk/
- Leatherhead & District Local History Society
  www.leatherheadlocalhistory.org.uk/
- Nonsuch Antiquarian Society
  www.nonsuchas.org.uk
- Richmond Archaeological Society
  www.richmondarchaeology.org.uk/

- Shere and Gomshall Local History Society
  www.gomshall.freeserve.co.uk/sglshhp.htm
- Woking History Society
  freespace.virgin.net/woking.history/

Sussex
- Sussex Archaeological Society
  www.sussexpast.co.uk/
  Includes a directory of local history societies, and abstracts from
  Sussex archaeological collections, etc.
- Sussex Industrial Archaeology Society
  www.snowing.co.uk/sias/
- Bolney Local History Society
  www.bolney history.co.uk/
- Brighton and Hove Archaeological Society
  www.brightonarch.org.uk/
- Chichester & District Archaeology Society
  www.cdas.info/
- H.A.A.R.G.: Hastings Area Archaeological Research Group
  www.1066.net/haarg/
- Worthing Archaeological Society
  www.worthingpast.co.uk/

Warwickshire
- Local History Societies Birmingham
  www.birminghamuk.com/localhistsocieties.htm
  Gateway to society web pages.
- Birmingham and Warwickshire Archaeological Society
  www.bwas.org.uk/
- Midlands History Forum
  www.mhforum.fsnet.co.uk/
  History teachers forum based in Birmingham.
- Local Past: Alcester & District Local History Society
  dialspace.dial.pipex.com/town/square/fk26/localpast/
  Includes articles from the society's journal.
- Birmingham & District Local History Association
  www.bdlha.org
  Includes index to the *Birmingham historian.*

Wiltshire
- Wiltshire Heritage
  www.wiltshireheritage.org.uk/
  Wiltshire Archaeological and Natural History Society website.
- South Wiltshire Industrial Archaeology Society
  www.southwilts.co.uk/site/south-wiltshire-industrial-archaeology-society/

Worcestershire
- South Worcestershire Archaeological Group
  swag.csamuel.org/
- Vale of Evesham Historical Society
  www.vehs.org.uk/

Yorkshire
- Yorkshire Archaeological Society
  www.laplata.co.uk/yas/
- Yorkshire Vernacular Buildings Study Group
  www.yvbsg.org.uk
- South Yorkshire Industrial History Society
  www.topforge.co.uk/SYIHS.htm
- Boston Spa and District Community Archaeology Group
  www.bsparh.org.uk/
- Bradford Historical and Antiquarian Society
  www.bradfordhistorical.fsnet.co.uk/
  Includes full-text of articles in the *Bradford antiquary.* In progress.
- Earby & District Local History Society
  www.earbylocalhistorysociety.co.uk/
- East Riding Archaeological Society
  www.hullcc.gov.uk/archaeology/eras.htm
- Fulford Battlefield Society
  www.fulfordbattlefieldsociety.org.uk/
- Halifax Antiquarian Society
  www.halifaxhistory.org.uk/
- Huddersfield & District Archaeological Society
  ichuddarch.co.uk/
- The Hunter Archaeological Society
  www.shef.ac.uk/~ap/hunter/
  Covers South Yorkshire and North Derbyshire.
- The Thoresby Society
  www.thoresby.org.uk/
  Leeds.

- Poppleton History Society
  freespace.virgin.et/susan.major/PHS/
- Saddleworth Historical Society
  www.saddleworth-historical-society.org.uk/
- Wakefield Historical Society
  www.wakefieldhistoricalsoc.org.uk/
- The Yorkshire Architectural and York Archaeological Society
  homepages.tesco.net/~hugh.murray/yayas/
- York Bibliographical Society
  www-users.york.ac.uk/~pml1/ybs.htm

Channel Islands
- La Société Guernesiaise
  www.societe.org.gg/
- The Société Jersiaise
  www.societejersiaise/org/

Isle of Man
- Isle of Man Natural History & Antiquarian Society
  iomnhas.iomonline.co.im/
- Peel Heritage Trust
  www.pht.iofm.net/

5. Journals and Newspapers

Many sites on the web include pages for historical journals and newspapers. An increasing number of these offer the full text of journals which are also available in print; a small number are only available on the web. More sites offer full contents listings; many others simply advertise the availability of published journals. The latter are not listed here. Many journals are issued by societies; details of these can be found on their web-sites listed in chapter 4.

- The History Journals Guide
  www.history-journals.de/
  Directory of 5400+ journals world-wide, including many British.
- Magazine Stacks: table of contents of historical journals, monographic series and occasional volumes / Stuart Jenks & Dieter Rübsamen (eds)
  www.phil-uni-erlangen.de/~p1ges/zfhm/zfhm__na.html
  International in scope, but indexes many British journals.

General information on a major project to microfilm old newspapers is provided by:
- The Newsplan 2000 Project
  www.newsplan2000.org

A gateway to electronic journals for archaeologists is provided by:
- Electronic Journals in Anthropology and Archaeology
  archnet.asu.edu/archnet/other/journals.html

See also:
- Archway
  ads.ahds.ac.uk/catalogue/ARCHway.html
  Online index to archaeological journals.

A number of sites provide full text of historic newspapers and journals. These include:
- British Library Online Newspaper Archive
  www.ukolivesoftware.com/
  Only a few at present, but likely to grow fast.

- History Cooperative
  www.historycoop.org/
  Full text of a number of American historical journals, some of which are of interest to British historians.
- Internet Library of Early Journals: a digital library of 18th and 19th Century Journals
  www.bodley.ac.uk/ilej/
  Includes runs of the *Gentleman's magazine,* the *Annual register, Philosophical transactions of the Royal Society, Notes and queries,* the *Builder,* and *Blackwood's Edinburgh magazine.*

The journals listed here are arranged alphabetically by title.
- *Anglo-Norman Studies*
  www.boydell.co.uk/ANGAN.HTM
  Includes contents listings.
- *Anglo-Saxon England*
  www.trin.cam.ac.uk/sdk13/asewww/
  Includes contents listing from 1972.
- *Anglo-Saxon England*
  titles.cambridge.org/journals/
  journal_catalogue.asp?historylinks=ALPHA&mnemonic=ASE
- *Anglo-Saxon Studies in Archaeology and History*
  users.ox.ac.uk/~assah/
  Includes contents lists.
- *Antiquity*
  antiquity.ac.uk
  Includes index, contents pages, and text of a few articles.
- *Archaeologia Aeliana*
  www.newcastle-antiquaries.org.uk/index.php?pageId=86
  Covers Northumberland and Durham; includes contents listings.
- *Archaeological Review from Cambridge: a graduate journal*
  www.cam.ac.uk/societies/arc/
- *Archaeology Abroad*
  www.britarch.ac.uk/archabroad/
  Information on fieldwork opportunities.
- *Archaeology Review* / English Heritage
  www.eng-h.gov.uk/ArchRev/
  Reviews of the work of English Heritage 1994/5-1998/9. Full text.
- *Assemblage: the Sheffield Graduate Journal of* Archaeology
  www.shef.ac.uk/assem/
  On-line journal.
- *At the Edge*
  www.indigogroup.co.uk/edge/
  Journal dealing with archaeology, folk-lore and mythology; includes full text.
- *The Athenaeum:* Index of Reviews and Reviewers 1830-1870
  www.sol.city.ac.uk/~asp/v2/home.html
- *Briefing* / Council for British Archaeology
  www.britarch.ac.uk/briefing/briefing.html
  Full text.
- *British Archaeology*
  www.britarch.ac.uk/ba/ba.html
  Full text.
- *Publications* [of the Society for the Promotion of Roman Studies]
  www.sas.ac.uk/icls/roman/publicat.htm
  Includes details of *Britannia,* including contents listings and some abstracts.
- Roman Britain: a bibliography of sources
  www.btinternet.com/~britannica/britart.html
  Contents listing for *Britannia* .
- *Catholic Archives*
  www.catholic-history.org.uk/catharch/catharch.htm
  Author index.
- *Chronique: the journal of chivalry*
  www.chronique.com/chrniq.htm
  Includes contents lists.
- *Contemporary British History*
  www.tandf.co.uk/journals/titles/13619462.asp
  Includes full text, pay per view.
- *Cornish history*
  www.marjon.ac.uk/cornish-history/
  Includes full text of articles.
- *Current Archaeology*
  www.archaeology.co.uk
  Includes contents listing.
- *The English Historical Review*
  www3.oup.co.uk/enghis/
  Full text of the journal since 1998 on subscription basis.
- *Essays in History*
  etext.lib.virginia.edu/journals/EH/
  Many online articles, some listed separately below.

- *Essays in medieval studies: proceedings of the Illinois Medieval Association*
  www.leu.edu/publications/medieval/
  Full text.
- Attributions of authorship in the *Gentleman's magazine.*
  etext.virginia.edu/bsuva/gm/
- *Guardian* (formerly *Manchester Guardian*) Archive
  rylibweb.man.ac.uk/data2/spcoll/guardian/
  Brief description of an archive at the John Rylands University Library of Manchester
- *The Heroic Age: a journal of early medieval north-western Europe*
  www.mun.ca/mst/heroicage/
  Online journal.
- *Historical Research*
  www.history.ac.uk/historical/index.html
  Brief note on a major journal.
- Articles published in the journal *Historical research* from May 1977 to February 1996
  www.history.ac.uk/projects/historical/index.html
  Listing only, not full text.
- *History Today*
  www.historytoday.com
  Includes articles published in the magazine since 1980; pay per view or subscription.
- *History Today*
  www.findarticles.com/m1373/6__49/issue.jhtml
  Full text of articles since 1995.
- *History Workshop journal*
  www3.oup.co.uk/hiwork/
  Full text of the journal on a subscription basis.
- Huntington Library Press
  www.huntington.org/HLPress/quarterly.html
  Includes contents listing of *Huntington Library quarterly*
- *Internet Archaeology*
  intarch.ac.uk/
  Online journal; fee-based.
- *Journal of Conservation & Museum Studies*
  www.ucl.ac.uk/archaeology/conservation/jcms/
  Online journal.
- *Journal of Social History*
  www.findarticles.com/cf__0/m2005/mag.jhtml
- *Local History Magazine*
  www.local-history.com
  Includes contents listing, forthcoming events.
- *London Archaeologist*
  www.np03.dial.pipex.com/la
  Includes contents listings.
- *The London Gazette*
  www.gazettes-online.co.uk/
  Click on title. Includes some full text
- *The London Gazette*
  www.history.rochester.edu/London__Gazette
  Includes transcripts of some 17th c. editions.
- *The London journal*
  www.history.ac.uk/cmh/londonjournal/
  Concerned with London's history. Includes contents listing and abstracts of articles in recent issues.
- *Papers from the Institute of Archaeology*
  www.ucl.ac.uk/archaeology/pia/whatis.html
  Journal; includes abstracts.
- *Parliamentary history*
  www.cup.ed.ac.uk/newweb/journals/Parliamentary/
  Includes some abstracts.
- *Past & present*
  www3.oup.co.uk/past/contents/
  Full text of the journal on subscription basis.
- *The Penny Magazine*
  www.history.rochester.edu/pennymag/
  Full text of a working class magazine, 1832-5. Other issues in progress.
- *Quadrat: a periodical bulletin on research in progress on the history of the British book trade*
  www.bbti.bham.ac.uk/Quadrat.htm
  Includes contents listing and full text of the latest issue.
- *Recusant History, formerly Biographical Studies*
  www.catholic-history.org.uk/crs/rechist.htm
  Contents listing.

- *Renaissance Forum: an electronic journal of early-modern literary and historical studies*
  www.hull.ac.uk/Hull/EL__Web/renforum
  Online journal.
- *Teaching history online*
  www.spartacus.schoolnet.co.uk/history.htm
  Online journal.
- Index to the *Times,* 1790-1980
  edina.ac.uk/times-index/
  Subscription service.
- *Twentieth Century British History*
  www3.oup.co.uk/tweceb/
  Full text of journal from 2002; pay per view.

6. Techniques

A. The Study of History

- Representations
  www.earlymodernweb.org.uk/emrepresentation.htm
  Gateway to pages on philosophy of history and historiography.
- History in Focus: What is History?
  www.history.ac.uk/ihr/Focus/Whatishistory/index.html
  With opinions from 14 historians.
- History and its post-modern critics
  www.history.ac.uk/projects/discourse/index.html
  Debate.
- BUTTERFIELD, HERBERT. *Man on his past: the study of the history of historical scholarship.* Cambridge University Press, 1955.
  www.questia.com/PM.qst?a=o&d=10909326
  Subscription based.
- Defender of the Faith: Geoffrey Elton and the Philosophy of History / Geoffrey Roberts
  www.ucc.ie/chronicon/elton.htm
- History Trail: How to Do History
  www.bbc.co.uk/history/lj/
  Includes:
  - The role of a historian / Dr. John Arnold
  - The Elusive Face of History / Dr. Ronald MacRaild
  - The Element of Choice: How to Work with Sources / Dr. John Arnold
- PHILLIPS, PAUL T. *Britain's past in Canada: the teaching and writing of British history.* Vancouver: University of British Columbia Press, 1989.
  www.questia.com/SM.quest
  Click on title.
- School History.co.uk
  www.schoolhistory.co.uk/
  For teachers and pupils.
- Studying History / Christopher Harrison
  www.keele.ac.uk/depts/hi/resources/Indexes/StudyingHistory.pdf
- Some Tips for Writing History Papers
  falcon.arts.cornell.edu/prh3/257/classmats/papertip.html
- Evaluating Information Found on the Web
  www.library.jhu.edu/elp/useit/evaluate/

- Citing Electronic Information in History Papers / Maurice Crouse
  cas.memphis.edu/~mcrouse/elcite.html

B. Archival Research
- Archives in Focus
  www.hmc.gov.uk/focus/focus.htm
  Beginner's guide to using archives.
- Archival Research Techniques and Skills
  www.arts-scheme.co.uk/

C. Palaeography
- An Introduction to Palaeography
  paleo.anglo-norman.org/
- English Handwriting 1500-1700: an online course
  www.english.cam.ac.uk/ceres/ehoc/
- Medieval Writing: history, heritage and data source
  medievalwriting.50megs.com/writing.htm

D. Medieval Latin
- White Trash Scriptorium: Latin E-books
  www.ipa.net/~magreyn/
  Includes glossary of Latin words in English manuscripts, Latin place names, *etc.,* from Charles T. Martin. *The record interpreter.* 1911.
- Dictionary of Medieval Latin from Celtic Sources
  journals.eecs.qub.ac.uk/DMLCS/DMLCS.html

E. Old English
- Old English Pages
  www.georgetown.edu/faculty/balle/oe/old__english.html
- Old English at the University of Calgary
  www.ucalgary.ca/UofC/eduweb/engl401/
  Includes introduction to the language.
- The Electronic Introduction to Old English / Peter S. Baker
  www.wmich.edu/medieval/research/rawl/IOE/index.html
- Old English Aerobics
  www.engl.virginia.edu/OE/OEA/index.html
- WENDERE Old English Dictionary
  www.spiritone.com/~mcrobins/mark/oldenglish/wendere.htm
- Modern English to Old English Vocabulary
  www.mun.ca/Ansaxdat/vocab/wordlist.html

- Hypertext Medieval Glossary
  www.netserf.org/glossary/

F. Dates
- Dates of Easter Sunday and Perpetual Calendar, 1550-2049 (for Great Britain and the Colonies / Brian Pears
  www.genuki.org.uk/big/easter
- Methods of Chronology
  www.history.org.uk/HTML/Members/stamp.htm
- English Calendar
  www.albion.edu/english/calendar/
- Medieval Calendar Calculator
  www.wallandbinkley.com/mcc/mcc__main.html
- On-line Calendar of Saints Days
  www.the-orb.net/encyclop/religion/hagiography/calendar/home.htm

G. Oral History
- East Midlands Oral History Archive
  www.le.ac.uk/emoha/
  Includes much advice on oral history techniques.

H. Computing for Historians
- Digitising History: a guide to creating digital resources from historical documents / Sean Townsend, Cressida Chappell and Oscar Struijvé.
  hds.essex.ac.uk/g2gp/digitising__history.index.asp
- Using Computer Technology to Teach Medieval Texts
  www.unc.edu/student/orgs/cams/techtoteach/

7. Maps and Cartography

Locating places is a fundamental task for most historians. Maps and gazetteers are vital tools for the task, but also have a much greater historical importance: they provide a pictorial representation of the relationship of places to each other, and often contain important historical information. For the development of mapping, see:

- Map History / History of Cartography
  www.maphistory.info/

The Ordnance Survey produces the authoritative topographical maps of the U.K. See:
- Ordnance Survey
  www.ordnancesurvey.co.uk/

It has also produced the authoritative gazetteer:
- Landranger
  www.ordsvy.gov.uk/products/Landranger

Other gazetteers include:
- Church Location Database
  www.genuki.org.uk/big/parloc/
  Lists churches within any specified distance of a particular place.
- Gazetteer of British Place Names
  www.abcounties.co.uk/newgaz/
- Gazetteer of British Place Names
  www.gazetteer.co.uk
- Genuki Gazetteer
  www.genuki.org.uk/big/eng/Gazetteers.html
- How to find a Present Day House, Street, or Place in the U.K.
  www.genuki.org.uk/big/ModernLocations.html

For historic administrative boundaries, consult:
- Great Britain Historical G.I.S. Project
  www.geog.port.ac.uk/gbhgis/

- Historic Parishes of England & Wales: an electronic map of boundaries before 1850 with a gazetteer and metadata / Roger J.P. Kain & Richard R. Oliver.
  hds.ac.uk/hpew/hpew.asp

An old but useful historical atlas has been digitised for the web at:
- Gardiners Atlas of English History
  www.livgenmi.com/gardinertitle.htm
  Maps from GARDINER, S.R. *A school atlas of English history.* Longmans, Green & Co., 1892.

A number of sites include facsimiles of old maps. These include:
- Genmaps: old and interesting maps of England, Wales and Scotland.
  freepages.genealogy.rootsweb.com/≈genmaps/
- Historical Maps
  www.britannia.com/history/histmaps.htm
  Mainly maps of the Roman and Anglo-Saxon period, and county maps by Thomas Moule published in 1830.
- [National Library of Scotland]: Maps from our collection
  www.nls.uk/maps/
  Over 3,000 historic maps on-line, not just from Scotland.
- Old Maps.co.uk
  www.old-maps.co.uk
- A survey of the History of English Placenames / Kristine Elliott
  www.sca.org/heraldry/laurel/names/engplnam.html

8. Archaeology

A. Gateways and Directories

There are a number of gateways and guides to archaeological websites. These include:

- Archnet
  archnet.asu.edu/archnet/
  American gateway with some British links.
- Archaeology on the Internet
  www.geocities.com/helen__albrow/archaeologyontheinternet
- Archaeology on the World Wide Web: a User's Field Guide
  intarch.ac.uk/antiquity/electronic/champion.html
- C.B.A. Guide to U.K. Archaeology Online
  www.britarch.ac.uk/info/uklinks.html
- The Amazing Worlds of Archaeology, Anthropology & Ancient Civilizations
  www.archaeolink.com/
  International gateway, with innumerable British links.

Many archaeological resources are catalogued at:

- HEIRPORT: Historic Environment Resources Portal
  ads.ahds.ac.uk:81/heirport/
  Catalogue of archaeological resources created by partner organisations.

Access to digital data on-line is provided by:

- A.D.S.: Archaeology Data Service
  ads.ahds.ac.uk
  Provides access to digital data online; some of its pages listed separately here.

For a specialist gateway on computers in archaeology, see:

- Computers in Archaeology
  www.gla.ac.uk/Acad/Archaeology/resources/computing/index.html

For a web-ring, see:

- Archaeology on the Net Web Ring
  www.serve.com/archaeology/ring/index.html

The authoritative guide to British archaeological publications is:

- B.I.A.B.: the British and Irish Archaeological Bibliography
  www.biab.ac.uk
  Subscription based.

For a union catalogue of archaeological journals, consult:

- Archway
  ads.ahds.ac.uk/catalogue/ARCHway.html

A project to record excavation and other archaeological projects is the subject of:

- A.I.P.: Archaeological Interventions Project
  www.csweb.bournemouth.ac.uk/consci/text__aip/aipintro.htm

For an excavations database consult:

- Arch Search: the A.D.S. Online Catalogue
  ads.ahds.ac.uk/catalogue/info/index.cfm

See also:

- Dig Reports
  www.bbc.co.uk/history/archaeology/dig__reports.shtml
  Collection of brief summaries of excavations.

The Council for British Archaeology has published many research reports. Most of the early ones are online, and individually listed here. For a full listing, visit:

- C.B.A. Research Reports
  www.britarch.ac.uk/pubs/resrep.html

For summaries of projects funded by English Heritage since 1996/7, see:

- Archaeology Commissions: English Heritage
  www.eng-h.gov.uk/archcom/projects/summarys/

A number of web-based directories are available; these include:

- Ancient Sites Directory
  www.henge.org.uk
- Archaeology Directory
  www.archaeologydirectory.co.uk/
  Directory of archaeological institutions, societies, units, *etc.*
- Current Archaeology Data Centre
  www.archaeology.co.uk/directory/index.htm
  Directory to digs, societies, education, and raw data.

- The Directory of British Archaeology
  www.cix.ac.uk/~archaeology/directory/
- HEIRNET: Historic Environment Information Resources Network
  ads.ahds.ac.uk/heirnet/index.cfm
  Lists information resources of archaeological units, *etc.*
- Online Archaeology
  www.online-archaeology.co.uk/
  News, books, links, forums, resources, *etc.*

A number of pages offer help with careers, education, training and voluntary work, *etc.* See:
- C.B.A. Fact Sheets
  www.britarch.ac.uk/cba/factshts.html
  Introductions to various aspects of education, training and careers.
- Profiling the Profession: a survey of archaeological jobs in the U.K.
  www.britarch.ac.uk/training/profile.html
- Survey of Archaeological Specialists / Kenneth Aitchison
  www.landward.dnet.co.uk/specialists/FrontPage.htm
- British Archaeological Jobs Resource Website
  www.archaeo.freeserve.co.uk/
- U.K. Archaeology Opportunities
  www.ukarchaeology.org.uk/
  List of volunteer opportunities, courses, work experience, *etc.*
- British Archaeological Awards
  www.britarch.ac.uk/awards/

B. Introductory Guides
- Archaeology: an introduction
  www.staff.ncl.ac.uk/kevin.greene/wintro/index.htm
  Website of links for a published book.
- The Archaeology of …
  www.thearchaeologyof.co.uk/
  Collection of essays, listed here individually.
- Archaeology
  www.fact-index.com/a/ar/archaeology.html
  Encyclopedia.
- Archaeology of Britain
  www2.sfu.ca/archaeology/museum/britain/archbr.html
  Photographs of neolithic, iron age, and Roman sites.

- Field Archaeology
  www.field-archaeology.info/
  General introduction to archaeological techniques.
- FOWLER, ELIZABETH. ed. *Field survey in British archaeology: papers given at a C.B.A. conference, 1071.* C.B.A. occasional paper, 1972.
  ads.ahds.ac.uk/catalogue/library/cba/op3.cfm
- Hidden Treasure
  www.bbc.co.uk/history/archaeology/treasure/
  Many introductory pages, some listed elsewhere in this directory. Also includes a directory of organisations, courses, *etc.*
- STEANE, JOHN M., & DIX, BRIAN F. *Peopling past landscapes: a handbook introducing archaeological fieldwork techniques in rural areas.* C.B.A. occasional paper. 1978.
  ads.ahds.ac.uk/catalogue/library/cba/op9.cfm
- CRACKNELL, STEVEN, & CORBISHLEY, MIKE, eds. *Presenting archaeology to young people.* C.B.A. research report **64.** 1986.
  ads.ahds.ac.uk/catalogue/library/cba/rr64.cfm
- Spoilheap: selected themes in archaeology
  www.spoilheap.co.uk/
  Includes pages on ' British archaeology', 'post-Roman pottery', 'finds', and 'human bones'.

C. History of Archaeology
- Birth of Archaeology / Julian Richards
  www.bbc.co.uk/history/lj/archaeologylj/origins__01.shtml
- A short History of Arthurian Archaeology / Michelle L. Biehl
  www.jammed.com/~mlb/arthur.html
- Piltdown Man: Britain's Greatest Hoax / Kate Bartlett
  www.bbc.co.uk/history/archaeology/piltdown__man__01.shtml
- A Mostly Complete Piltdown Man Bibliography
  www.talkorigins.org/faqs/piltdown/piltref.html

D. Archaeological Policy
- *Archaeology and government: a plan for archaeology in Britain.* C.B.A. occasional paper. 1974.
  ads.ahds.ac.uk/catalogue/library/cba/op7.cfm
- DARVILL, TIMOTHY, & RUSSELL, BRONWEN, et al. *Archaeology after PPG16: archaeological investigations in England 1990-1999.* Bournemouth: Bournemouth School of Conservation Sciences, 2002.
  csweb.bournemouth.ac.uk/consci/text__aip/ppg16/
  Archaeology and planning.

- THOMAS, CHARLES. *Research objectives in British archaeology.* C.B.A. occasional paper. 1983.
  ads.ahds.ac.uk/catalogue/library/cba/op14.cfm
- MELLARS, PAUL, ed. *Research priorities in archaeological science.* C.B.A. occasional paper. 1987.
  ads.ahds.ac.uk/catalogue/library/cba/op17.cfm
- HAWKES, CHRISTOPHER, & PIGGOT, STUART, eds. *Survey and policy of field research in the archaeology of Great Britain. 1. The prehistoric and early historic ages to the 7th century A.D.* C.B.A. occasional paper. 1948.
  ads.ahds.ac.uk/catalogue/library/cba/op1.cfm
- The Monuments at Risk Survey
  csweb.bournemouth.ac.uk/consci/text_mars/marsint.htm
- Monuments at Risk in England's Wetlands / Robert Van de Noort, *et al.*
  www.ex.ac.uk/marew/findreport.pdf
  Report for English Heritage, covering the wetlands of the Somerset Levels, the Humber, the Fens, and the North West.
- Sacred Sites: Contested Rights/Rites Project: Paganisms, Archaeological Monuments, and Access
  sacredsites.org.uk/
  Scholarly examination of modern paganism and religious use of prehistoric sites.
- The East Midlands Archaeological Research Framework Project
  www.le.ac.uk/ar/east_midlands_framework.htm
- North East Regional Research Framework for the Historic Environment
  www.durham.gov.uk/durhamcc/usp.nsf/pws/
  Archaeology+2001++Regional+Research+Framework

E. Archaeological Techniques
- Guides to Good Practice
  ads.ahds.ac.uk/project/goodguides/g2gp.html

i. *Finds*
- mda Archaeological Objects Thesaurus
  www.mda.org.uk/archobj/archcon.htm
- Advice for Finders of Archaeological Objects
  www.bbc.co.uk/history/archaeology/treasure/faq.shtml
- Finding Our Past: the Portable Antiquities Scheme
  www.finds.org.uk/
  For reporting finds; includes database of 60,000 finds.

- Guidelines for the Care of Waterlogged Archaeological Leather
  www.eng-h.gov.uk/guidelines/leather.html

ii. *Digital Technology*
- DigIT: Digital Information Technology in Field Archaeology
  www.landscaperesearchcentre.org/digit/Introduction.htm
- Strategies for Digital Data: findings and recommendations from Digital Data in Archaeology: a survey of user needs / Frances Condron, *et al*
  ads.ahds.ac.uk/project/strategies/
- Digital Archives from Excavation and Fieldwork: a guide to good practice / Julian Richards & Damian Robinson
  ads.ahds.ac.uk/project/goodguides/excavation/

iii. *Mapping*
- English Heritage National Mapping Programme
  ads.ahds.ac.uk/catalogue/projArch/NMP/
  Project to map all archaeological sites.
- PHILLIPS, C.W. *Archaeology in the Ordnance Survey, 1791-1965.* C.B.A. occasional paper. 1980.
  ads.ahds.ac.uk/catalogue/library/cba/op11.cfm
- Digital Mapping and Archaeology
  www.casa.ucl.ac.uk/dma/dma.htm

iv. *Archaeology in the Laboratory*
- PHILLIPS, PATRICIA, ed. *The archaeologist and the laboratory.* C.B.A. research report **58.** 1985.
  ads.ahds.ac.uk/catalogue/library/cba/rr58.cfm
- Direct Evaluation of Archaeological Immigration, Population Dynamics and Lead Exposure by Isotope Biogeochemistry
  www.dur.ac.uk/p.d.budd/isogeochem/
- Archaeometallurgy in Archaeological Projects
  www.eng-h.gov.uk/guidelines/archmet.html
- Experimental Archaeology / Barrie Andrian
  www.bbc.co.uk/history/lj/archaeologylj/experimental_01.shtml
  Evidence based on re-construction of ancient conditions.

v. *Geophysical Surveys*
- The English Heritage Geophysical Survey Database
  www.eng-h.gov.uk/reports/
  Includes 77 reports.

- Geophysical Data in Archaeology: a guide to good practice / Armin Schmidt
  ads.ahds.ac.uk/project/goodguides/geophys/

vi. *Dating Techniques*
- Dating Techniques
  www.mnsu.edu/emuseum/archaeology/dating/
- Interpreting Stratigraphy
  www.york.ac.uk/depts/arch/strat/pastpub.htm
  Conference proceedings, 1992-6.
- Archaeological Site Index to Radiocarbon Dates from Great Britain and Ireland
  ads.ahds.ac.uk/catalogue/specColl/c14__cba/index.cfm
- Dendrochronology Database / Vernacular Architecture Group
  ads.ahds.ac.uk/catalogue/specColl/vag__dendro/
  Tree-ring dated sites.
- Ceramic Petrology
  www.postex.demon.co.uk/index.html

vii. *Aerial Archaeology*
- Aerial Archaeology / Dave MacLeod
  www.bbc.co.uk/history/archaeology/time__flyers__01.shtml
- WILSON, D.R., ed. *Aerial reconnaissance for archaeology.* 1975. C.B.A. research report 12. 1975.
  ads.ahds.ac.uk/catalogue/library/cba/rr12.cfm
- Aerial Survey for Archaeology: report of a British Academy Working Party
  www.britac.ac.uk/news/reports/archaeology/asfa.html
  Report on the institutional framework.
- Archiving Aerial Photography and Remote Sensing Data: a guide to good practice / Robert Bewley, *et al.*
  ads.ahds.ac.uk/project/goodguides/apandrs/
- MAXWELL, G.S., ed. *The impact of aerial reconnaissance on archaeology.* C.B.A. research report 49. 1983.
  ads.ahds.ac.uk/catalogue/library/cba/rr49.cfm
- Cambridge University Collection of Air Photos (CUCAP)
  venus.aerial.cam.ac.uk

viii. *Environmental Archaeology*
- Environmental Archaeology Bibliography
  ads.ahds.ac.uk/catalogue/specColl/eab__eh__2004/
- Environmental Archaeology Bibliography
  www.eng-h.gov.uk/EAB/
- Discussing the Range of Environmental Data that might be obtained on an Archaeological Excavation
  thearchof.topcities.com/Scientific/environmental.htm
  Very brief introductory essay.
- HALL, A.R., & KENWARD, H.K., eds. *Environmental archaeology in the urban context.* C.B.A. research report 43. 1982.
  ads.ahds.ac.uk/catalogue/library/cba/rr43.cfm
  The web version is incomplete.
- EVANS, J.G., LIMBREY, SUSAN, & CLEERE, HENRY, eds. *The effect of man on the landscape: the Highland zone.* C.B.A. research report 11. 1973.
  ads.ahds.ac.uk/catalogue/library/cba/rr11.cfm
- LIMBREY, SUSAN, & EVANS, J.G., ed. *The effect of man on the landscape: the Lowland zone.* C.B.A. research report 21. 1978.
  ads.ahds.ac.uk/catalogue/library/cba/rr21.cfm
- Landscape Mysteries / Professor Aubrey Manning
  www.open2.net/landscapemysteries/
- LAMBRICK, GEORGE. *Archaeology and agriculture: a survey of modern cultivation methods and the problems of assessing plough damage to archaeological sites.* C.B.A. occasional paper. 1977.
  ads.ahds.ac.uk/catalogue/library/cba/op8.cfm
- BROWN, A.E., ed. *Garden archaeology.* C.B.A. research report 78. 1991.
  ads.ahds.ac.uk/catalogue/library/cba/rr78.cfm
- A review of the Archaeological Evidence for Food Plants from the British Isles: an example of the use of the Archaeobotanical Computer Database / Philippa Tomlinson & Alan R. Hall
  interarch.ac.uk/journal/issue1/tomlinson__toc.html
- Living Under a Medieval Field / John Letts
  www.britarch.ac.uk/ba/ba58/feat1.shtml
  Using the evidence of burnt medieval thatch.

ix. *Metal Detecting*
- Archaeology and Metal Detecting / Alex Hunt
  www.bbc.co.uk/history/archaeology/treasure/metal__detect__01.shtml
- U.K. Detector.net
  www.ukdetector.net
  Metal detecting activities.

F. Urban Archaeology

- HEIGHWAY, CAROLYN M., ed. *The erosion of history: archaeology and planning in towns: a study of historic towns affected by modern development in England, Wales and Scotland.* C.B.A. occasional paper. 1972.
  ads.ahds.ac.uk/catalogue/library/cba/op4.htm
- SCHOFIELD, JOHN, & LEECH, ROGER, eds. *Urban archaeology in Britain.* C.B.A. research report 61. 1987.
  ads.ahds.ac.uk/catalogue/library/cbarr61.cfm
- SCHOFIELD, JOHN, PALLISER, DAVID, *et al.* eds. *Recent archaeological research in English towns.* C.B.A. occasional paper. 1981.
  ads.ahds.ac.uk/catalogue/library/cba/op12.cfm
- GOOD, G.L., JONES, R.H., & PONSFORD, M.W., eds. *Waterfront archaeology: proceedings of the third international conference held at Bristol, 23-26 September, 1988.* C.B.A. research report **74.** 1988.
  ads.ahds.ac.uk/catalogue/library/cba/rr74.cfm
- MILNE, GUSTAV, & HOBLEY, BRIAN, eds. *Waterfront archaeology in Britain and Northern Europe.* C.B.A. research report **41.** 1981.
  ads.ahds.ac.uk/catalogue/library/cba/rr41.cfm
  Medieval.
- KENYON, JOHN R. *Castles, town defences and artillery fortifications in Britain and Ireland: a bibliography. Volume 2.* C.B.A. research report **53** & **72.** 1983-91.
  ads.ahds.ac.uk/catalogue/library/cba/rr53.cfm
  Supplement to a bibliography not available on the web. Continued by vol.3 at **/rr72.cfm**

G. Church Archaeology

- ADDYMAN, PETER, & MORRIS, RICHARD, eds. *The archaeological study of churches.* C.B.A. research report 13. 1976.
  ads.ahds.ac.uk/catalogue/library/cba/rr13.cfm
- JESSON, MARGARET. *The archaeology of churches: a report from the Churches Committee of the C.B.A. presented to the conference on the archaeology of churches held at Norwich on April 13-15, 1973.* C.B.A. occasional paper. 1973.
  ads.ahds.ac.uk/catalogue/library/cba/op5.cfm
- MORRIS, RICHARD. *The church in British archaeology.* C.B.A. research report **47.** 1983.
  ads.ahds.ac.uk/catalogue/library/cba/rr47.cfm

H. Industrial Archaeology

- FALCONER, KEITH, & HAY, GEOFFREY. eds. *The recording of industrial sites: a review.* C.B.A. occasional paper, 1981.
  ads.ahds.ac.uk/catalogue/library/cba/op13.cfm
- I.A. Recordings
  www.iarecordings.org/
  Recording industrial archaeology on film and video.

I. Marine Archaeology

- An Introduction to Marine Archaeology / Colin Martin
  www.bbc.co.uk/history/archaeology/marine__1.shtml
- Wreck Database
  www.ukdiving.co.uk/
  Click on title. Details of shipwrecks around the coast.
- [Wreck Sites around Britain]
  www.bbc.co.uk/history/archaeology/marine__map1.shtml

J. Numismatics

- Early Medieval Corpus of Coin Finds: Sylloge of coins of the British Isles
  www-cm.fitzmuseum.cam.ac.uk/Coins/emc__search.php

K. Miscellaneous Sites

- Battlefield Archaeology / Neil Oliver and Tony Pollard
  www.bbc.co.uk/history/archaeology/two__men.01.shtml
- Deliberately Concealed Garments Project: Clothes found hidden in Buildings
  www.concealedgarments.org/

9. Archaeological Institutions

A. General

- The Battlefields Trust
  www.battlefieldstrust.com/
  Concerned with the preservation and study of battlefields.
- Council for British Archaeology
  www.britarch.ac.uk
  Extensive and important site; some pages listed here separately.
- Council for Independent Archaeology
  www.independents.org.uk
- Institute of Field Archaeologists
  www.archaeologists.net/
  Professional organisation; includes AITCHISON, KENNETH. *Profiling the profession: a survey of archaeological jobs in the U.K.* Council for British Archaeology, *et al*, 1999.
- National Council for Metal Detecting
  www.ncmd.co.uk/
- National Monuments Record
  www.english-heritage.org.uk/default.asp?WCI=webItem&WCE=2131
- The National Trust: Archaeology
  www.nationaltrust.org.uk/environment/html/archeaol/_fs/fs_arch.htm
  Includes *Annual Archaeological review,* with many papers.
- Time Team Website
  www.channel4.com/history/timeteam/

B. University Departments and Centres

- University of Birmingham: the Institute of Archaeology and Antiquity
  www.arch-ant.bham.ac.uk
- Archaeology and the Historic Environment
  csweb.bournemouth.ac.uk/consci/text/archgrp.htm
  At the University of Bournemouth.
- University of Bradford. Department of Archaeological Sciences
  www.bradford.ac.uk/archsci/
- University of Bristol. Department of Archaeology
  www.bris.ac.uk/Depts/Archaeology/
- University of Cambridge. Department of Archaeology
  www.arch.cam.ac.uk/
- University of Durham. Department of Archaeology
  www.dur.ac.uk/Archaeology/
- Archaeological Services. University of Durham
  www.dur.ac.uk/archaeologicalservices/
- Department of Archaeology. University of Exeter
  www.ex.ac.uk/schools/geogarch/archaeology/
- The Exeter Centre for Wetland Research
  www.ex.ac.uk/schools/geogarch/wetlandresearch/
- Wetland Archaeology and Environments Research Centre
  www.hull.ac.uk/wetlands/
  At the University of Hull
- University of Leicester: Archaeology and Ancient History
  www.le.ac.uk/archaeology/
- University of Leicester Archaeological Services
  www.le.ac.uk/ulas
- University of Liverpool: School of Archaeology, Classics and Egyptology
  www.liv.ac.uk/sacos/
- Institute of Archaeology, University College, London
  www.ucl.ac.uk/archaeology/
- Historical Studies / University of Newcastle upon Tyne
  historical-studies.ncl.ac.uk/archaeology.asp
  Includes archaeology.
- Archaeology at Oxford
  athens.arch.ox.ac.uk/schoolarch/index.phtml
- Oxford Dendrochronology Laboratory
  www.dendrochronology.com/
  Includes much information on dendrochronological dating techniques.
- Archaeology at Reading
  www.rdg.ac.uk/archaeology/
- Archaeology @ Sheffield
  www2.shef.ac.uk/uni/academic/A-C/ap/index.html
- Archaeology: University of Southampton
  www.arch.soton.ac.uk/
- Centre for Maritime Archaeology
  cma.soton.ac.uk
  At the University of Southampton.
- University of York: Department of Archaeology
  www.york.ac.uk/depts/arch/

C. Archaeological Units, Sites & Monuments Records, *etc.*

Berkshire
- Archaeology in West Berkshire
  www.westberks.gov.uk/WestBerkshire/tourism.nsf/
  pages.archaeology140802
  Includes information on the sites and monuments record.

Buckinghamshire
- Buckinghamshire County Council: County Archaeological Service
  www.buckscc.gov.uk/archaeology/index.htm

Cambridgeshire
- Cambridge Archaeological Unit
  www-cau.arch.cam.ac.uk/

Cheshire
- Cheshire Archaeology Homepage
  www.cheshire.gov.uk/archolgy/
  Includes details of sites & monuments record.
- Chester City Council: Archaeology
  www.chestercc.gov.uk/heritage/archaeology/archaeology.html

Cornwall
- Cornwall County Council Archaeology & Historic Environment
  www.cornwall.gov.uk/history/ab-hi30.htm

Derbyshire *see also* Nottinghamshire
- Anglo-Saxon Derbyshire: site database
  www.ccc.nottingham.ac.uk/~aczkdc/asd/database.html

Devon
- Torbay Archaeology Service
  www.torbay.gov.uk/main.asp?page=95

Durham
- Durham County Council: Archaeology
  www.durham.gov.uk/durhamcc/usp/nsf/pws/
  archaeology2001++archaeology+Introduction

Gloucestershire
- Gloucester Archaeology Unit
  www.mylife.gloucester.gov.uk/archaeology/gloarcun.htm
  See also:
  www.glos-city.gov.uk/libraries/templates/page.asp?URN=934
- Forest of Dean Archaeological Survey
  www.gloucestershire.gov.uk/index.cfm?articleID=1950/

Herefordshire
- Herefordshire Sites & Monuments Record
  www.smr.herefordshire.gov.uk/

Kent
- Canterbury Archaeological Trust
  www.canterburytrust.co.uk/
- Canterbury Archaeological Trust
  www.hillside.co.uk/arch/archaeology.html
  Includes annual reports, but an unofficial site.

Lancashire
- Field Archaeology at National Museums Liverpool
  www.liverpoolmuseums.org.uk/livmus/humanities/fieldarch.asp

London & Middlesex
- London Archaeological Archive and Research Centre
  www.museumoflondon.org.uk/laarc/new/
- Greater London Sites and Monuments Record
  www.british-history.ac.uk/source.asp?pubid=34
  In progress.
- Museum of London Archaeology Service
  www.molas.org.uk/
- Newham Museum Service Archaeology Centre: Digital Archive
  ads.ahds.ac.uk/catalogue/projArch/newham/newham__intro.cfm
  Work of a local government archaeological unit that has been closed down.

Nottinghamshire
- Trent & Peak Archaeological Unit
  www.nottingham.ac.uk/tpau/

Oxfordshire
- Oxfordshire Buildings Record
  www.obr.org.uk/

Somerset
- Somerset Historic Environment Record
  webapp1.somerset.gov.uk/her/sop.asp?flash=true

Suffolk
- Suffolk County Council: Archaeology
  www.suffolkcc.gov.uk/e-and-t/archaeology/
  Suffolk Archaeology Service reports, *etc.*

Warwickshire
- Birmingham Archaeology
  www.arch-ant.bham.ac.uk/bufau/
  Archaeological unit of Birmingham University.

Worcestershire
- Worcestershire County Council: Historic Environment & Archaeology
  Service
  www.worcestershire.gov.uk/home/index/cs-index/cs-archeo.htm
  Includes the 'historic environment record' database.

Yorkshire
- Humber Sites and Monuments Record
  www.hullcc.gov.uk/archaeology/smrindex.htm
  Covers the East Riding.
- West Yorkshire Archaeology Service
  www.arch.wyjs.org.uk/
- Archaeology in York
  www.york.ac.uk/depts/arch/yccweb/welcome.htm
  Includes the Urban Archaeology Database, the Sites and Monuments
  record, *etc, etc.*
- York Archaeological Trust for Excavation and Research Ltd.
  www.yorkarchaeology.co.uk/index.htm
- York Archaeological Trust
  www.jorvik-viking-centre.co.uk/trialsplash2.htm
  Includes details of the Jorvik Centre.

9. British History: Long Periods

A. General Sites
- Britannia
  www.britannia.com
  One of the most extensive sites for British history; many articles are
  individually cited in this directory.
- British History
  www.great-britain.co.uk/history/history.htm
  Brief popular outline.
- England: a narrative history / Peter N. Williams
  www.britannia.com/history/narintrohist.html
- History
  www.bbc.co.uk/history/
  Popular but authoritative pages on many subjects, some of them
  separately listed here; includes 'timelines' (i.e.chronologies).
- eHistory
  www.ehistory.com
  International in scope, but includes some pages on British history.
- History Study Stop
  www.historystudystop.co.uk
  Articles for G.C.S.E. and A level students, some listed here individually.
- *The Cambridge history of English and American literature.* 18 vols.
  New York: Putnam, 1907-21
  www.bartleby.com/cambridge/
  Includes much information of general historical interest.
- Encyclopaedia of British History 1500-1980
  www.spartacus.schoolnet.co.uk/Britain.html
  For schools; many pages, some of which are listed here individually.
- G.C.S.E. History Pages
  www.historygcse.org/
- History Learning Site
  www.historylearningsite.co.uk/
  Includes many pages on British history for schools, some individually
  listed here.
- The Making of the United Kingdom
  www.spartacus.schoolnet.co.uk/UnitedKingdom.htm
  Includes numerous biographies 1485-1750, and articles on events and
  issues, *etc.* For schools.

- The National Archives Learning Curve
  www.learningcurve.gov.uk/default.asp
  On-line teaching resources from the National Archives; including facsimiles of original sources.
- School History.co.uk
  www.schoolhistory.co.uk
  Many lesson plans.

Encyclopedias

- British and Irish History Articles
  reference.allrefer.com/encyclopedia/categories/ukhist.html
  Encyclopedia.
- CANNON, JOHN. *The Oxford companion to British history.* Oxford: Oxford University Press, 1997.
  www.questia.com/PM.qst?a=o&d=72417955
  Subscription based. Encyclopedia.
- Catholic Encyclopedia
  www.newadvent.org/cathen/
  Extensive; includes many articles relevant to British history, some of which have separate entries here.
- Columbia Encyclopedia. 6th edition
  www.bartleby.com/65/
  Includes many articles on British history.
- Encarta
  encarta.msn.com
  Encyclopedia with many articles of British interest. Subscription based.
- Encyclopedia.com
  www.encyclopedia.com
  Many articles providing basic information on British history.
- Encyclopedia Britannica
  www.britannica.org
  The web version of the best-known encyclopedia; many British articles. Subscription based (but free for 72 hours).
- Infoplease
  www.infoplease.com
  Encyclopedia including basic information on British history.
- The New Schaff-Herzog Encyclopedia of Religious Knowledge / Philip Schaff
  www.ccel.org/s/schaff/encyc/home.html
  Facsimile; many articles of British historical interest.

- Wikipedia: the free encyclopedia
  en.wikipedia.org/wiki/Main__Page
  Many articles providing basic information on British history.

Chronologies & Time Lines

- Timelines
  www.bbc.co.uk/history/timelines/
  Many pages providing a brief summary of British history.
- Timelines of British History
  www.britannia.com/history/timelines.html

Miscellaneous Pages

- Eyewitness to History
  www.eyewitnesstohistory.com/
  Extracts from many sources, mainly American, but including some English material.
- Voices of the Powerless
  www.bbc.co.uk/radio4/history/voices/index.shtml
  Contemporary accounts of major events in British history.
- HOSKINS, W.G. *Provincial England: essays in social and economic history.* Macmillan & Co., 1963
  www.questia.com/PM.qst?a=o&d=1755230
  Subscription based.
- Medieval England / Steven Muhlberger
  www.the-orb.net/textbooks/muhlberger/muhlindex.html
  Introductory history, c.500-1500.
- SAYLES, G.O. *The medieval foundations of England.* Philadelphia: University of Pennsylvania Press, 1950.
  www.questia.com/PM.qst?a=o&d=3806266
  Subscription based.
- Medieval World
  www.spartacusschoolnet.co.uk/Medieval.htm
  Includes many pages on Anglo-Saxon and Norman England, *etc.* especially biographies. For schools.
- BROOKE, CHRISTOPHER. *From Alfred to Henry III, 871-1272.* Edinburgh: T. Nerlson, 1961.
  www.questia.com/PM.qst?a=o&d=93517765
  Subscription based.
- The origins of English Individualism: some surprises / Alan Macfarlane
  www.alanmacfarlane.com/TEXTS/Origins__HI.pdf
  From *Theory and society* 6(2), 1978.

- Individualism Reconsidered, or, the craft of the historian / Alan Macfarlane
  www.alanmacfarlane.com/TEXTS/CRAFT.pdf
- The Cradle of Capitalism: the case of England / Alan Macfarlane
  www.alanmacfarlane.com/TEXTS/CRADLE.pdf
  Published as chapter 8 of *The culture of capitalism*. Blackwell, 1987.
- Reformation and Restoration 1485-1689 A.D.
  www.britannia.com/history/h70.html
- Union of the Crowns 1603-2003
  www.unionofthecrowns.com
- PREST, WILFRID. *Albion ascendant: English history, 1660-1815*. Oxford: Oxford University Press, 1998.
  www.questia.com/PM.qst?a=o&d=13654090
  Subscription based.
- FIRTH, CHARLES, SIR. *A commentary on Macaulay's History of England*. Macmillan, 1938.
  www.questia.com/PM.qst?a=o&d=14713002
  Subscription based.
- The Age of Empire, 1689-1901 A.D.
  www.britannia.com/history/h80.html
  Many pages.

B. Sources
The authoritative online guide to sources for British history is:
- Manuscript Sources for British History / R.J. Olney
  www.history.ac.uk/projects/manuscripts/index.html

See also:
- Surveys of Historical Manuscripts in the United Kingdom: a select bibliography / C.J. Kitching (ed.)
  www.hmc.gov.uk/pubs/surveys3rd.htm

Many major sources were officially published in the 19th century 'Rolls series'. These are listed in:
- Index to the Rolls Series / Steven H. Silver
  www.the-orb.net/rolls.html

Many original sources are available online, and listed in appropriate chapters below. A number of sites offer important collections of sources, or provide gateways to them: These include:
- History of the United Kingdom: Primary Documents
  library.byu.edu/~rdh/eurodocs/uk.html
  Gateway.
- Internet History Sourcebooks Project
  www.fordham.edu/halsall/
  International in scope, but with much British material.
- Internet Modern History Sourcebook
  www.fordham.edu/halsall/mod/modsbook.html
  Gateway, international in scope, with many links to British source-material.
- Sources of British History
  www.britannia.com/history/docs/
  Translations of many original sources.
- The ORB: on-line reference book for medieval studies
  www.the-orb.net/
- The Avalon Project at Yale Law School: Documents in Law, History and Diplomacy
  www.yale.edu/lawweb/avalon/avalon.htm
- Original Historical Texts
  www.adelpha.com/~davidco/History/histinde.htm
  16-17th c. at present, although some Napoleonic war texts are promised.

For statistics, visit:
- Great Britain Historical Database Online
  hds.essex.ac.uk/gbh.asp
  19-20th c. statistics collection.

C. Biography, Genealogy and Diaries
i. *Biographies*
- Oxford Dictionary of National Biography
  www.oup.com/oxforddnb/info/
  Discussion of the authoritative biographical dictionary; on-line edition forthcoming.

- Historic Figures
  www.bbc.co.uk/history/historic__figures/
  Includes many brief biographies.
- Biographies & Profiles
  www.britannia.com/bios/
  Many famous people.
- The Mac Tutor History of Mathematics Archives: Biographies Index
  turnbull.mcs.st-and.ac.uk/history/BiogIndex.html
  Many scientific biographies; international in scope but including some British entries.
- Channel 4's Portrait Gallery
  www.channel4.com/history/microsites/R/real-lives/
  Brief biographies, mainly 19-20th c., but some earlier.

ii. *Genealogy*
The listing which follows is very basic. For a full listing, consult the present author's *Family history on the web: a directory for England and Wales,* and the other relevant volumes in the present series (see back cover for details).
- Genuki: U.K. & Ireland Genealogy
  www.genuki.org.uk
  Thousands of pages on this and associated web-sites.
- Cyndis List
  www.CyndisList.com
- British Isles Genweb Project
  www.britishislesgenweb.org
- First Steps in Family History
  www.ffhs.org/General/Help/First.htm
- Family History in England and Wales
  www.catalogue.nationalarchives.gov.uk/rdleaflet.asp?sleafletID=84
  Click on title.
- Family Records.gov.uk
  www.familyrecords.gov.uk
  Consortium of 10 national institutions holding primary sources for family history.
- Historical Text Archive: Genealogy
  historicaltextarchive.com/sections.php
  Click on 'Genealogy'.

iii. *Diaries*
- British and Irish Women's Letters and Diaries
  www.alexanderstreet2.com/BWLDlive/
  c.100,000 pages planned; pay per view.

D. Government & Politics

i. *General*
- National Politics Webguide
  lego70.tripod.com/
  Click on 'nations' and scroll down to 'England and United Kingdom' for pages on early British monarchs and on leading politicians with some information on politics and government.

ii. *Constitutional History*
- STEPHENSON, CARL, & MARCHAM, FREDERICK GEORGE. *Sources of English constitutional history: a selection of documents from A.D.600 to the present.* Harper & Row, 1937.
- BURTON, GEORGE, ed. *Select documents of English constitutional history.* Macmillan & Co., 1901.
  www.questia.com/PM.qst?a=o&d=6081828
  Subscription based.
- Liberty Library of Constitutional Classics
  www.constitution.org/liberlib.htm
  Many texts of constitutional documents, British and American, some listed individually here.
- COSTIN, W.C., & WATSON, J. STEVEN, eds. *The law and working of the constitution: documents, 1660-1914.* Adam & Charles Black, 1952.
  www.questia.com/PM.qst?a=o&d=7951632
  Subscription based.
- SMITH, GOLDWIN. *A constitutional and legal history of England.* New York: Charles Scribner's Sons, 1955.
  www.questia.com/PM.qst?a=o&d=27896456
  Subscription based.
- KNAPPEN, M.M. *Constitutional and legal history of England.* New York: Harcourt Brace & Co., 1942.
  www.questia.com/PM.qst?a=o&d=553904
  Subscription based.

- POCOCK, J.G.A. *The ancient constitution and the feudal law: a study of English historical thought in the seventeenth century.* New York: W.W.Norton & Co., 1957.
  www.questia.com/PM.qst?a=o&d=61637692
  Subscription based.
- MAY, THOMAS ERSKINE, SIR. *The constitutional history of England from the accession of George III, 1760-1860.* Longmans Green & Co., 1861.
  home.freeuk.net/don-aitken/emayvols.html
- KEITH, ARTHUR BERRIEDALE. *The constitutional history of England from Queen Victoria to George VI.* Macmillan, 1940.
  www.questia.com/PM.qst?a=o&d=95054936
  Subscription based. Continued at /95108779
- Citizenship: a History of People, Rights and Power in Britain
  www.nationalarchives.gov.uk/pathways/citizenship/default.htm

iii. *The Monarchy*
- The British Monarchy
  www.royal.gov.uk/
  The official website; includes history pages.
- Englands Royal History
  www.royalty.nu/Europe/England/
  Pages on each dynasty, *etc.*
- History of the Monarchy
  www.royalinsight.gov.uk/Page5.asp
  Includes chronological lists of the monarchs of England, Scotland, and the United Kingdom, with pages on each dynasty.
- The Monarchy, 1042-1952
  www.spartacus.schoolnet.co.uk/monarchy.htm
  For schools.
- Monarchs
  www.britannia.com/history/history/h6.html
- List of British Monarchs
  www.fact-index.com/L/li/list__of__british__monarchs.html
  With brief biographies; includes Scottish monarchs.
- BROOKE, CHRISTOPHER. *The Saxon and Norman Kings.* B.T.Batsford, 1963.
  www.questia.com/PM.qst?a=o&d=6171724
  Subscription based.

iv. *Office Holders*
- Office Holders in Modern Britain
  www.history.ac.uk/office/index.html
  Chronological lists of the holders of many crown appointments, medieval - 20th c.
- Britain's Prime Ministers
  www.britannia.com/gov/primes/
  Pages on each Prime Minister, 1721-2004.
- Prime Ministers in History
  www.number-10.gov.uk/output/page123.asp
  Brief biographies of prime ministers.
- Prime Ministers 1760-1960
  www.spartacus.schoolnet.co.uk/pm.htm
  Brief biographies. For schools.

v. *Parliament*
- POLLARD, A.F. *The evolution of Parliament.* 2nd ed. Longmans Green & Co., 1926
  www.questia.com/PM.qst?a=o&d=14833042
  Subscription based.
- A Brief Chronology of the House of Commons
  www.parliament.uk/documents/upload/g03.pdf
- The History of Parliament
  www.history.ac.uk/hop/
  Details of a major prosopographical project.
- Women in the House of Commons
  www.parliament.uk/documents/upload/m04.pdf
  19-21st c.
- PIKE, LUKE OWEN. *A constitutional history of the House of Lords.* Macmillan, 1894.
  www.questia.com/PM.qst?a=o&d=78385747
  Subscription based.
- TURBERVILLE, A.S. *The House of Lords in the age of reform, 1784-1837, with an epilogue on aristocracy and the advent of democracy, 1837-1867.* Faber & Faber, 1958.
  www.questia.com/PM.qst?a=o&d=685589
  Subscription based.

vi. *Political Parties*
- Conservative Party Web Sites
  www.conservative-party.net/
  Click on 'History' for gateway to many sites on Conservative history.

- History of the Conservative Party / Stuart Ball
  www.conservatives.com/party/history.cfm
- HARLING, PHILIP. *The waning of old corruption: the politics of economical reform in Britian, 1779-1846.* Oxford: Clarendon Press, 1946.
  www.questia.com/PM.qst?a=o&d=22934056
  Subscription based.
- Conservatism
  www.spartacus.schoolnet.co.uk/conservatives.htm
  Many pages, mainly biographical sketches. For schools
- Liberalism
  www.spartacus.schoolnet.co.uk/Liberal.htm
  Biographies of 18-20th c. politicians; for schools

E. The Church

i. *Directories & Bibliographies*
- English Literature and Religion / William S. Peterson
  www.english.umd.edu/englfac/WPeterson/ELR/elr.htm
  Detailed bibliography; 8000+ entries.
- Mundus: Gateway to Missionary Collections in the United Kingdom
  www.mundus.ac.uk/
  Directory
- Missionary Periodicals Database
  research.yale.edu:8084/missionperiodicals/
  Union list of periodicals published in the U.K., 18-20th c.

ii. *General History Sites*
- Church History
  www.britannia.com/history/church/
  Many essays, some listed individually here; also includes lists of the holders of various ecclesiastical offices.
- History [of the Church]
  www.request.org.uk/main/history/history.htm
  General history of the church, for schools, primarily English history.
- Religion in Britain
  www.spartacus.schoolnet.co.uk/religion.htm
  For schools.
- Church and State
  www.bbc.co.uk/history/lj/churchlj/preview.shtml
  Includes, amongst much else:
  - Ely Cathedral / Carol Davidson Cragoe
  - Kirtling Parish Church / Carol Davidson Cragoe

- Abbeys and Cathedrals / Carol Davidson Cragoe
- The Wider Community / Carol Davidson Cragoe
- The Palace of Westminster / Jacqueline Riding
- St. Stephens Chapel / Jacqueline Riding
- Reformation and Reform / Carol Davidson Cragoe
- The Parochial Revolution / Carol Davidson Cragoe
- MOORMAN, JOHN R.H. *A history of the church in England.* New York: Morehouse-Gorham Co., 1954.
  www.questia.com/PM.qst?a=o&d=10766255
  Subscription based.
- The Development of Christian Society in Early England / Tim Bond
  www.britannia.com/church/bond1.html
  Roman and Anglo-Saxon period.
- The Clergy of the Church of England Database 1540-1835
  www.personal.rdg.ac.uk/~lhstalrs/cced.htm
- Biographical Sketches of Memorable Christians of the Past / James E. Keifer
  justus.anglican.org/resources/bio/
  Includes many British names.
- CADMAN, S. PARKES. *The three religious leaders of Oxford and their movements; John Wycliffe, John Wesley, John Henry Newman.* Macmillan, 1916.
  www.questia.com/PM.qst?a=o&d=2044944
  Subscription based.

iii. *Church of England*
- England, Church of
  www.bartleby.com/65/en/EnglandCh.html
  From the *Columbia encyclopedia.* 6th ed. 2001.
- Anglicanism
  www.newadvent.org/cathen/01498a.htm
  From the *Catholic encyclopedia.*
- Project Canterbury
  justus.anglican.org/resources/pc/
  Original texts relating to the Church of England, 6-19th c.
- *The Book of Common Prayer*
  justus.anglican.org/resources/bcp/
  Includes full text of various editions, 1549-1979.

- *Fasti ecclesiae Anglicanae:* the higher clergy list
  www.history.ac.uk/fasti/index.html
  Includes index, to the printed editions for 1300-1541 and 1541-1837.

iv. *Roman Catholicism*
- T.A.S.C: the Trans-National Database and Atlas of Saints Cults
  www.le.ac.uk/elh/grj1/intro.html
- The Rule of Benedict: an index to texts on-line and gateway to RB: bibliographic index.
  www.osb.org/rb/index.html
- The Catholic Historian's Handbook 1829-1965 / Brian Plumb
  www.catholic-history.org.uk/nwchs/plumb/contents.html

v. *The History of Dissent*
- English Dissenters
  www.exlibris.org/nonconform/engdis/
  Bibliography, with brief notes on each sect.
- Fire and Ice: Puritan and Reformed Writings
  www.puritansermons.com/index.htm
  Includes text of many works by Richard Baxter, Thomas Goodwin, Jonathan Edwards, Robert Hawker, Charles Spurgeon, *etc.,* 17-19th c., also many articles, historical and biographical, *etc.*
- Quaker Electronic Archive and Meeting Place
  www.qis.net/~daruma/
  Includes historical texts 17-20th c., *etc.*
- Quaker Historical Texts
  www.users.voicenet.com/~kuenning/qhp/index.html
  Writings by George Fox, Margaret Fell, *etc.*
- The Quaker Writings Home Page
  www.qhpress.org/quakerpages/qwhp/qwhp.htm
  17-20th c. texts.
- Quaker Women, 17-19th Century / Tina Helfrich
  www.users.globalnet.co.uk/~helfrich/

v. *Jewish History*
- Survey of Jewish Archives in the U.K. and Eire
  www.archives.lib.soton.ac.uk/jewish.shtml

F. Economic History
i. *General*
- CLAPHAM, JOHN, SIR *A Concise economic history of Britain, from the earliest times to 1750.* Cambridge: Cambridge University Press, 1949.
  www.questia.com/PM.qst?a=o&d=5458279
  Subscription based.

ii. *Agricultural & Garden History*
Agriculture
- Ecological Aspects of Agricultural Sustainability c.1576-1946: the archives (study numer 4537)
  hds.essex.ac.uk/studybrowse/showabstract.php?sn=4537
  Database derived from estate records.
- Farming: New Landscapes, New Technologies
  www.rdg.ac.uk/NOF/index.html
  Project to digitise records relating to the Victorian mechanisation of agriculture, and to the 18th c. enclosure of Berkshire.
- Agricultural Revolution in England 1500-1800 / Mark Overton
  www.bbc.co.uk/history/society__culture/industrialisation/
  agricultural__revolution__01.shtml

Garden
- Sources for Garden History
  www.hmc.gov.uk/sheets/14__gardn.htm
- Study Garden History
  www.studygardenhistory.freeserve.co.uk/
- U.K. Database of Historic Parks and Gardens
  www.york.ac.uk/depts/arch/landscapes/ukpg/database/
  Academic listing.

iii. *Labour History*
- Sources for Labour History
  www.hmc.gov.uk/sheets/1__labour.htm
- James Edwin Thorold Rogers 1823-1890
  www.ecn.bris.ac.uk/het/rogers/index.htm
  Includes text of *Six centuries of work and wages: the history of English labour.* 1884.
- Child Labour
  www.spartacus.schoolnet.co.uk/IRchild.htm
  1750-1900; many pages. For schools.

iv. *Business & Financial History*
- Sources for Business History
  www.hmc.gov.uk/business/busarchives.htm
- The Rothschild Archives
  www.rothschildarchive.org/ta/
  Guide to a bank's archives, and to a family's papers, 18-20th c.
- History of Money
  www.ex.ac.uk/~RDavies/arian/llyfr.html
  Includes several pages on British numismatics.
- Course of the Exchange, London, 1698-1823
  www.icpsr.umich.edu:8080/ICPSR-STUDY/01008.xml
  Stock market prices database.

v. *Transport History*
- Transport 1750 to 1900
  www.historylearningsite.co.uk/transport__1750__to__1900.htm
  Pages on roads, canals, coaches, railways, & navvies. For schools
- Milestonesweb: Counting Down the Miles
  www.milestonesweb.com/types.htm
  Includes a gazetteer.

vi. *Specific Industries*
- The Mills Archive
  www.millarchive.com/
  Resources for the history of traditional mills and milling.
- Coal Mining Records in the National Archives
  www.catalogue.nationalarchives.gov.uk/Leaflets/ri2142.htm
  Click on title.
- Mining History Network
  www.ex.ac.uk/~RBurt/MinHistNet
  International in scope, but with some British pages.

vii. *Urban History*
- Small Towns Project
  www.le.ac.uk/urbanhist/urstp.html
- Towns & Cities
  www.spartacus.schoolnet.co.uk/towns.htm
  Very brief notes on the histories of 44 places; for schools
- Portcities U.K.
  www.portcities.org.uk/
  Maritime history of Bristol, Hartlepool, Liverpool, London and Southampton.

viii. *History of Science and Medicine*
- The B.S.H.S. Guide to History of Science Courses in the United Kingdom and Republic of Ireland
  www.bshs.org.uk/
- H.O.S.T: the History of Science and Technology 1801-1914
  www.kcl.ac.uk/depsta/iss/library/speccoll/host/
  Project to catalogue printed and archival resources.
- A History of Photography from its beginnings till the 1920's / Dr. Robin Leggat
  www.rleggat.com/photohistory/
- Med Hist: the guide to History of Medicine Resources on the Internet
  medhist.ac.uk/
- Hospital Records Database
  www.nationalarchives.gov.uk/hospitalrecords/
  Information on the existence and location of hospital records.
- Medical Archives and Manuscripts Survey
  library.wellcome.ac.uk/resources/db__mams.shtml
  Lists manuscripts at 100 record offices, 17-20th c.
- Medical Heritage of Great Britain
  www.medicalheritage.co.uk/
  Gazetteer of historical hospitals and other buildings.
- History in Focus: Medical History
  www.history.ac.uk/ihr/Focus/Medical/index.html
- Whonamedit.com: the world's most comprehensive dictionary of medical eponyms
  www.whonamedit.com
  Biographical dictionary.
- A Chronology of State Medicine, Public Health, Welfare and Related Services in Britain, 1066-1999 / Michael Warren
  www.chronology.org.uk/
- The Plague in England / Anne Roberts
  www.education.guardian.co.uk/higher/humanities/partner/story/
  0,9885,585086,00.html
  Covers 1348-1679.
- Nursing and Midwifery History, U.K. / David J. Wright
  www.shef.ac.uk/~nmhuk/
- Mental Health History Timeline
  www.mdx.ac.uk/www/study/mhhtm.htm
- World of Asylums
  www.worldofasylums.co.uk
  History of lunatic asylums.

- The Hospice History Project
  www.hospice-history.org.uk/
  Project to study the modern hospice movement.
- London's Museums of Health and Medicine
  www.medicalmuseums.org/

G. Social History
i. *Social Customs*
- HUTTON, REGINALD. *The rise and fall of merry England: the ritual year 1400-1700.*
  www.questia.com/PM.qst?a=o&d=23621357
  Subscription based.
- HOULBROOKE, RALPH. *Death, religion, and the family in England, 1480-1750.* Oxford: Oxford University Press, 1998.
  www.questia.com/PM.qst?a=o&d=29320196
  Subscription based.
- To Picture a Plot
  www.geocities.com/Paris/LeftBank/9314/fawkespic2.html
  Images of Gunpowder Plot, 17-20th c., and social history.
- Ten Ages of Christmas / Christine Lalumia
  www.bbc.co.uk/history/society__culture/society/ ten__ages__gallery.shtml
  History of the ways in which Christmas has been celebrated.
- SCHOR, ESTHER. *Bearing the dead: the British culture of mourning from the enlightenment to Victoria.* Princeton: Princeton University Press, 1994.
  www.questia.com/PM.qst?a=o&d=99843997
  Subscription based.
- What Contribution was made by the Alehouse to the life of early modern towns?
  www.elizabethi.org/us/essays/alehouses.htm
- The Pub in Literature
  www.shu.ac.uk/schools/cs/teaching/sle/indexalt.htm
  13-20th c.
- British Society of Sports History World Wide Web Service and Sports History Gateway
  www2.umist.ac.uk/sport/index2.html

ii. *Demography*
- Illegitimacy and illegitimates in English History / Alan Macfarlane
  www.alanmacfarlane.com/TEXTS/BASTARDY.PDF
  Originally published in LASLETT, PETER, *et al. Bastardy and its comparative history.* Arnold, 1980.
- SPRING, EILEEN. *Law, land and family: aristocratic inheritance in England, 1300 to 1800.* Chapel Hill: University of North Carolina Press, 1993.
  www.questia.com/PM.qst?a=o&d=72484289
  Subscription based.

iii. *Womens History*
- Genesis: Developing Access to Women's History Sources in the British Isles
  www.genesis.ac.uk/
  Database listing of resources.
- Emanicipation of Women 1750-1920
  www.spartacus.schoolnet.co.uk/women.htm
  Many pages, especially biographies. For schools.

iv. *Immigrants*
- Black Presence: Asian and Black History in Britain, 1500-1850
  www.nationalarchives.gov.uk/pathways/blackhistory/
- Black People in Britain
  www.spartacus.schoolnet.co.uk/BlackPeople.htm
  Brief biographies, 18-20th c.
- Every Generation
  www.everygeneration.co.uk
  Black history in Britain.
- Black and Asian History Map
  www.channel4.com/history/microsites/B/blackhistorymap/
  Gateway.
- The First Black Britons / Sukhdev Sandhu
  www.bbc.co.uk/history/society__culture/multicultural/ black__britons__01.shtml
- Moving Here: 200 years of Migration to England
  www.movinghere.org.uk

- Bedfordshire and Luton Archives and Records Service: Research Resources for Caribbean Studies and the History of Black and Asian people in the U.K.
  www.casbah.ac.uk/surveys/archivereportBLARS.stm

v. *Education*
- Sources for the History of Education
  www.hmc.gov.uk/sheets/4__educat.htm
- The U.K. Schools History Site
  chrisb.4ce.co.uk/schools__site/index.php
  History of education site for genealogists; gives details of individual schools.
- Education, 1750-1950
  www.spartacus.schoolnet.co.uk/education.htm
  Many pages; for schools

vi. *Newspapers, Pamphlets & Books*
- Concise History of the British Newspaper since 1620
  www.bl.uk/collections/britnews.html
- Sources for the History of the Press
  www.hmc.gov.uk/sheets/10__press.htm
- Book History Online: International Bibliography of the History of the Printed Book and Libraries
  www.kb.nl/kb/bho/index2.html
  International in scope, but much British material.
- BOOKHAD: support for nationwide research in book history and design
  www.bookhad.ac.uk:9080/
- Chez La Veuve: Women Printers in Great Britain 1475-1700: an exhibition at the University of Illinois Library
  gateway.library.uiuc.edu/rbx/exhibit/
- Library History: the British Isles to 1850
  www.r-alston.co.uk/contents.htm
- The British Book Trade Index
  www.bbti.bham.ac.uk/
  List of people in the book trades to 1851.
- Women and Books: from the Sixteenth Century to the Suffragettes
  special.lib.gla.ac.uk/exhibns/women/women.html
- Pamphlet and Polemic: pamphlets as a guide to the controversies of the 17th-19th Centuries
  specialcollections.st-andrews.ac.uk/projpamph.htm
  Description of collections at Lampeter and St. Andrews.

vii. *The Law, Crime and Policing*
- English Legal History Materials / Robert Palmer
  vi.uh.edu/pages/bib/elhone/elhmat.html
- HALE, MATTHW. *The history of the common law of England.* 1713
  socserv2.socsci.mcmaster.ca/=econ/ugcm/3ll3/hale/common
- Sources for the History of Crime and the Law in England
  www.hmc.gov.uk/sheets/9__crime.htm
- Legislation 1760-1960
  www.spartacus.schoolnet.co.uk/legislation.htm
  Brief notes for schools on the history of many pieces of legislation, from the Riot Act 1715 to the National Health Service Act, 1948
- Early Modern Bibliographies: Crime, Law and Order
  www.earlymodernweb.org.uk/embiblios/emcrimebib.htm
- Crime and Punishment
  www.learningcurve.gov.uk/candp/default.htm
  Includes facsimiles of original sources, medieval-20th c.
- Outlaws and Highwaymen: the history of the highwaymen and their predecessors, the medieval outlaws
  www.outlawsandhighwaymen.com/
  Includes original sources.
- The History of Police and Policing in the United Kingdom: an annotated searchable bibliography / Stanley D. Nash
  www.scc.rutgers.edu/policeBiblio/policeintro.html

G. Historic Buildings & Vernacular Architecture
- Sources for Architectural History
  www.hmc.gov.uk/sheets/11__archi.htm
- Sources for Building History: a guide to researching historic buildings in the British Isles / Jean Manco
  www.building-history.pwp.blueyonder.co.uk/
- Bibliography of the Vernacular Architecture Group
  ads.ahds.ac.uk/catalogue/library/vagbiblio/
- PEACE, DAVID. *Historic buildings and planning policies.* C.B.A. occasional paper, 1979.
  ads.ahds.ac.uk/catalogue/library/cba/op10.cfm
- A History of British Architecture / Adrian Tinniswood
  www.bbc.co.uk/history/society__culture/architecture/architecture__01.shtml

- The Great Buildings Collection
  www.greatbuildings.com
  International in scope, but including much information on particular British buildings.
- Pevsner Architectural Guides and the Buildings Books Trust
  www.pevsner.co.uk/
  Details of Pevsner's series of guides.
- Looking at Buildings
  www.lookingatbuildings.org.uk/
- The recording of architecture and its publication
  ads.ahds.ac.uk/catalogue/library/cba/rr2.cfm
  Reprinted from *Archaeologia Cambrensis,* **104,** 1955.
- ALCOCK, N.W. *Cruck construction: an introduction and catalogue.*
  C.B.A. research report **42.** 1981.
  ads.ahds.ac.uk/catalogue/library/cba/rr42.cfm
- Notes on the Investigation of smaller domestic buildings.
  ads.ahds.ac.uk/catalogue/library/cba/rr3.cfm
  Reprinted from *Archaeologia Cambrensis,* **104,** 1955.
- Survey of the Jewish Built Heritage in the United Kingdom and Ireland
  www.mucjs.org/HERITAGE/
- Sources for Architectural History at Lambeth Palace Library
  www.lambethpalacelibrary.org
  Click on 'source guides' and 'architectural history'.
- Church Crawler
  www.churchcrawler.co.uk
  Church architecture.
- Abbeys and Cathedrals / Carol Davidson Cragoe
  www.bbc.co.uk/history/lj/churchlj/cathedral__01.shtml
  Church architecture, 11-16th c.
- The History of Plumbing: Roman and English legacy
  www.theplumber.com/eng.html
- The Men that Made the Water Closet
  www.theplumber.com/closet.html

H. Military & Naval History
- Military History: Your Guide to Resources
  www.nationalarchives.gov.uk/militaryhistory/
- Naval History: Great Britain
  www.bruzelius.info/Nautica/Naval-History/GB/TOC.html
  Original sources, 16-19th c.

- Survey of the Papers of Senior U.K. Defence Personnel, 1793-1975
  archive.lib.soton.ac.uk/military/shtml
- LLOYD, CHRISTOPHER. *The nation and the Navy: a history of naval life and policy.* Cresset Press, 1961.
  www.questia.com/PM.qst?a=o&d=5388608
  Subscription based.
- Battles and Major Skirmishes in Great Britain 55 B.C. - 1797 / John E. Muter
  www.geocities.com/Broadway/Alley/5443/bloody1.htm
  List of battles.
- British Battles
  www.britainexpress.com/History/battles/index.htm
  Discussion of many battles, 878-1746.
- The Threat of Invasion 1066-1789: an overview
  www.bbc.co.uk/history/war/invasion__threat__01.shtml
- English Battles and Sieges
  web.ukonline.co.uk/glenn.foard/contents.htm
  Pages on the Wars of the Roses, the English Civil War, Battlefield Archaeology, *etc.*
- History Trails: Wars & Conflict
  www.bbc.co.uk/history/lj/preview.shtml
  Includes:
  - Towards a Standing Army / Professor Richard Holmes
  - Gone for a Soldier / Professor Richard Holmes
  - From Musket to Breech Loader / Professor Richard Holmes
  - From the Field Gun to the Tank / Professor Richard Holmes
  - Women at War / Peter Caddick-Adams
  - The Home Front / Peter Caddick-Adams
  - Art from the Frontline / Roger Tolson
- Trafalgar to Korea: Five British Battles, 1805 to 1951
  www.nationalarchives.gov.uk/pathways/battles/default.htm
  Trafalgar 1805; Crimea 1854; Egypt 1882; D-Day 1944; Korea 1951
- Land Forces of Britain, the Empire and Commonwealth
  www.regiments.org/milhist/
  Many pages on regiments, particular wars and rebellions, and military history in general.

I. Discovery & Empire

i. *Reference Resources*

- The English and British Empires, c.1497-1800
  cbss26.ucs.edu/britem.html
  Gazetteer of territories
- Discoverers Web
  www.win.tue.nl/cs/fm/engels/discovery/
  Gateway, international in scope, but linking to many pages on British explorers.
- The British Empire: an internet gateway / Jane Sansom
  www.ualberta.ca/~janes/EMPIRE.HTM
  Many broken links.
- British Empire Studies
  pages.britishlibrary.net/empirehist/
  Includes gateway, mailing list, directory of scholars, select bibliography, and introductory survey.
- Internet African History Sourcebook
  www.fordham.edu/halsall/africa/africasbook.html
  Includes much on the British Empire in Africa.
- Internet Indian History Sourcebook
  www.fordham.edu/halsall/india/indiabook.html
  Includes much on British rule.
- Sources for Imperial and Commonwealth History
  www.hmc.gov.uk/sheets/2__colony.htm
- The English and British Empires, c.1497-1800
  www.cbsr.ucr.edu/britem.html
  Gazetteer of territories.
- Sources for Maritime History
  www.hmc.gov.uk/sheets/12__marit.htm
- The Maritime History Virtual Archive
  www.bruzelius.info/Nautica/Nautica.html
  Many pages; international in scope, with some British content

ii. *Discovery*

- Exploration and Settlement
  www.heritage.nf.ca/exploration/es__contents.html
  General history of exploration in the North Atlantic.
- Voyages of Discovery
  www.nhm.ac.uk/museum/tempexhib/voyages/index.html
  Pages on the voyages of famous explorers.

iii. *Empire*

- WINKS, ROBIN W., ed. *The historiography of the British Commonwealth.* Durham, N.C.: Duke University Press, 1966.
  www.questia.com/PM.qst?a=o&d=95979809
  Subscription based.
- The British Empire
  www.britishempire.co.uk/
- British Empire
  www.learningcurve.nationalarchives.gov.uk/empire/default.htm
  Includes facsimiles of original sources.
- History in Focus: Empire
  www.history.ac.uk/ihr/Focus/Empire/
  The study of British Empire history.
- LLOYD, T.O. *The British Empire 1558-1995.* 2nd ed. Oxford. Oxford University Press, 1995.
  www.questia.com/PM.qst?a=o&d=27709944
  Subscription based.
- THORNTON, A.P. *The Imperial idea and its enemies: a study in British power.* Macmillan, 1959.
  www.questia.com/PM.qst?a=o&d=94910304
  Subscription based.
- CAIN, P.J., & HOPKINS, A.G. *British imperialism: innovation and expansion, 1688-1914.* Longman, 1993.
  www.questia.com/PM.qst?a=o&d=24219275
  Subscription based.
- Trade and the British Empire: a Symbiotic Relationship / Professor Kenneth Morgan
  www.bbc.co.uk/history/state/empire/trade__empire__01.shtml
- LAWS, PHILIP. *The East India Company: a history.* Longman, 1993.
  www.questia.com/PM.qst?a=o&d=14109194
  Subscription based.
- GRIFFITHS, PERCIVAL, SIR. *The British impact on India.* Macdonald, 1952.
  www.questia.com/PM.qst?a=o&d=6504181
  Subscription based.

11. Prehistory

1. General
- The Prehistoric Period
  www.britannia.com/history/h20.html
  Many pages.
- Earth Mysteries: an introduction
  witcombe.sbc.edu/earthmysteries/EMIntro.html
  Includes many pages on prehistoric sites; takes topics such as ley-lines and geomancy more seriously than academics would.

2. Palaeolithic
- A.H.O.B: Ancient Human Occupation of Britain
  www.nhm.ac.uk/hosted__sites/ahob/index__2.html
  Project to determine when men first occupied Britain.
- ROE, DEREK A. *A gazetteer of British lower and middle palaeolithic sites.* C.B.A. research report 8. 1968.
  ads.ahds.ac.uk/catalogue/library/cba/rr8.cfm
- BARTON, N., ROBERTS, A.J., & ROE, D.A., eds. *The late glacial in north-west Europe: human adaptation and environmental change at the end of the Pleistocene.* C.B.A. research report 77. 1991.
  ads.ahds.ac.uk/catalouge/library/cba/rr77.cfm

3. Mesolithic
- WYMER, J.J., ed. *Gazetteer of Mesolithic sites in England and Wales.* C.B.A. research report 20. 1977.
  ads.ahds.ac.uk/catalogue/library/cbarr20.cfm
- Flint Shaping Techniques / Daniel Beesley
  thearchof.topcities.com/Prehistoric/flint__tech.htm
- Chert Use in the Mesolithic of Northern England / D. Hind
  www.shef.ac.uk/assem/4/4hind.html
- Living with the Dead: Unparalleled Behaviour in Britain and Ireland from the early tenth to the late fifth millenium B.P. / Martin King.
  ads.ahds.ac.uk/catalogue/specColl/lwtd/
  Database of prehistoric human remains.

4. Neolithic
- Human Bones from the Southern British Neolithic / Alasdair Whittle
  www.cf.ac.uk/hisar/archaeology/projects/bones/
- Outlining the Major Changes that Occurred during the Late Neolithic in England / David Beesley
  thearchof.topcities.com/Prehistoric/late__neo.htm
- C.B.A. Database of Implement Petrology for Britain
  ads.ahds.ac.uk/catalogue/projArch/petro__cba__1999/
  Records of stone implements.
- CLOUGH, T.H.McK., & CUMMINS, W.A., eds. *Stone axe studies.* C.B.A. research report 23. 1979.
  ads.ahds.ac.uk/catalogue/library/cba/rr23.cfm
- CLOUGH, T.H.McK., & CUMMINS, W.A. eds. *Stone axe studies, volume 2: the petrology of prehistoric stone implements from the British Isles.* C.B.A. research report 67. 1988.
  ads.ahds.ac.uk/catalogue/library/cba/rr67.cfm

Megaliths
- The Megalithic Portal
  www.megalithic.co.uk/
  For the layman.
- BRADLEY, RICHARD. *Altering the earth: the origins of monuments in Britain and continental Europe.* Society of Antiquaries of Scotland monograph series 8. 1993.
  ads.ahds.ac.uk/catalogue/library/psas/monograph08.cfm
- Beyond Stonehenge: exploring Britain's other megalithic mysteries / Marcus Wohlsen
  gorp.away.com/gorp/location/europe/uk/uk__mega.htm
- Ancient Stones - a photographic guide to the stone circles of Britain
  www.ancientstones.co.uk/
- Megalithia
  www.anima.demon.co.uk/
  Photographs of standing stones.
- Megalithics
  www.ukonline.co.uk/megalithics/
  4,000 photographs of British megaliths.
- The Megalith Map, in association with Aubrey Burl: a resource for finding any stone circle or row in England, Ireland, Scotland or Wales
  www.megalith.ukf.net/bigmap.htm
- Prehistoric Stone Circles & Rows: a dowsers perspective
  www.sover.net/~ihoneywo/
- Rock Art in the British Landscape
  groups.msn.com/rockartinthebritishlandscape/
  homepage.msnw?pgmarket=en-us

5. Bronze Age

- The British Bronze Age
  www.angelfire.com/me/ij/britishBA.html
  Introductory.
- Assessing the Evidence for Chieftains in the Early Bronze Age of Southern England and Brittany / Daniel Beesley
  thearchof.topcities.com/Prehistoric/EBA.htm
- Later Prehistoric Pottery Gazetteer
  www.arch.soton.ac.uk/Research/PotteryGazetteer/index.html
- Bronze Age Craft
  www.bronze-age-craft.com/

6. Iron Age

- Burials as Indicators of Social Status with special reference to Iron Age Britain / Daniel Beesley
  thearchof.topcities.com/Prehistoric/IA__burials.htm
- World of the Celts
  www.gallica.co.uk/celts/index.htm
  Pages on ancient Britain.
- Celtic Inscribed Stones: Language, Location and Environment
  www.ucl.ac.uk/archaeology/cisp/database/
  Includes database of stones.
- The Development of Fortification through the First Millenium B.C. / Daniel Beesley
  thearchof.topcities.com/Prehistoric/fortification.htm
- Vitrification of Hill Forts: gazetteer of vitrified fires
  www.brigantesnation.com/VitrifiedForts/VitrifiedForts.htm
  i.e. destroyed by fire.
- Brigantes Nation
  www.brigantesnation.com/
- CUNLIFFE, BARRY. *Coinages and society in Britain and Gaul: some current problems.* C.B.A. research report, **38**, 1981.
  ads.ahds.ac.uk/catalogue/library/cba/rr38.cfm
  Pre-Roman iron age.
- The Celtic Coin Index
  www.writer2001.com/cciwriter2001/

12. Roman Britain

1. General

- The Roman Period, 55 B.C.-410 A.D.
  www.britannia.com/history/h30.html
  Many pages
- The Romans in Britain
  www.open2.net/romans/
- The Romans in Britain: the history of the Romans in Britain 100 B.C. to 450 A.D.
  www.romans-in-britain.org.uk/
  Many pages, including details of sites to visit.
- Roman Britain.ORG
  www.roman-britain.org/
  Extensive amateur site; includes gazetteer of sites (click on 'maps of Roman Britain').
- COLLINGWOOD, R.G.F.B.A., & MYRES, J.N.L. *Roman Britain and the English settlements.* New York: Biblo & Tannen, 1990.
  www.questia.com/PM.qst?a=o&d=22805683
  Subscription based. Authoritative.
- Roman Britain: a Bibliography of Sources
  www.btinternet.com/~britannica/
  Not updated since 1999, but still a useful bibliography, with some links.
- BLAIR, PETER HUNTER. *Roman Britain and early England, 55 B.C. - A.D. 871.* Edinburgh: T. Nelson, 1963.
  www.questia.com/PM.qst?a=o&d=54400068
  Subscription based.
- Celtic Peoples of Roman Britain
  www.britannia.com/history/tribes.html
  Map.
- Romano-British Place Names
  users.breathe.com/kmatthews/RB__placenames.html

2. The Conquest

- Roman Influence in Britain before the Conquest
  thearchof.topcities.com/Roman/roman__influence.htm
- Comparing the Likely Motives of Caesar and Claudius invading Britain: what sort of archaeological evidence might we find? / Daniel Beesley
  thearchof.topcities.com/Roman/caesar__and__claudius.htm

- The Life of Gnaeus Julius Agricola / Tacitus
  www.unrv.com/tacitus/tacitusagricola.php
  In English translation. Partly on the Roman subjection of Britain.
- TACITUS. *Annals*. Book XIV. Chapters 29-37
  www.britannia.com/history/docs.tacitus.html
  Account of Boudicca's rebellion
- In Boudicea's Footsteps
  www.channel4.com/history/microsites/H/history/heads/footnotes/
                                                                footboud.html

3. Roman Towns

- GREEP, STEPHEN J. *Roman towns: the Wheeler inheritance. A review of 50 years research*. C.B.A. research report **93**. 1993.
  ads.ahds.ac.uk/catalogue/library/cba/rr93.cfm
- The Evidence for the Development of Urban Fortifications in Roman Britain / Daniel Beesley.
  thearchof.topcities.com/Roman/roman__urban.htm
- MALONEY, JOHN, & HOBLEY, BRIAN. eds. *Roman urban defences in the West*. C.B.A. research report **51**. 1983.
  ads.ahds.ac.uk/catalogue/library/cba/rr51.cfm
  Includes papers on Britain.
- GREW, FRANCIS, & HOBLEY, BRIAN. eds. *Roman urban topography in Britain and the Western Empire*. C.B.A. research report **59**. 1985.
  ads.ahds.ac.uk/catalogue/library/cba/rr59.cfm
- JOHNSON, PETER, *et al*, eds. *Architecture in Roman Britain*. C.B.A. research report **94**. 1996.
  ads.ahds.ac.uk/catalogue/library/cba/rr94.cfm

4. Roman Villas & Rural Settlement

- THOMAS, CHARLES, ed. *Rural settlement in Roman Britain*. C.B.A. research report **7**. 1966.
  ads.ahds.ac.uk/catalogue/library/cba/rr7.cfm
- Ancient Landscapes, Information Systems and Computers
  www2.cmp.ueaa.ac.uk/Research/researchareas/JWMP/
  Study of Roman cadastral systems, i.e. land surveys.
- Romano-British Villas: some current problems. Report of a conference held by the Council for British Archaeology, July 1955
  ads.ahds.ac.uk/catalogue/library/cba/rr1.cfm
  From the *Archaeological newsletter,* 6(2), 1955, 28-55.
- Roman Villas in the North of England / Martin Burroughs
  ads.ahds.ac.uk/catalogue/projArch/villas__na__2003/

- What Evidence is there to indicate that the Villa Estates of Roman Britain represent State-of-the-art Farming Enterprise? / Daniel Beesley
  thearchof.topcities.com/Roman/villas.htm

5. Military History

- Britannia: the Roman Army & Navy in Britannia 55 B.C. - 410 A.D.
  www.morgue.demon.co.uk/
- JOHNSTON, D.E. *The Saxon Shore*. C.B.A. research report **18**. 1977.
  ads.ahds.ac.uk/catalogue/library/cba/rr18.cfm
- The Saxon Shore Forts
  www.ee.surrey.ac.uk/Personal/R.Clarke/ShoreForts/
- The Saxon Shore: How reasonable is the view that there is a 'parity of hard facts' about it? / Daniel Beesley
  thearchof.topcities.com/Roman/saxon__shore.htm

6. Pottery

- WEBSTER, GRAHAM, ed. *Romano-British coarse pottery: a students guide*. C.B.A. research report **6**. 3rd ed. 1976.
  ads.ahds.ac.uk/catalogue/library/cba/rr6.cfm
- DETSICAS, ALEC, ed. *Current research in Romano-British coarse pottery*. C.B.A. research report **10**. 1973.
  ads.ahds.ac.uk/catalogue/library/cba/rr10.cfm
- Structure of Romano-British pottery kilns / Philip Corder
  ads.ahds.ac.uk/catalogue/library/cba/rr5.cfm
  Reprinted from *The archaeological journal* **114**, 1957, 10-27.
- Potsherd
  www.potsherd.uklinux.net/
  Roman pottery in Britain.

7. *Writing Tablets*

- A Corpus of Writing Tablets from Roman Britain (A British Academy Research Project)
  www.csad.ox.ac.uk/RIB/RIBIV/
- Vindolanda / Dr. Mike Ibeji
  www.bbc.co.uk/history/ancient/romans/vindolanda__01.shtml
  Study of Roman writing tablets.
- Vindolanda Tablets Online
  vindolanda.csad.ox.ac.uk/
  Includes text of writing tablets.

8. Miscellaneous Sites

- TAYLOR, JOAN DU PLAT, & CLEERE, HENRY, eds. *Roman shipping and trade: Britain and the Rhine provinces.* C.B.A. research report **24**. 1978.
  ads.ahds.ac.uk/catalogue/library/cba/rr24.cfm
- The Roman Shipwrecks Project
  www.arch.soton.ac.uk/Research/PuddingPan/
  Project to locate wrecks.
- Birmingham Roman Roads Project
  web.bham.ac.uk/leathepd/
- REECE, RICHARD, ed. *Burial in the Roman world.* C.B.A. research report **22**.
  ads.ahds.ac.uk/catalogue/library/cba/rr22.cfm

13. Britain c.400-600

A. Bibliography *etc.*

- [Britain (sub-Roman)]: Bibliography
  www.the-orb.net/encyclop/early/origins/rom-celt/biblio1.html
- Bibliographies: Arthur's Britain / Lynn Nelson
  www.the-orb.net/bibliographies/arthur.html
- A Gazetteer of Sub-Roman Sites
  intarch.ac.uk/journal/issue3/snyder__index.html
  Subscription based.

B. General History

- Adventus Saxonum / Michael Veprauskas
  www.britannia.com/history/ebk/articles/adventus1.html
  The Anglo-Saxon invasion.
- The Ruin and Conquest of Britain 400 A.D.-600 A.D: a reconstruction / Howard Wiseman
  www.cit.gu.edu.au/~sctwiseh/DECB/DECB.html
- The Dark Origins of Britain
  www.bbc.co.uk/radio4/history/dark__origins.shtml
  5-6th c. history.
- The End of Roman Britain: assessing the Anglo-Saxon invasions of the fifth century / William Bakken
  www.mnsu.edu/emuseum/prehistory/vikings/asinv.html
- MYRES, J.N.L. *The English settlements.* Oxford: Oxford University Press, 1989.
  www.questia.com/PM.qst?a=o&d=54426042
  Subscription based.

C. The Britons and their Kingdoms

- Anglo-Celtic Relations in the Early Middle Ages
  www.mun.ca/mst/heroicage/issues/4/toc.html
  Collection of articles in *The heroic age,* issue 4.
- Ancient Celts Page / Simon James
  www.ares.u-net.com/celtindx.htm
- Early British Kingdom / David Nash Ford
  www.earlybritishkingdoms.com/
- Early British Kingdoms / David Nash Ford
  www.britannia.com/history/ebk/
  6th c. Extensive.

D. The Arthurian Tradition
- The Quest: an Arthurian resource
  www.uidaho.edu/student_orgs/arthurian_legend/
- Arthurian Resources
  www.arthuriana.co.uk/
  Arthur in legend and history; includes bibliography.
- King Arthur
  www.britannia.com/history/h12.html
  Many pages on the legend and its historical background.
- Early Arthurian Tradition: text and context
  www.mun.ca/mst/heroicage/issues/1/hatoc.htm
  Collection of articles in *The heroic age*, issue 1, on Britain, 5-6th c.
- Royal Interest in Glastonbury and Cadbury: two Arthurian itineraries, 1278 and 1331 / Caroline Shenton
  www.findarticles.com/cf_dls/m0293/459_114/58282445/p1/article.jhtml
  From the *English historical review*, 11/1999.
- Vortigern Studies: British History 400-600
  www.vortigernstudies.org.uk/
- Vortigern
  www.britannia.com/history/biographies/vortig.html

E. Written Evidence: Gildas
- St. Gildas 504 A.D. - 570 A.D.
  www.webmesh.co.uk/gildashomepage.htm
  English translation of *De excidio Britanniae.*
- Gildas (c.504-570): Works
  www.fordham.edu/halsall/basis/gildas-full.

14. The Anglo-Saxons

A. *Gateways, Bibliographies, etc.*
- Early British and Viking Resource Pages
  www.lauraloft.com/history/history.htm
  Gateway to Anglo-Saxons, Viking, and Norman conquest web-sites.
- Electronic Medievalia: Anglo-Saxonica / L.J.Swain
  www.mun.ca/mst/heroicage/issues/2/ha2webcol.htm
- WWW-VL History: Anglo-Saxon Britain
  www.ku.edu/kansas/uk-med/anglo-saxons.html
  Gateway.
- The Independent Scholar: Internet Resources in Medieval Studies / Brad Eden
  www.mun.ca/mst/heroicage/issues/4/eden.html
- Anglo-Saxon History: a select bibliography / Simon Keynes
  www.wmich.edu/medieval/research
- Anglo-Saxon Studies: a select bibliography / C.P.Biggam. 3rd edition
  bubl.ac.uk/docs/bibliog/biggam/

B. General Studies
- Early Medieval Britain and Ireland
  www.postroman.info/index.htm
  Includes text of the *Anglo-Saxon chronicle*, Gildas's *De excidio Britanniae*, and Nennius's *Historia Brittonum*, plus much else.
- Anglo-Saxons.net: England c.450-1066 in a Nutshell / Sean Miller
  www.anglo-saxons.net/
- The Saxon Period, 597-1066 A.D.
  www.britannia.com/history/h50.html
  Many pages, including lists of the kings of numerous kingdoms.
- Anglo-Saxon England
  www.britainexpress.com/History/dark_ages_index.htm
  Basic information only.
- Anglo-Saxon Attitudes
  www.mun.ca/mst/heroicage/issues/3/toc/html
  Collection of articles in *The heroic age*, issue 3.
- Octavia, her Domain
  www.octavia.net
  Essays on various aspects of Anglo-Saxon life

- DANIEL, GLYN. *The Anglo-Saxons.* Ancient people and places. New York: Praeger, 1960.
  www.questia.com/PM.qst?a=o&d=89176591
  Subscription based.
- ROSENTHAL, JOEL T. *Angles, Angels and conquerors, 400-1154.* New York: Knopf, 1973.
  www.questia.com/PM.qst?a=o&d=9370127
  Subscription based.
- Connections and interconnections: the British Isles and the Continent 400-1000
  www.mun.ca/mst/heroicage/issues/6/toc.html
  Collections of articles in *The Heroic age,* issue 6.
- Why did the Anglo-Saxons not become more British? / Bryan Ward-Perkins
  www.findarticles.com/cf__dls/m0293/462__115/62980101/p1/article.jhtml
  From the *English historical review,* 6/2000.
- History Trail: Conquest
  www.bbc.co.uk/history/lj/conquestLj/preview.shtml
  Includes, amongst much else:
  - The Sermon of the Wolf / Michael Wood (on the pre-Conquest identity of England)
  - Keeping Order / Michael Wood (in Anglo-Saxon England)
  - Loot and Land / Dr. Anna Ritchie (Viking invasions, 8-9th c.)
  - Alcuin of York / Dr. Anna Ritchie
  - Legacy of the Vikings / Dr. Elaine Treharne
  - Conquest / Michael Wood (1066)
  - Conquered / Michael Wood (11th c. Anglo-Saxons under Norman Rule)
- The Norman Yoke / Michael Wood
- Anglo-Saxon England
  www.musu.edu/emuseum/prehistory/vikings/angsaxe.html
  Includes thesis, 'King Cnut and the Anglo-Saxon church'/ William Bakken, *etc.*.
- Anglo-Saxonists from the 16th through the 20th Century
  www.u-arizona.edu/~ctb/saxon.html
  Bibliography.

C. Archaeological Evidence
- Anglo-Saxon Archaeology
  www.gla.ac.uk/Acad/Archaeology/resources/Anglo-Saxon/
  Links page.

- Anglo-Saxon Cemeteries
  www.gla.ac.uk/Acad/Archaeology/resources/Anglo-Saxon/cemeteries/index.html
  Database.
- Missing, presumed Buried? Bone diagenesis and the under-representation of Anglo-Saxon children / Jo Buckberry
  www.shef.ac.uk/assem/5/buckberr.html
- Pottery
  www.regia.org/pottery.htm
  Introduction to Anglo-Saxon pottery studies.
- Anglo-Saxon pottery: a symposium / G. C. Dunning, *et al.*
  ads.ahds.ac.uk/catalogue/library/cba/rr4.cfm
  Reprinted from *Medieval archaeology* 3, 1959.
- Corpus of Anglo-Saxon Stone Sculpture
  www.dur.ac.uk/corpus/
- Jean Mary Cook: Early Anglo-Saxon Buckets: a corpus of copper alloy and iron bound stave-built vessels
  ads.ahds.ac.uk/catalogue/projArch/buckets__var__2003/

D. Written Evidence
i. *The Anglo-Saxon Chronicle*
- The Anglo-Saxon Chronicle
  www.georgetown.edu/labyrinth/library/oe/texts/asc/index.html
  Details of the various versions, with some transcriptions, *etc.* In progress.
- The Anglo-Saxon Chronicle
  www.yale.edu/lawweb/avalon/angsax/angsax.htm
  Includes a translation.
- The Anglo-Saxon Chronicle
  sunsite/berkeley.edu/OMACL/Anglo/
  Translation as published by Everyman Press, 1912.
- The Anglo-Saxon Chronicle
  www.britannia.com/history/docs/asintro2.html
  Full translation, originally published in this version. Everyman Press, 1912.

ii. *Annales Cambriae*
- The *Annales Cambriae,* 447-954 (the *annals of Wales*)
  www.fordham.edu/halsall/source/annalescambriae.html
  English translation.

iii. *Historia Brittonum*

- Historia Brittonum / Nennius. Keith J. Matthews (ed.)
  historicaltextarchive.com/sections.php?op=viewarticle&artid=69
  See also =68

iv. Anglo-Saxon Charters & Laws

- British Academy / Royal Historical Society Joint Committee on Anglo-Saxon Charters
  www.trin.cam.ac.uk/chartwww/charthome.html
- Anglo-Saxon charters: the new *Regesta regum Anglorum*. A searchable edition of the corpus of Anglo-Saxon royal diplomas 670-1066 / Dr. Sean Miller
  www.trin.cam.ac.uk/chartwww/NewRegReg.html
- STENTON, F. M. *The Latin charters of the Anglo-Saxon period*. Oxford: Clarendon Press, 1955.
  www.questia.com/PM.qst?a=o&d=10271247
  Subscription based.
- The Tribal Hidage
  www.georgetown.edu/labyrinth/library/oe/texts/hidage.html
- Medieval Sourcebook: the Anglo-Saxon Dooms
  www.fordham.edu/halsall/source/560-975dooms.html
  Anglo-Saxon law codes.
- Anglo-Saxon Law: Extracts from Early Laws of the English
  www.yale.edu/lawweb/avalon/medieval/saxlaw.htm
- Laws of Alfred and Ine
  www.georgetown.edu/labyrinth/library/oe/texts/prose/laws.html
  In Old English.

v. *Ecclesiastical Sources*

- The Durham Liber Vitae Project
  www.kcl.ac.uk/humanities/cch/dlv/
  9th c. manuscript, added to until 16th c., listing names associated with Lindisfarne or possibly Monkwearmouth / Jarrow.
- Old English Homilies (Homily), 600(?)-1200(?)
  www.litencyc.com/php/stopics.php?rec=true&UID=1269
- The Old English Martyrology: an annotated bibliography / Christine Rauer
  www.st-andrews.ac.uk/~cr30/martyrology/
- The Lindisfarne Gospels
  www.bl.uk/whatson/exhibitions/lindisfarne/lind__hi/htm?top
  Facsimile of an 8th c. manuscript.
- The Lindisfarne Gospels
  www.lindisfarnegospels.org/
  Gateway to web resources.
- The Book of Deer
  www.lib.cam.ac.uk/book__of__deer/
  10th century gospel book; the earliest surviving Scottish manuscript.

E. Kingdoms & Kings

- Chronicle of the Kings of England: the Anglo-Saxon Kings / William of Malmesbury, d.1143?
  www.fordham.edu/halsall/source/malmsbury-chronicle1.html
  Selections; translated from Latin.
- Regnal Lists
  hometown.aol.com/rdavidh218/britishroyalty.html
  Of British kings and queens, pre 1000, including mythical monarchs such as Albion, Brutus, *etc.*
- HOLLISTER, C. WARREN. *Anglo-Saxon military institutions.* Oxford: Clarendon Press, 1962.
  www.questia.com/PM.qst?a=o&d=89045237
- The Anglo-Saxon Fyrd c.400-878 A.D.
  www.regia.org/fyrd1.htm
  Continued to 1066 at **/fyrd2.htm**
- The Battle of Maldon 991 A.D.
  www.airflow.net/maldon/
- Dr. Sam Newton's Wuffings Website
  www.wuffings.co.uk/
  Anglo-Saxon Kingdom of the Wuffings in East Anglia
- Anglo Saxon Suffolk: Kingdom of East Anglia
  www.visit-suffolk.org.uk/anglo__saxon__suffolk/
- Edmund of East Anglia / Paul E. Szarmach (ed.)
  www.wmich.edu/medieval/research/rawl/edmund/index.html
  Anglo-Saxon King; includes original sources.
- ABBO OF FLEURY. *The martyrdom of St. Edmund, King of East Anglia.* 870.
  www.fordham.edu/halsall/source/870abbo-edmund.html
- Alfred the Great
  www.ogdoad.force9.co.uk/alfred/alfredintro.htm
- DUCKETT, ELEANOR SHIPLEY. *Alfred the Great.* Chicago: University of Chicago Press, 1956.
  www.questia.com/PM.qst?a=o&d=9697592
  Subscription based.

- King Alfred the Great / Ken Roberts
  www.mirror.org/people/ken.roberts/king.alfred.html
  Essay; many links.
- A Biographical Sketch of Cnut the Great, Emperor of the North / William Bakken
  www.mnsu.edu/emuseum/prehistory/vikings/cnutaut.html
- The Life of King Edward the Confessor
  www.lib.cam.ac.uk/MSS/Ee.3.59/
  Facsimile of a 13th c. manuscript.
- The Lands and Revenues of Edward the Confessor / J. L. Grassi
  www.findarticles.com/cf__dls/m0293/471__117/86230452/pl/article.jhtml
  From the *English historical review*, 4/2002.

F. Religion
- Anglo-Saxon Heathenism
  www.englishheathenism.homestead.com
- BUTLER, L.A.S. & MORRIS, R.K., eds. *The Anglo-Saxon church: papers on history, architecture and archaeology in honour of Dr. H. M. Taylor.* C.B.A. research report **60**. 1986.
  ads.ahds.ac.uk/catalogue/library/cba/rr60.cfm
- GODFREY, JOHN. *The church in Anglo-Saxon England.* Cambridge: Cambridge University Press, 1962.
  www.questia.com/PM.qst?a=o&d=3737110
  Subscription based.
- The Naming of Bishop Ithamar / R. Sharpe
  www.findarticles.com/cf__dls/m0293/473__117/92203927/pl/article.jhtml
  From the *English historical review*, In 644.
- Finding the Forger: an alleged decree of the 679 Council of Hatfield / Catherine Cubitt
  www.findarticles.com/cf__dls/m0293/459__114/58282444/pl/article.jhtml
  From the *English historical review*, 11/1999. Ecclesiastical government.
- Corpus Christi College ms.197
  image.ox.ac.uk/show?collection=corpus&manuscript=ms197
  Facsimile of a 10th c manuscript containing the rule of St. Benedict in Latin and Old English.
- Church
  www.britannia.com/bios/saints/
  Biographies of Anglo-Saxon and Celtic saints.

G. Social & Economic History
- RACKHAM, JAMES. *Environment and economy in Anglo-Saxon England: a review of recent work on the environmental archaeology of rural and urban Anglo-Saxon settlements in England.* C.B.A. research report **89**. 1994.
  ads.ahds.ac.uk/catalogue/library/cba/rr89.cfm
- Anglo-Saxon England: settlement - rural and town life / G. R. Jones
  www.le.ac.uk/elh/grj1/asl.html
- Anglo-Saxon Plant Name Survey
  www2.arts.gla.ac.uk/SESLL/EngLang/ihsl/projects/plants.htm
- Cattle-tracking in the Fonthill Letter / Carol Hough
  www.findarticles.com/cf__dls__m0293/463__115/66274347/pl/article.jhtml
  From the *English historical review*, 9/2000. Anglo-Saxon legal dispute.
- The Kings Thegns of England on the Eve of the Norman Conquest / David Roffe
  www.roffe.freeserve.co.uk/thegns.htm
  Includes lists for some counties; ongoing project.
- English and Norman Society / Dr. Mike Ibeji
  www.bbc.co.uk/history/war/normans/society__01.shtml
  Comparison on the eve of the Conquest.
- HODGES, RICHARD, & HOBLEY, BRIAN, eds. *The rebirth of towns in the West A.D.700-1050.* C.B.A. research report **68**.
  ads.ahds.ac.uk/catalogue/library/cba/rr68.cfm
  Includes 7 papers on British towns.

H. The Vikings
- The Viking Network
  viking.no
  For schools.
- The Vikings in the British Isles / Nicola Cook
  www.bbc.co.uk/history/programmes/bloodofthevikings/british__isles__01.shtml
- The Vikings and Money / Roy Davies
  viking.no/e/heritage/emoney.htm
  Includes 'The Vikings and money in England', and 'Minting coins in Jorvik'.
- Viking Women / Judith Jesch
  www.bbc.co.uk/history/ancient/viking/women__01.shtml

I. Anglo-Saxon People and Authors

- Prosopography of Anglo-Saxon England
  www.kcl.ac.uk/humanities/cch/pase/
  Index to biographical information in selected reference works; includes articles.
- Fontes Anglo-Saxonici: a register of written sources used by Anglo-Saxon authors
  fontes.english.ac.uk/
- The Old English Manuscripts Database
  www.georgetown.edu/labyrinth/subjects/mss/oe/oldeng.html
  Project to list Anglo-Saxon manuscripts.
- Old English Pages: Texts & mss.
  www.georgetown.edu/faculty/ballc/oe/oe-texts.html
  Edited original sources.

Aelfric

- Aelfric's Homilies on Judith, Esther, and the Maccabees / Stuart D. Lee (ed.)
  users.ox.ac.uk/~stuart/kings/
  In Old English.

Alcuin

- Alcuin
  www.newadvent.org/cathen/01276a.htm
  Article from the *Catholic encyclopedia*
- Alcuin of York / Dr. Anna Ritchie
  www.bbc.co.uk/history/lj/conquestlj/alcuin__01.shtml
  Late 8th c.

Alfred the Great

- King Alfred's Preface and the Teaching of Latin in Anglo-Saxon England / Malcolm Godden
  www.findarticles.com/cf__dls/m0293/472__117/89379226/pl/article.jhtml
  From the *English historical review*, 6/2002.

Asser

- ASSER. *The life of King Alfred,* ed. D.A. Giles. 1847.
  sunsit.berkeley.edu/OMACL/KingAlfred/
- Unmasking Alfred's False Biographer / A.P. Smyth
  www.britarch.ac.uk/ba/ba7/ba7feat.html#smyth

Bede

- The Venerable Bede
  www.newadvent.org/cathen/02384a.htm
  Article from the *Catholic encyclopedia*.
- BEDE. *Bede's ecclesiastical history,* ed. R.A.B. Mynors & Bertram Colgrave. Oxford: Clarendon Press, 1969.
  www.questia.com/PM.qst?a=o&d=85662878
  Subscription based.
- BEDE. *Ecclesiastical history of the English nation.*
  www.fordham.edu/halsall/basis/bede-book1.html
- Bede.net
  www.geocities.com/~jarrow/Welcome.htm
- BEDE. *The lives of the holy abbots of Weremouth and Jarrow: Benedict, Ceolfrid, Eosterwine, Sigfrid and Huetberht.*
  www.fordham.edu/halsall/basis/bede-jarrow.html
- St. Bede the Venerable, Hieromonk of Wearmouth and Jarrow
  www.ocf.org/OrthodoxPage/reading/St.Pachomius/Xbede-vener.html
  Includes texts of his works, and many articles.
- Observing Bede's Anglo-Saxon Calendar / John Robert Stone
  www.kami.demon.co.uk/gesithas/calendar/obs__bede.html

Boniface

- Medieval Sourcebook: the correspondence of St. Boniface
  www.fordham.edu/halsall/basis/boniface-letters.html
- St. Boniface and the Conversion of Germany
  www.fordham.edu/halsall/source/boniface1.html

Cuthbert

- St. Cuthbert
  www.newadvent.org/cathen/04578a.htm
- BEDE. *The life and miracles of St. Cuthbert, Bishop of Lindisfarne.* (721)
  www.fordham.edu/halsall/basis/bede-cuthbert.html

15. The Medieval Period, 1066-1485

A. Gateways and Reference

- Medieval Resources on the Internet
  www.york.ac.uk/inst/cms/research/gateway/
  Intended for members of the University of York, but also of general relevance.
- Internet Medieval Sourcebook: Help!
  www.fordham.edu/halsall/help.html
  Guide to internet use for medieval students.
- Foundation for Medieval Genealogy
  fmg.ac
- Internet Medieval Sourcebook
  www.fordham.edu/halsall/sbook.html
  Many pages of original texts, some listed in appropriate places in this directory.
- The Labyrinth: Resources for Medieval Studies
  labyrinth.georgetown.edu/
- The Anglo-Norman On-Line Hub
  and4.anglo-norman.net/
- Late Medieval England: suggested reading list / A. Compton Reeves
  www.the-orb.net/bibliographies/late-eng.html
- Fifteenth Century Life: an annotated bibliography
  www.r3.org/life/biblio/biblio.html
- Feudal Terms of England / Michael Adams
  eserver.org/langs/feudal-dictionary.txt
  Brief dictionary of terms.
- Feudal Terms of England (and other places) / Michael Adams
  www.geocities.com/abrigon/terms.html

B. Overviews

- Medieval England
  www.historylearningsite.co.uk/Year%207.htm
  Many pages for schools
- The Medieval Period 1066-1485 A.D.
  www.britannia.com/history/h60.html
  Many Pages

- Uniting the Kingdoms? 1066-1603
  www.nationalarchives.gov.uk/pathways/utk/
- Medieval England 1066-1399
  www.the-orb.net/wales/h3h03/h3h03bib.htm
  Tutorial.
- BARROW, G.W.S. *Feudal Britain: the completion of the medieval kingdoms 1066-1314*. E. Arnold, 1956.
  www.questia.com/PM.qst?a=o&d=8931587
  Subscription based.
- DAVIS, H.W.C. *England under the Normans and Angevins, 1066-1272*. Methuen & Co., 1905.
  www.questia.com/PM.qst?a=o&d=13885133
  Subscription based.
- FRAME, ROBERT. *The political development of the British Isles, 1100-1400*. Oxford: Clarendon Press, 1995.
  www.questia.com/PM.qst?a=o&d=74411768
  Subscription based.
- POWICKE, MAURICE. *The thirteenth century, 1216-1307*. 2nd ed. Oxford: Clarendon Press, 1962.
  www.questia.com/PM.qst?a=o&d=9288319
  Subscription based.
- HOLMES, GEORGE. *The later middle ages 1272-1485*. Edinburgh: Thomas Nelson & Sons, 1962.
  www.questia.com/PM.qst?a=o&d=293609
  Subscription based.
- Fifteenth-Century Life
  www.r3.org/life/
  Includes bibliography.
- JACOB, E.F. *The fifteenth century, 1399-1485*. Oxford: Clarendon Press, 1961.
  www.questia.com/PM.qst?a=o&d=9005175
  Subscription based.

C. Constitutional & Administrative History

i. *Constitutional History*

- JOLLIFFE, J.E.A. *The constitutional history of medieval England, from the English settlement to 1485*. A. & C. Black, 1937.
  www.questia.com/PM.qst?a=o&d=58561865
  Subscription based.

- RICHARDSON, H.G., & SAYLES, G.O. *The governance of medieval England from the Conquest to Magna Carta.* Edinburgh: Edinburgh University Press, 1963.
  www.questia.com/PM.qst?a=o&d=54319342
  Subscription based.
- HOWELL, MARGARET. *Regalian right in medieval England.* Athlone Press, 1962.
  www.questia.com/PM.qst?a=o&d=3568116
  Subscription based.
- CHRIMES, S.B. *An introduction to the administrative history of medieval England.* New York: Macmillan, 1952.
  www.questia.com/PM.qst?a=o&d=5973111
  Subscription based.
- HOYT, ROBERT S. *The royal demesne in English constitutional history 1066-1272.* Ithaca: Cornell University Press, 1950.
  www.questia.com/PM.qst?a=o&d=10795665
  Subscription based.
- WILKINSON, B. *Studies in the constitutional history of the thirteenth and fourteenth centuries.* Manchester: Manchester University Press, 1937.
  www.questia.com/PM.qst?a=o&d=35615477
  Subscription based.
- The Queens Council in the Middle Ages / Anne Crawford.
  www.findarticles.com/cf__dls/m0293/469__116/82469639/pl/article.jhtml
  From the *English historical review,* 11/2001.
- Sub-keepers and Constables: the role of local officials in keeping the peace in fourteenth-century England / A.J. Musson.
  www.findarticles.com/cf__dls/m0293/470__117/84302832/pl/article.jhtml
  From the *English historical review,* 2/2002.
- CUTTINO, G.P. *English medieval diplomacy.* Bloomington: Indiana University Press, 1985.
  www.questia.com/PM.qst?a=o&d=91359339
  Subscription based.
- Crowner: History of the Medieval English coroner system / Prof. Bernard Knight
  www.britannia.com/history/articles/coroner1.html

ii. *Legal History*
- POLLOCK, FREDERICK, SIR, & MAITLAND, F.W. *The history of English law before the time of Edward I.* 1908.
  www.constitution.org/cmt/poll-mait/poll-mait.htm

- History in Deed: medieval society and the law in England, 1100-1600
  www.law.harvard.edu/library/special/exhibitions/history__in__deed/index.php.
  Calendar of deeds and charters held in Harvard University Law Library.
- English Legal History: Materials
  vi.uh.edu/pages/bob/elhone/elhmat.html
  Medieval.
- Ordinance of William I Separating the Spiritual and Temporal Courts
  www.yale.edu/lawweb/avalon/medieval/ordwill.htm
- Constitutions of Clarendon,1164
  www.constitution.org/eng/consclar.pdf
- Bracton Online
  hlsl.law.harvard.edu/bracton/index.htm
  Full text, with translation, of Henry de Bracton, *De legibus et consuetudines Angliae.*
- The Early History of the Court of Chancery: a comparative study / P.Tucker.
  www.findarticles.com/cf__dls/m0293/463__115/66274344/pl/article.jhtml
  From the *English historical review,* 9/2000.
- Statute of Mortmain, November 15, 1279
  www.yale.edu/lawweb/avalon/medieval/mortmain.htm
- Statute of Edward I concerning the buying and selling of land (Quia Emptores) 1290
  www.yale.edu/lawweb/avalon/medieval/land.htm
- Tales of Justice and Vengeance
  falcon.arts.cornell.edu/prh3/bktales.html
  Medieval case law.
- Murder, Motive, and Punishment in Fifteenth-Century England: two gentry case studies / S.J. Payling.
  www.findarticles.com/cf__dls/m0293/n450__v113/20572944/p1/article.jhtml
  From the *English historical review,* 2/1998.

iii. *Domesday Book*
- FINN, R. WELLDON. *An introduction to Domesday Book.* New York: Barnes & Noble, 1963.
  www.questia.com/PM.qst?a=o&d=10575685
  Subscription based.
- Domesday Book
  www.nationalarchives.gov.uk/museum/
  Click on 'Middle Ages' and title

- The Domesday Book Online
  www.domedaybook.co.uk
- The Purpose of Domesday Book: a quandary / William E. Kapelle
  www.domesdaybook.net/domesday__homeframe.htm
- Domesday: the Inquest and the Book / David Roffe
  www.roffe.freeserve.co.uk/prolecture.htm
  See also **/imc.htm**
- The Digital Domesday / David Roffe
  www.roffe.freeserve.co.uk/ddb.htm
  See also **/dbdatabases.htm**
  Reviews of Domesday databases on CD
- The Domesday Book
  www.domesdaybook.co.uk
- Domesday Book Explorer
  www.domesdaybook.net/hs10.htm
  Details of a CD version. Click on 'Domesday Book', 'here', and 'online help manual' for useful historical background.
- The Domesday Book Index and Search Engine
  www.infokey.com/hon/domesday.htm

iv. *Magna Carta*
- King John and the Magna Carta / Dr. Mike Ibeji
  www.bbc.co.uk/history/state/monarchs__leaders/magna__01.shtml
- Magna Carta
  www.bl.uk/collections/treasures/magna/
  Includes facsimile and translation.
- The Magna Carta (the Great Charter)
  www.magnacar.htm
  Text
- The Magna Carta (the Great Charter)
  historicaltextarchive.com/sections/php?op-viewarticle&artid=72
  English translation.
- Magna Carta
  www.britannia.com/history/magna2.html
  Full text in English, 1215.
- The 1215 Magna Carta
  www.magnacartaplus.org/magnacarta

v. *The Exchequer & Taxation*
- Medieval Source Book: the *Dialogue concerning the Exchequer.* Late 12th c.
  www.fordham.edu/halsall/source/excheq1.html
  Full translation of book 1.

- The Dialogue Concerning the Exchequer, circa.1180
  www.yale.edu/lawweb/avalon/medieval/excheq.htm
  English translation.
- Records of Central Goverment Taxation in England, c.1190-1690 / R. Glasscock
  hds.essex.ac.uk/abstract.asp?study__number=4338
  Brief description of a database.
- The Taxation Database
  www.taxatio.man.ac.uk
  The Pope Nicholas IV taxation, 1291.
- The Hundred Rolls / David Roffe
  www.roffe.freeserve.co.uk/rolls.htm
  Study of 13th c. inquests.

D. **Government & Politics**

i. *The Normans*
- The Normans: A European People: the Norman Heritage, 10th-12th Century
  www.norman-world.com/angleterre/index.htm
- Essential Norman Conquest
  www.essentialnormanconquest.com
  Includes the Bayeux Tapestry, a day by day account of the 1066 campaign, *etc.*
- What Did the Normans Do for Us? / Dr. John Hudson
  www.bbc.co.uk/history/war/normans/hudson__norman__01.shtml
- William I, the Conqueror (1066-1087 A.D.)
  www.britannia.com/history/monarchs/mon22.html
- 1066 and the Norman Conquest
  members.tripod.com/~GeoffBoxell/1066.htm
- 1066: the effects of the Norman Conquest
  www.geocities.com/Athens/Aegean/3532/1066.htm
  Links page.
- Key Events of the Conquest / Dr. Mike Ibeji
  www.bbc.co.uk/history/war/normans/key__events__01.shtml
- 11th Century Vikings and their Involvement in the Norman Conquest of England / Geoff Boxell
  www.britannia.com/history/articles/normvik.html
- The Norwegian Invasion of England, September 1066 / William Bakken
  www.mnsu.edu/emuseum/prehistory/vikings/norinv.html

- Battle of Fulford, 20 September 1066
  www.battleoffulford.org.uk
- Battle of Hastings, 1066
  www.battle1066.com
- Secrets of the Norman Invasion
  www.secretsofthenormaninvasion.com/
  Discussion of the actual invasion and battle of Hastings.
- The Battle of Hastings
  members.tripod.com/~Battle__of__Hastings/index.html
- The Battle of Hastings (October 14, 1066) / Stephen Beck
  www.geocities.com/beckster05/Hastings/HaMain.html
- The Bayeux Tapestry: primary source for the Battle of Hastings, William the Conqueror, Harold II and the Norman Conquest
  www.angelfire.com/rnb/bayeux__tapestry/
- The Full Bayeux Tapestry
  www.hastings1066.com/baythumb.html
- The Reading Bayeux Tapestry
  www.bayeuxtapestry.org.uk
- Frederic William Maitland
  www.ecn.bris.ac.uk/het/maitland/index.htm
  Includes text of *Domesday book and beyond: three essays in the early history of England.* 1897.
- The Significance and Fate of the Native Landholders of 1086.
  www.findarticles.com/cf__dls/m0293/476__118/102139249/pl/article.jhtml
  From the *English historical review,* 4/2003.
- Statutes of William the Conqueror
  www.yale.edu/lawweb/avalon/medieval/lawwill.htm
- William Rufus and Henry I / Peter of Blois
  www.fordham.edu/halsall/source/blois1.html
- William II, Rufus the Red (1087-1100 A.D.)
  www.britannia.com/history/monarchs/mon23.html
- Extraordinary Privilege: the Trial of Penenden Heath and the Domesday Inquest / Alan Cooper
  www.findarticles.com/cf__dls/m0293/469__116/82469638/pl/article.jhtml
  From the *English historical review,* 11/2001
  11-12th c. property dispute involving Archbishop Lanfranc.
- Henry I, Beauclerk (1100-1135 A.D.)
  www.britannia.com/history/monarchs/mon24.html
- King Stephen (1135-54 A.D.)
  www.britannia.com/history/monarchs/mon25.html

- Empress Matilda (1141 A.D.)
  www.britannia.com/history/monarchs/mon25a.html
- New Charters of King Stephen with some reflections upon the Royal Forests during the Anarchy / Nicholas Vincent
  www.findarticles.com/cf__dls/m0293/458__114/55979087/pl/article.jhtml
  From the *English historical review,* 9/1999.
- Henry of Blois and the Lordship of Glastonbury / N.E. Stacy
  www.findarticles.com/cf__dls/m0293/455__114/54050231/pl/article.jhtml
  From the *English historical review,* 2/1999.

ii. *The Plantagenets*
- NORGATE, KATE. *England under the Angevin Kings.* New York: Haskell House, 1969.
  www.questia.com/PM.qst?a=o&d=86049679
  Subscription based.
- JOLLIFFE, J.E.A. *Angevin Kingship.* Adam & Charles Black, 1955.
  www.questia.com/PM.qst?a=o&d=7801666
  Subscription based.
- Henry II (1154-1189)
  www.britannia.com/history/monarchs/mon26.html
- The Character and Legacy of Henry II / Dr. Mike Ibeji
  www.bbc.co.uk/history/state/monarchs__leaders/
              henryii__character__01.shtml
- Common Law: Birth of a State, Henry II and the Angevins / Dr. John Hudson
  www.bbc.co.uk/history/state/monarchs__leaders/henryii__law__01.shtml
- Henry II's Heir: the Acta and Seal of Henry the Young King, 1170-83.
  www.findarticles.com/cf__dls/m0293/466__116/74691873/pl/article.jhtml
  From the *English historical review,* 4/2001.
- Richard I Coeur de Lion (1189-99 A.D.)
  www.britannia.com/history/monarchs/mon27.html
- The English Revenue of Richard I / Nick Barratt
  www.findarticles.com/cf__dls/m0293/467__116/76650910/pl/article.jhtml
  From the *English historical review,* 6/2001.
- Abbot Ralph of Coggeshall's Account of the Last Years of King Richard and the First Years of King John / D.A. Carpenter
  www.findarticles.com/cf__dls/m0293/454__113/53706851/pl/article.jhtml
  From the *English historical review,* 11/1998.
- APPLEBY, JOHN T. *John, King of England.* New York: Knopf, 1959.
  www.questia.com/PM.qst?a=o&d=5957055
  Subscription based.

- John Lackland (1199-1216 A.D.)
  www.britannia.com/history/monarchs/mon28.html
- King John, the Lusignan Affair and the Early Years / Dr. Mike Ibeji
  www.bbc.co.uk/history/state/monarchs__leaders/lusig__01.shtml
- TURNER, RALPH V. *The King and his courts: the rule of John and Henry III in the administration of justice, 1199-1240.* Ithaca: Cornell University Press, 1968.
  www.questia.com/PM.qst?a=o&d=9457931
  Subscription based.
- The Robin Hood Project: texts, images, bibliographies and basic information
  www.lib.rochester.edu/camelot/rh/rhhome.stm
- Robin Hood and his Historical Context / Dr.Mike Ibeji
  www.bbc.co.uk/history/state/monarchs__leaders/robin__01.shtml
- Henry III (1216-72 A.D.)
  www.britannia.com/history/monarchs/mon29.html
- Justice and the Bureaucracy: the English royal writ and 1258 / Andrew Hershey
  www.findarticles.com/cf__dls/m0293/n453__v113/21226615/p1/article.jhtml
  From the *English historical review,* 9/1998.
- Edward I, Longshanks (1272-1307 A.D.)
  www.britannia.com/history/monarchs/mon30.html
- Edward I: his ancestors and descendants
  www.angelfire.com/mi/RedBearsDream/EdwardI.html
- Knights of the Shire in the Parliaments of Edward I / J.S.Illsley
  www.the-orb.net/wales/esknights/knights.htm
- Essex Knights and the Parliaments of Edward I / J.S. Illsley
  www.the-orb.net/wales/esknights/genframe.htm
  Extensive study.
- Edward II (1307-27 A.D.)
  www.britannia.com/history/monarchs/mon31.html
- The Deposition and Abdication of Edward II / Claire Valente
  www.findarticles.com/cf__dls/m0293/n453__v113/21226616/p1/article.jhtml
  From the *English historical review,* 9/1998.
- Edward III (1327-1377 A.D.)
  www.britannia.com/history/monarchs/mon32.html
- Edward III's Prisoners of War: the Battle of Poitiers and its Context / Chris Given-Wilson & Francoise Beriac
  www.findarticles.com/cf__dls/m0293/468__116/79334667/p1/article.jhtml
  From the *English historical review,* 9/2001.
- Edward III's Entail and the Succession to the Crown, 1376-1471 / Michael Bennett
  www.findarticles.com/cf__dls/m0293/n452__v113/20920711/p1/article.jhtml
  From the *English historical review,* 6/1998.
- Chronicles of the Revolution 1397-1400: the Reign of Richard II / Chris Given-Wilson (ed.)
  www.medievalsources.co.uk/revolution.htm
  Subscription based. Sources.
- The Reign of Richard II 1377 to 1399 / Ian Bremner
  www.bbc.co.uk/history/state/monarchs__leaders/richardii__reign__01.shtml
- Richard II (A.D. 1377-1399)
  www.britannia.com/history/monarchs/mon33.html
- Richard II and the Crisis of Authority / Professor Nigel Saul
  www.bbc.co.uk/history/state/monarchs__leaders/richardii__crisis__01.shtml
- Peasants' Revolt: 14th century poll tax riots / Jeff Hobbs
  www.britannia.com/history/articles/peasantsrevolt.html

iii. *The Lancastrians*
- Henry IV (1399-1413 A.D.)
  www.britannia.com/history/monarchs/mon34.html
- Henry V (1413-1422 A.D.)
  www.britannia.com/history/monarchs/mon35.html
- The Myth of Henry V / Felipe Fernandez-Armesto
  www.bbc.co.uk/history/state/monarchs__leaders/henry__v__01.shtml
- KINGSFORD, CHARLES LETHBRIDGE. *Henry V: the typical medieval hero.* New York: G.E.Putnams Sons, 1901.
  www.questia.com/PM.qst?a=o&d=33432472
  Subscription based.
- The Battle of Agincourt (October 25, 1415) / Stephen Beck
  www.geocities.com/beckster05/Agincourt/Agmain.html
- The Hundred Years War: final phase (1422-1453)
  xenophongroup.com/montjoie/hyw__fp.htm

- Henry VI (1422-61, 1470-71 A.D.)
  www.britannia.com/history/monarchs/mon36.html
- ROSKELL, J.S. *The Commons in the Parliament of 1422.* Manchester: Manchester University Press, 1954.
  www.questia.com/PM.qst?a=o&d=3611981
  Subscription based.
- The Commission De Mutuo Faciendo in the Reign of Henry VI
  www.findarticles.com/cf__dls/m0293/465__116/78678850/pl/article.jhtml
  From the *English historical review,* 2/2001. Governmental borrowing and its problems, mid-15th c.
- Armed Force and Civil Legitimacy in Jack Cade's Revolt, 1450 / Montgomery Bohna
  www.findarticles.com/cf__dls/m0293/479__118/104728588/pl/
  article/jhtml
  From the *English historical review,* 6/2003.

iv. *The House of York*
- Wars of the Roses History Guide
  www.geocities.com/Athens/Oracle/2719/
- Wars of the Roses
  www.warsoftheroses.com/
- The Croyland Chronicle Continuations, 1453-1486
  www.r3.org/bookcase/croyland/index.html
  Originally published as: RILEY, HENRY T., ed. *Ingulphs chronicle of the Abbey of Croyland ...* Henry G. Bohn, 1854. A key source for the Wars of the Roses
- Edward IV (1461-70, 1471-83 A.D.)
  www.britannia.com/history/monarchs/mon37.html
- *Historie of the arrivall of Edward IV in England and the finall recoverye of his kingdomes from Henry VI*
  www.blackmask.com/books44c/arrivaleddex.htm.
- NICOLAS, NICHOLAS HARRIS, ed. *Privy purse expenses of Elizabeth of York: wardrobe accounts of Edward IV.* 1830.
  wwwr3.org/bookcase/wardrobe.ward1.html
- WARKWORTH, JOHN, *The Warkworth chronicle, part 1: a chronicle of the first thirteen years of the reign of King Edward IV,* ed. James Orchard Halliwell. Camden Society, 1839.
  www.r3.org/bookcase/warkwort/worthi.html
- Richard III (1483-5 A.D.)
  www.britannia.com/history/monarchs/mon39.html

- The Richard III Foundation
  www.richardiii.com
- MORE, THOMAS, SIR. *The history of King Richard the Third.* 1557.
  darkwing.uoregon.edu/%7Erbear/r3.html
- Richard III: the making of a legend / Roxane C. Murph
  www.r3.org/bookcase/murph1.html
- The Battle of Bosworth: August 22, 1485
  www.r3.org/bosworth/
- The Battle of Bosworth: contemporary and Tudor accounts
  www.r3.org/bosworth/chronicl.html

C. The Medieval Church
  The Wider Community / Carol Davidson Cragoe
  www.bbc.co.uk/history/lj/churchlj/community__01.shtml
  The church and the community, 11-16th c.
- THOMPSON, A. HAMILTON. *The English clergy and their organization in the later middle ages.* Oxford: Clarendon Press, 1947.
  www.questia.com/PM.qst?a=o&d=8577639
  Subscription based.
- GREENAWAY, DIANA E. *Fasti ecclesiae Anglicanae 1066-1300.* Vol. 6. 1999.
  www.british-history.ac.uk/source.asp?pubid=29
  Biographical dictionary of senior clergy of York Minster, with the archbishops of York.
- English Monastic Archive
  www.ucl.ac.uk/history/monastic
  Project to re-construct the archives of every English monastery.
- POWER, EILEEN. *Medieval English nunneries c.1275 to 1535.* New York: Biblo & Tannen, 1964.
  www.questia.com/PM.qst?a=o&d=23556422
  Subscription based.
- The Household Chapel in Medieval England c.1250-c.1450 / Kent Rawlinson
  www.dur.ac.uk/k.a.c.rawlinson/index.htm
  Includes a gazetteer.
- St. Anselm
  www.newadvent.org/cathen/01546a.htm
  Article from the *Catholic encyclopedia.* Archbishop of Canterbury 1093-1109.

- CHENEY C.R. *From Becket to Langton: English church government, 1170-1213.* Manchester: Manchester University Press, 1956.
  www.questia.com/PM.qst?a=o&d=10830297
  Subscription based.
- St. Thomas Becket
  www.newadvent.org/cathen/14676a.htm
  From the *Catholic encyclopedia.*
- Becket, the Church, and Henry II / Dr. Mike Ibeji
  www.bbc.co.uk/history/state/church__reformation/becket__01/shtml
- Thomas Becket, Archbishop of Canterbury, martyred 29 December 1170 / Scott McLetchie
  www.loyno.edu/~letchie/becket/
- Thomas Becket: a preliminary bibliography / Carolyn Schriber
  www.the-orb.net/bibliographies/becket.html
- Churchmen in Late Fourteenth Century England / Jeff Hobbs
  www.britannia.com/history/articles/14churchmen.html
- Bibliographies for Lollard Studies
  home.att.net/~lollard/bibhome.html
- John Wyclif
  www.newadvent.org/cathen/15722a.htm
  Catholic Encyclopedia article.
- John Wycliffe and the Lollards
  www.courses.fas.harvard.edu/~chaucer/special/varia/lollards/ lollards.html
  Includes bibliography.
- A Radical Preacher's Handbook c.1383 / J.I. Catto
  www.findarticles.com/cf__dls/m0293/463__115/66274348/pl/article.jhtml
  From the *English historical review,* 9/2000. The Wycliffe controversy.
- Notes of an Early Fifteenth Century Research Assistant, and the Emergence of the 267 Articles against Wyclif / Anne Hudson
  www.findarticles.com/cf__dls/m0293/477__118/104728592/pl/ article.jhtml
  From the *English historical review,* 6/2003.
- Adam Easton and the Condemnation of John Wyclif, 1377 / Margaret Harvey
  www.findarticles.com/cf__dls/m0293/n451__v113/20555552/pl/ article.jhtml
  From the *English historical review,* 4/1998.

- Pope Gregory XI: the Condemnation of Wycliffe 1382, *and* Wycliffe's reply
  www.fordham.edu/halsall/source/1382wycliffe.html
  From the *Medieval sourcebook* web site.
- Lollards / Dr. Mike Ibeji
  www.bbc.co.uk/history/state/church__reformation/lollards__01.shtml
- Catholic England: Faith, Religion, and Observance before the Reformation / R.N. Swanson (ed.)
  www.medievalsources.co.uk/catholic.htm
  Subscription based. Sources.
- Some Ambiguities of late Medieval Religion in England / Dr. Dave Postles
  www.history.ac.uk/projects/elec/sem20.html
- The Website of Unknowing: celebrating the lives and writings of the medieval English mystics / Carl McColman
  www.anamchara.com/mystics/
  Includes pages on individual mystics, and a bibliography.
- The British Medieval Mystics: a bibliography
  www.carlmccolman.com/wsu-bibliography.htm
- Jews and the Law in England, 1275-90 / Paul Brand
  www.findarticles.com/cf__dls/m0293/464__115/69064672/pl/article.jhtml
  From the *English historical review,* 11/2000.

D. **Medieval Society**

i. *General*
- STENTON, DORIS MARY. *English society in the early middle ages 1066-1307.* Harmondsworth: Penguin, 1952.
  www.questia.com/PM.qst?a=o&d=60031604
  Subscription based.
- SALZMAN, L.F. *English life in the middle ages.* Oxford University Press, 1926.
  www.questia.com/PM.qst?a=o&d=833902
  Subscription based.
- LENNARD, REGINALD. *Rural England, 1086-1135: a study of social and agrarian conditions.* Oxford: Clarendon Press, 1959.
  www.questia.com/PM.qst?a=o&d=6230620
  Subscription based.
- RAZI, ZVI, ed. *Medieval society and the manor court.* Oxford: Oxford University Press, 1996.
  www.questia.com/PM.qst?a=o&d=91899332
  Subscription based.

- Manor Courts
  www.keele.ac.uk/depts/hi/resources/manor__courts/
  Includes extensive bibliography and glossary.
- The Dating of Medieval English Private Charters of the twelfth and thirteenth centuries / Michael Gervers
  www.utoronto.ca/deeds/pubs/doc2/page1a.htm
- DEEDS Project, University of Toronto
  www.utoronto.ca/deeds
  Project to compile a database of Essex deeds pre-1300.
- Medieval Estates and Orders: making and breaking rules
  www.wwnorton.com/nael/middleages/topic__1/welcome.htm
  Social stratification.
- Mostly Medieval
  www.skell.org
  Social life: ballads, festivals, medicine, religion, *etc.*

ii. *Food*
- Medieval / Renaissance Food Homepage
  www.pbm.com/~lindahl/food.html
  Gateway
- Medieval / Renaissance Brewing Homepage
  www.pbm.com/~lindahl/brewing.html

iii. *Medicine & Disease*
- The Black Death 1347-1350: Culprit, Oriental Rat Flea
  www.insecta__inspecta.com/fleas/bdeath/
- Black Death: the Disease
  www.bbc.co.uk/history/society__culture/welfare/blackdisease__01.shtml
- Black Death: the effect of the Plague / Dr. Mike Ibeji
  www.bbc.co.uk/history/society__culture/welfare/plague__countryside__01.shtml
- Black Death: Political and Social Changes / Dr. Mike Ibeji
  www.bbc.co.uk/history/society__culture/welfare/blacksocial__01.shtml
- The Black Death's Lasting Impact on British Society / Tom James
  www.bbc.co.uk/history/society__culture/welfare/black__impact__01.shtml
- The Physicians Handbook
  library.wellcome.ac.uk/resources/etexts/ms8004/
  Fasimile of a 15th c. manuscript in English, including directions for pilgrims travelling from London to Jerusalem.

v. *Women & Marriage*
- Marriage in fifteenth century England: Primary Sources / Sharon Michalove
  www.the-orb.net/bibliographies/marriag1.html
  Continued at/marriage2.html
- Women in England c.1275-1525 / P.J.P. Goldberg (ed.)
  www.medievalsources.co.uk/womeneng.htm
  Subscription based.
- Women of the English Nobility and Gentry 1066-1500 / Jennifer Ward
  www.medievalsources.co.uk/womenof.htm
  Subscription based. Sources.
- KARRAS, RUTH MAZO. *Common women: prostitution and sexuality in medieval England.* New York: Oxford U.S., 1996.
  www.questia.com/PM.qst?a=o&d=96562574
  Subscription based.
- ROSENTHAL, JOEL T. *Old age in late medieval England.* Philadelphia: University of Pennsylvania Press, 1996.
  www.questia.com/PM.qst?a=o&d=7976155

iv. *The Elite*
- HUDSON, JOHN. *Land, law and lordship in Anglo-Norman England.* Oxford. Clarendon Press, 1994.
  www.questia.com/PM.qst?a=o&d=72297921
  Subscription based.
- Rural and Urban Elites in England during the later Middle Ages / Richard Britnell
  www.dur.ac.uk/r.h.britnell/articles/Elites.htm
- ROSENTHAL, JOEL T. *Nobles and the noble life, 1295-1500.* George Allen & Unwin, 1976.
  www.questia.com/PM.qst?a=o&d=57162741
  Subscription based.
- The Knighthood, Chivalry & Tournament Resource Library
  www.chronique.com/
- On a ms. Collection of Ordinances of Chivalry of the 15th century belonging to Lord Hastings
  www.chronique.com/Library/Medhistory/Archaeologia-chivalry.htm
- Deeds of Arms: a collection of accounts of formal deeds of arms of the fourteenth century
  www.nipissingu.ca/department/history/muhlberger/chroniqu/texts/deedsch.htm
  Study of tournaments.

vi. *The Peasantry*
- Paul Vinogradoff 1854-1925
  www.ecn.bris.ac.uk/het/vinogradoff/index.htm
  Includes text of *Villainage in England*. 1892
- Statute of Labourers, 1351
  www.fordham.edu/halsall/seth/statute-labourers/
  English translation.
- The Statute of Labourers, 1351
  www.yale.edu/lawweb/avalon/medieval/statlab.htm

vii. *Urban History & Trade*
- Medieval English Towns
  www.trytel.com/~tristan/towns/towns.html
- English Medieval Boroughs
  www.le.ac.uk/elh/pot/borough/borfram.html
- MILLER, EDWARD & HATCHER, JOHN. *Medieval England: towns, commerce and crafts 1086-1348*. Longman, 1995.
  www.questia.com/PM.qst?a=o&d=54365963
  Subscription based.
- BARLEY, M.W., ed. *The plans and topography of medieval towns*. C.B.A. research report, 14. 1976.
  ads.ahds.ac.uk/catalogue/library/cba/rr14.cfm
- Market Towns and the Countryside in Late Medieval England / Christopher Dyer
  www.usask.ca/history/cjh/dyer__496.htm
  From the *Canadian journal of history* 31, 1996, pp.17-35.
- Gazetteer of Markets and Fairs in England and Wales to 1516 / Dr. Samantha Letters
  www.history.ac.uk/cmh/gaz/gazweb2.html
- Markets and Fairs in Britain and Ireland before 1216 / Richard Britnell
  www.dur.ac.uk/r.h.britnell/articles/Earlymarkets.htm
- The rise and fall of markets in South East England / Mavis Mates
  www.usask.ca/history/cjh/mate__496.htm
  Late medieval.
- Urban Economic Regulation and Economic Morality in Medieval England / Richard Britnell
  www.dur.ac.uk/r.h.britnell/articles/Morality.htm
- Price Setting in English Borough Markets, 1349-1500
  www.dur.ac.uk/r.h.britnell/cjh/brit__496.htm
  From the *Canadian journal of history* 31, 1996, pp.1-15.

- Medieval Trade and Industry: Seminar Assignments
  www.the-orb.net/wales/mtib/mtifola.htm
  Students reports and bibliographies.
- The Marketing of Grain in England 1250-1350 / Richard Britnell
  www.dur.ac.uk/r.h.britnell/articles/Grainframe.htm
- POWER, EILEEN. *The wool trade in English medieval history*. 1941.
  socserv2.mcmaster.ca/~econ/ugcm/3ll3/power/WoolTrade.pdf

viii. *Medieval Industry & Technology*
- Medieval Technology Pages
  scholar.chem.nyu.edu/tekpages/Technology.html
  European focus, but includes Britain.
- CROSSLEY, D.W. ed. *Medieval industry*. C.B.A. research report, 40. 1981.
  ads.ahds.ac.uk/catalogue/library/cba/rr40.cfm
- MATHESON, LISTER M., ed. *Popular and practical science of medieval England*. East Lansing: Colleagues Press, 1994.
  www.questia.com/PM.qst?a=o&d=14467651
  Subscription based.

ix. *Buildings & Architecture*
- WEBB, GEOFFREY. *Architecture in Britain: the middle ages*. Baltimore: Penguin Books, 1956.
  www.questia.com/PM.qst?a=o&d=869512
  Subscription based.
- The English Medieval Castle / David Dawson
  www.britannia.com/history/david1.html
- ABERG, F.A. *Medieval moated sites*. C.B.A. research report, 17.
  ads.ahds.ac.uk/catalogue/library/cba/rr17.cfm
- The Age of Carpentry: the new art and society in Plantagenet England / C.R.J. Currie
  eserver.org/medieval-carpentry.txt
  Study of wooden house building.
- The Corpus of Romanesque Sculpture in Britain and Ireland
  www.crsbi.ac.uk/
  12th c.

x. *Medieval Archaeology*
- Medieval Pottery Research Group bibliography
  ntserver002.liv.ac.uk/mprg/

- Corpus of Early Medieval Coin Finds
  www-cm.fitzmuseum.ac.uk/emc
  Database.

xi. *Education & Literacy*
- LEACH, A.F. *The schools of medieval England.* New York: Benjamin Blom, 1968.
  www.questia.com/PM.qst?a=o&d=6584328
  Subscription based.
- A Medieval Education and its implications
  www.upf.com/content/RussellChap1.pdf
  Discussion of how Chaucer may have been educated.
- Urban Manuscripts Project: privately owned urban manuscripts 1300-1476: a database
  www.york.ac.uk/inst/cms/resources/manuscripts/About
  Study of the urban culture of literacy.

E. *Medieval Texts & Ideas*
- Early Manuscripts at Oxford University: Digital Facsimiles of Complete Manuscripts, Scanned directly from the Originals
  image.ox.ac.uk
- Repertorium Chronicarum: a bibliography of the manuscripts of medieval Latin chronicles
  www.chronica.msstate.edu/chronica/
  Listing locations.
- LOWE, BEN. *Imagining peace: a history of early English pacifist ideas, 1340-1560.* Pennsylvania State University Press, 1997.
  www.questia.com/PM.qst?a=o&d=10781040
  Subscription based.

Chronicles
- *Brut* Chronicle
  images.umdl.umich.edu/cgi/i/image/image-idx?c=brut&page=index
  Medieval chronicle.
- Imagining History Project: medieval texts, contents, and communities in the English *Brut* tradition
  www.qub.ac.uk/imagining-history/
- ROTHWELL, HARRY. ed. *The chronicle of Walter of Guisborough.* Royal Historical Society, 1957.
  www.questia.com/PM.qst?a=o&d=100082718
  Subscription based.

Psalters & Missals
- The St. Albans Psalter
  www.abdn.ac.uk.stalbanspsalter/
  Facsimile of a medieval manuscript associated with Christina of Markyat.
- Exploring the Sherborne Missal
  www.bl.uk/collections/treasures/digitisation.html
  Click on 'Sherborne missal'. Facsimile of a 15th c. missal.

Cely Family
- MALDEN, HENRY ELLIOT, ed. *The Cely papers: selections from the correspondence and memoranda of the Cely family, merchants of the staple, A.D. 1475-1488.* Longmans, Green & Co., 1900.
  www.r3.org/bookcase/cely/

Geoffrey of Monmouth
- Geoffrey of Monmouth
  www.britannia.com/history/geofmon.html

Grosseteste, Robert
- The Electronic Grosseteste: Who was Robert Grosseteste?
  www.grosseteste.com
  Bishop of Lincoln, 1235-53.

Hilton, Walter
- Hilton, Walter (d.1396): English Mystic
  www.ccel.org/h/hilton/
  Includes article from the *Catholic encyclopedia,* and texts of his devotional works.
- Walter Hilton and his *Scale of perfection*
  www.gloriana.nu/hilton.html
  14th c. mystic; includes links to his works.

Julian of Norwich
- Julian of Norwich (ca.1342-ca.1416)
  www.luminarium.org/medlit/julian.htm/
  Includes some of her works.
- Julian of Norwich (c.1342-c.1413)
  www.ccel.org/j/julian/
  Includes *Catholic encyclopedia* article, and text of her *Revelations of Divine Love.*

Kempe, Margery
- Explaining Margery Kempe: a review of the literature / Jennifer C. Lane
  fac.cgu.edu/~torjesek/matristics/kempereview.html
  See also **/margery.html**
- Margery Kempe (ca.1373-1438)
  www.luminarium.org/medlit/margery.htm
- Mapping Margery Kempe: a guide to Late Medieval Material and Spiritual Life
  www.holycross.edu/departments/visarts/projects/kempe/
  Includes her *Book*
- Margery Kempe (1373-post 1438) / Lynn Harry Nelson
  www.ukans.edu/kansas/medieval/108/lectures/margery.html
  Essay
- *The Book of Margery Kempe* (1996) edited by Lynne Staley
  www.lib.rochester.edu/camelot/teams/staley.htm
  Written c. 1430's.

Kempis, Thomas
- Thomas Kempis (c.1380-1471); ascetical writer
  www.ccel.org/k/kempis/
  Includes article from the *Catholic encyclopedia.* and text of the *Imitation of Christ.*

Lydgate, John
- The Canon of John Lydgate Project / Stephen R. Reimer
  www.ualberta.ca/~sreimer/
  Includes some works.

Paston Family
- Paston Family Letters / Dr. Mike Ibeji
  www.bbc.co.uk/history/society__culture/welfare/pastonletters__01.shtml
- Paston Letters and Papers of the Fifteenth Century
  etext.lib.virginia.edu/mideng/browse.html
  Click on title.

Reginald of Durham
- REGINALD OF DURHAM. *Life of St. Goderic.* [12th cent.]
  www.fordham.edu/halsall/source/goderic.html

Rolle, Richard
- Rolle of Hampole, Richard (c.1290-c.1349): English hermit and mystic
  www.ccel.org/r/rolle/

16. Tudor History, 1485-1603

A. Gateways, Bibliography, *etc.*
- Early Modern Resources
  www.earlymodernweb.org.uk
  Gateway
- READ, CONYERS. *Bibliography of British History: Tudor period.* Oxford: Clarendon Press, 1959.
  www.questia.com/popularSearches/british__history.jsp
  Subscription based. Scroll to bottom of page, add 'Bibliography' in search box, search, and click on title.
- Early Modern England Source
  www.quelle.org/emes/index.html
  Notices of events, new books, research resources, *etc.*

B. General Introductions and Histories
- Time Travellers Guide to Tudor England
  www.channel4.com/history/microsites/H/history/guide16/
- Tudor England
  www.historylearningsite.co.uk/tudors.htm
  Many pages for schools
- Tudor Times (1485-1603) / Jean Mason
  www.likesbooks.com/tudor.html
  Brief overview for students.
- Tudor World
  historicaltimes.co.uk/new__folder/
  Deals with the Wars of the Roses and the early Tudor dynasty.
- Tudors.org / John Guy
  www.tudors.org/
  Many lectures and papers
- Who's Who in Tudor History
  tudorhistory.org/people/
- Tudor England 1485-1603
  www.englishhistory.net/tudor.htm
  General introduction to the period.
- Tudor History
  www.tudorhistory.org/
- HARRISON, DAVID. *Tudor England.* Cassell, 1953.
  www.questia.com/PM.qst?a=o&d=89176844
  Continued at /6710002. Subscription based.

- RUSSELL, CONRAD. *The crisis of Parliaments: English history 1509-1660*. Oxford: Oxford University Press, 1971.
  www.questia.com/PM.qst?a=o&d=14845605
  Subscription based.
- MACKIE, J.D. *The earlier Tudors 1485-1558*. Oxford: Clarendon Press, 1952.
  www.questia.com/PM.qst?a=o&d=8546253
  Subscription based.
- POLLARD, A.F. *The history of England from the accession of Edward VI to the death of Elizabeth (1547-1603)*. Longmans, Green & Co., 1911.
  www.questia.com/PM.qst?a=o&d=58544100
  Subscription based.
- WILLIAMS, PENRY. *The later Tudors: England 1547-1603*. Oxford: Clarendon Press, 1995.
  www.questia.com/PM.qst?a=o&d=9824769
  Subscription based.

C. Politics & Government

i. *General*

- *House of Commons journal.* Volume 1. 1802
  www.british-history.ac.uk/source.asp?pubid=14
  For 1547-1629.
- SLAVIN, ARTHUR J., ed. *Tudor men and institutions: studies in English law and government.* Baton Rouge: Louisiana State University Press, 1972.
  www.questia.com/PM.qst?a=o&d=14508137
  Subscription based.
- FLETCHER, ANTHONY. *Tudor rebellions.* Seminar studies in history. Longmans, 1968.
  www.questia.com/PM.qst?a=o&d=59672264
  Subscription based.
- FEILING, KEITH. *A history of the Tory Party 1640-1714.* Oxford: Clarendon Press, 1924.
  www.questia.com/PM.qst?a=o&d=6610420
  Subscription based.
- ALLEN, J.W. *A history of political thought in the sixteenth century.* Methuen & Co., 1951.
  www.questia.com/PM.qst?a=o&d=463083
  Subscription based.

- MORRIS, CHRISTOPHER. *Political thought in England, Tyndale to Hooker.* Oxford University Press, 1953.
  www.questia.com/PM.qst?a=o&d=7953801
  Subscription based.

ii. *The Royal Family*

- The Courtly Lives of Royalty, Peerage, Saints, Knights and their Genealogy: The Tudor Family / Margaret Odrowaz-Sypniewsk
  www.angelfire.com/mi/RedBearsDream/TudorTable.html
  Pages on each member of the family.
- The History of the Tudors
  www.geocities.com/henry8jane/Tudor.html
  A page for each monarch and for other members of the family.
- It's all about the Tudors
  www.tudors.youngbiz.com/
  The dynasty.
- Tudor Court
  www.tudorplace.com.ar/
  Pages on each monarch. Also includes a 'who's who in Tudor History', pages on the peerage, and many articles and sources *etc.*
- The Tudors
  www.spartacus.schoolnet.co.uk/Tudors.htm
  For schools.

iii. *Henry VII*

- BACON, FRANCIS, SIR. *Historia regni Henrici Septimi regis Anglioe.* 1622.
  eee.uci.edu/~papyri/henry/
  With introduction by Dana F. Sutton.
- Henry VII (1485-1509 A.D.)
  www.britannia.com/history/monarchs/mon40.html
- GAIRDNER, JAMES. *Henry VII.* Macmillan & Co., 1899.
  tudorhistory.org/secondary/henry7/title.htm
- ROUTH, E.M.G. *Lady Margaret: a memoir of Lady Margaret Beaufort, Countess of Richmond & Derby, mother of Henry VII.* Oxford University Press, 1924.
  tudorhistory.org/secondary/beaufort/contents.html

iv. *Henry VIII*

- Henry VIII (1509-47 A.D.)
  www.britannia.com/history/monarchs/mon41.html

- Henry VIII: destruction and renewal
  www.historystudystop.co.uk/php/displayarticle.php?article=12&topic=emb
- Henry VIII: Majesty with Menace / Professor Ronald Hutton
  www.bbc.co.uk/history/state/monarchs_leaders/
  majesty_menace_01.shtml
- The Six Wives of Henry VIII
  www.pbs.org/wnet/sixwives/
- SMITH, LACEY BALDWIN. *Henry VIII: the mask of royalty.* Boston:
  Houghton Mifflin, 1973.
  www.questia.com/PM.qst?a=o&d=85955080
  Subscription based.
- Anne Boleyn and the Downfall of Her Family / Richard Bevan
  www.bbc.co.uk/state/monarchs_leaders/anne_boleyn_01.shtml
- ELTON, G.R. *The Tudor revolution in government: administrative changes in the reign of Henry VIII.* Cambridge: Cambridge University Press, 1962.
  www.questia.com/PM.qst?a=o&d=2993196
  Subcription based.
- ANGLO, SYDNEY. *Spectacle, pageantry, and early Tudor policy.* Oxford: Clarendon Press, 1997.
  www.questia.com/PM.qst?a=o&d=41401745
  Subscription based.
- Cardinal Wolsey: Model Answer
  www.historystudystop.co.uk/php/displayarticle.php?article=13&topic=emb
  For A level students.
- Sir John Gage, Tudor Courtier and Soldier (1479-1556)
  www.findarticles.com/cf_dls/m0293/474_117/95912936/pl/article.jhtml
  From the *English historical review,* 11/2002.
- A Lost Source for the Rising of 1536 in North-West England / R.W.Hoyle & A.J.L. Winchester
  www.findarticles.com/cf_dls/m0293/475_118/98413767/pl/article.jhtml
  From the *English historical review,* 2/2003.
- The Mary Rose: a Great Ship of King Henry VIII
  www.bbc.co.uk/history/war/mary_rose_01.shtml

v. *Edward VI*
- Edward VI (1547-1553 A.D.)
  www.britannia.com/history/monarchs/mon42.html

- Hans Eworth's Portrait of the Earl of Arundel and the Politics of 1549-50 / Andrew Boyle
  www.findarticles.com/cf_dls/m0293/470_117/84302833/pl/article.jhtml
  From the *English historical review,* 2/2002.
- Protector Somerset and the 1549 Rebellions: new sources and new perspectives / Ethan H. Shagan
  www.findarticles.com/cf_dls/m0293/455_114/54050233/pl/article.jhtml
  From the *English historical review.* 2/1999.
- Popularity and the 1549 Rebellions Revisited / Ethan H. Shagan
  www.findarticles.com/cf_dls/m0293/60_115/60104296/pl/article.jhtml
  See also **/60104295/pl/article.jhtml** and **/60104293/pl/article.jhtml**
  From the *English historical review,* 2/2000.

vi. *'Queen' Jane*
- Lady Jane Grey Reference Site
  members.aol.com/ladyjanegreyref/
  Queen for a few days in 1553.
- The Lady Jane Grey Internet Museum
  www.bitterwisdom.com/ladyjanegrey/main.html
- Jane the Quene
  www.geocities.com/jane_the_quene/
- Lady Jane Grey
  www.ladyjanegrey.org/
- Lady Jane / Jennifer Halligan
  www.britannia.com/history/ladyjane/janefram.html

vii. *Queen Mary*
- Mary I (1553-1558 A.D.)
  www.britannia.com/history/monarchs/mon44.html
- Mary Tudor
  www.historystudystop.co.uk/php/displayarticle.php?article=6&topic=emb
  For A level students.
- Mary Tudor
  home.earthlink.net/~elisale/
- Mary Tudor
  www.newadvent.org/cathen/09766a.htm
  From the *Catholic encyclopedia.*

viii. *Elizabeth I*

- 'As True a Subject being Prysoner': John Foxe's notes on the imprisonment of Princess Elizabeth 1554-5 / Thomas S. Freeman
  www.findarticles.com/cf__dls/m0293/470__117/84302837/pl/article.jhtml
  From the *English historical review*, 2/2002.
- Elizabeth I (1558-1603 A.D.)
  www.britannia.com/history/monarchs/mon45.html
- Elizabeth R.
  www.elizabethi.org/
- Elizabethan Geek: resources for the Elizabethan History Fanatic
  elizabethgeek.com/
- CAMDEN, WILLIAM. *Annals rerum gestarum Angliae et Hiberniae Regnante Elizabetha* (1615 and 1625)
  e3.uci.edu/~papyri/camden/
- HAYWARD, JOHN, SIR. *Annals of the first four years of Queen Elizabeth*, ed. John Bruce. Camden Society, 1840.
  www.questia.com/PM.qst?a=o&d=9069771
  Subscription based.
- Elizabeth I: an assessment
  www.historystudystop.co.uk/php/displayarticle.php?article=95&topic=higher
  For schools.
- Elizabeth I: an overview / Alexandra Briscoe
  www.bbc.co.uk/history/state/monarchs__leaders/elizabeth__i__01.shtml
- Gloriana: the life and reign of Elizabeth I
  elizabethtudor.150m.com/
- History in focus: Elizabeth I and James VI and I
  www.history.ac.uk/ihr/Focus/Elizabeth/index.html
- LEVIN, CAROLE. *The Heart and stomach of a king: Elizabeth I and the politics of sex and power.* Philadelphia: University of Pennsylvania Press, 1994.
  www.questia.com/PM.qst?a=o&d=45651936
  Subscription based.
- PALMER, MICHAEL. *Reputations: Elizabeth.* B.T.Batsford, 1988.
  www.questia.com/PM.qst?a=o&d=66063093
- READ, CONYERS. *Lord Burghley and Queen Elizabeth.* New York: Alfred A. Knopf, 1960.
  www.questia.com/PM.qst?a=o&d=65990877
  Subscription based.

- SMITH, LACEY BALDWIN. *Elizabeth Tudor: portrait of a queen.* Boston: Little Brown & Co., 1975.
  www.questia.com/PM.qst?a=o&d=65399420
  Subscription based.
- LEHMBERG, STANFORD E. *Sir Walter Mildmay and Tudor Government.* Austin: University of Texas Press, 1964.
  www.questia.com/PM.qst?a=o&d=9455370
  Subscription based.
- Office of Justice of the Peace in England, 1600 / Earl B. Brand
  historicaltextarchive.com/sections.php?op=viewarticle&artid=644

D. Ecclesiastical History

- The Reformation Guide
  www.educ.msu.edu/homepages/laurence/reformation/index.htm
  Gateway, international in scope, but with many British sites.
- English Reformation Sources
  www.members.shaw.ca/reformation/
  Mid-16th c. Primary sources
- English Reformation
  www.educ.msu.edu/homepages/laurence/reformation/English/English.htm
- An Overview of the Reformation / Bruce Robinson
  www.bbc.co.uk/history/state/church__reformation/reformation__overview__01.shtml
- Reformation and Reform / Carol Davidson Cragoe
  www.bbc.co.uk/history/lj/churchlj/reform__01.shtml
- The Human Reformation / Bruce Robinson
  www.bbc.co.uk/history/state/church__reformation/human__reformation__01.shtml
- The Legacy of the Reformation / Bruce Robinson
  www.bbc.co.uk/history/state/church__reformation/reformation__debate__01.shtml
- The English Reformation / Professor Andrew Pettegree
  www.bbc.co.uk/history/state/church__reformation/english__reformation__01.shtml
- The Reformation in England / Dr. E.L.Skip Knox
  history.boisestate.edu/westciv/reformat/england01.htm
- Henry & Religion: the religious policy of Henry VIII 1530-1547 / Jeff Hobbs
  www.britannia.com/history/articles/relpolh8.html

- Dissent, Doubt, and Spiritual Violence in the Reformation
  www.wwnorton.com/nael/16century/topic__3/welcome.htm
- Redefining the Sacred in Early Modern England
  www.folger.edu/institute/sacred/
- CARLSON, JOSEF. *Religion and the English people 1500-1640: new voices, new perspectives.* Kirksville: Truman State University Press, 1998.
  www.questia.com/PM.qst?a=o&d=43055900
  Subscription based.
- HAIGH, CHRISTOPHER. *English reformations: religion, politics and society under the Tudors.* Oxford: Clarendon Press, 1993.
  www.questia.com/PM.qst?a=o&d=16221552
  Subscription based.
- SLAVIN, ARTHUR J. *Henry VIII and the English Reformation.* Lexington: Heath, 1968.
  www.questia.com/PM.qst?a=o&d=97615499
  Subscription based.
- HUGHES, PHILIP. *The Reformation in England.* New York. Macmillan, 1951.
  www.questia.com/PM.qst?a=o&d=161423
  Subscription based.
- The Taming of Reformation: preachers, pastors and parishioners in Elizabethan and early Stuart England / Christopher Haigh
  www.nd.edu/~dharley/Histideas/texts/TamingEngRef.pdf
- The Elizabethan Parish: a collection of documents / C.J. Harrison
  www.keele.ac.uk/depts/hi/resources/reformation/
  Illustrating how the reformation affected local church life.
- TITTIER, ROBERT. *The Reformation and the towns in England: politics and political culture 1540-1640.* Oxford: Clarendon Press, 1998.
  www.questia.com/PM.qst?a=o&d=97692767
  Subscription based.
- HILL, CHRISTOPHER. *Economic problems of the church from Archbishop Whitgift to the Long Parliament.* Oxford: Clarendon Press, 1956.
  www.questia.com/PM.qst?a=o&d=3768547
  Subscription based.
- TRUEMAN, CARL R. *Luther's legacy: salvation and English reformers, 1525-1556.* Oxford: Clarendon Press, 1994.
  www.questia.com/PM.qst?a=o&d=74343285
  Subscription based.

- Suppression of the English Monasteries during the reign of King Henry VIII
  www.peterwestern.f9.co.uk/monasteries.htm
- The Thirty-Nine Articles of Religion
  www.singnet.com.sg/~kohfly/articles.htm
- The Other Black Legend: the Henrician Reformation and the Spanish People / Peter Marshall
  www.findarticles.com/cf__dls/m0293/465__116/78678851/pl/article.jhtml
  From the *English historical review,* 2/2001.
- EMERSON, EVERETT H. *English puritanism from John Hooper to John Milton.* Durham, N.C.: Duke University Press, 1968.
  www.questia.com/PM.qst?a=o&d=9256957
  Subscription based.
- The History of the English *Book of Common Prayer* / Jeff Hobbs
  www.britannia.com/history/articles/prayerbk.html
- The Genevan Book of Order: the form of prayers and ministration of the sacraments *etc.* used in the English congregation at Geneva (1556)
  www.swrb.ab.ca/newslett/actualnls/GBO__ch00.htm
- The Recusant Historians Handbook / J.A. Hilton
  www.catholic-history.org.uk/nwchs/recushandbook.htm
- What happened to English Catholicism after the Reformation?
  www.nd.edu/~dharley/Histideas/texts/post-RefEngCatholicism.pdf
- The Bishop's Census of 1563: a re-examination of its reliability / Dr. Nigel Goose
  www.history.ac.uk/projects/elec/sem1.html
- Magic, Witchcraft and Popular Culture in Early Modern England / Dr. Michael Zell
  www.gre.ac.uk/~zm01/Magic/magic.html
  Undergraduate course.

E. **Social & Economic History**
- WAGNER, JOHN A. *Historical dictionary of the Elizabethan world: Britain, Ireland, Europe and America.* Phoenix: Oryx Press, 1999.
  www.questia.com/PM.qst?a=o&d=8999727
  Subscription based.
- Life in Elizabethan England: a compendium of common knowledge
  renaissance.dm.net/compendium/home.html
  Social history.
- Renaissance: the Elizabethan World
  renaissance.dm.net/
  Includes much information on Elizabethan society.

- Society and Culture in Early Modern England / Dr. Michael Zell
  www.gre.ac.uk/~zm01/preind/soc%20cult.html
  Undergraduate course.
- CRESSY, DAVID. *Birth, marriage and death: ritual, religion and the life-cycle in Tudor and Stuart England.* Oxford: Oxford University Press, 1997.
  www.questia.com/PM.qst?a=o&d=15467814
  Subscription based.
- Searchers of the Dead: authority, marginality and the interpretation of plague in England, 1574-1665 / Richelle Munkhoff
  www.nd.edu/~dharley/HistIdeas/texts/searchers-plague.pdf
  From *Gender & history*, 11(1), 1999, pp.1-29.
- WRIGHT, LOUIS B. *Middle class culture in Elizabethan England.* Chapel Hill: University of North Carolina Press, 1935.
  www.questia.com/PM.qst?a=o&d=892012
  Subscription based.
- SCHMIDT, ALBERT F. *The Yeoman in Tudor and Stuart England.* Washington, D.C.: Folger Shakespeare Library, 1961.
  www.questia.com/PM.qst?a=o&d=243350
  Subscription based.
- EMERSON, KATHY LYNN. *Wives and daughters: the women of sixteenth century England.* Troy, N.Y.: Whitson Publishing Co., 1984.
  www.questia.com/PM.qst?a=o&d=59429201
  Subscription based.
- MENDELSON, SARA, & CRAWFORD, PATRICIA. *Women in early modern England 1550-1720.* Oxford: Clarendon Press, 1998.
  www.questia.com/PM.qst?a=o&d=9827569
  Subscription based.
- Rereading Rape and Sexual Violence in Early Modern England / Garthine Walker
  www.nd.edu/~dharley/HistIdeas/texts/rape-earlyModEng.pdf
  From *Gender & history* 10(1), 1998, pp.1-25.
- Huswifery
  web.uvic.ca/shakespeare/Library/SLT/society/huswiferysubj.html
  16th c.
- TAWNEY, R.H. *The agrarian problem in the sixteenth century.* Longmans Green & Co., 1912
  www.questia.com/PM.qst?a=o&d=5791162
  Subscription based.

- TAWNEY, R.H., ed. *Tudor economic documents, being select documents illustrating the economic and social history of Tudor England.* Longmans Green & Co., 1924.
  www.questia.com/PM.qst?a=o&d=6848126
- Elizabethan Food: a page of references and links for students
  members.aol.com/renfrowcm/elizabethan.html
- Poverty in Elizabethan England / Alexandra Briscoe
  www.bbc.co.uk/history/state/monarchs__leaders/poverty__01.shtml
- Tyburn Tree: Public Execution in Early Modern England
  www.evergreen.loyola.edu/=cmitchell/
- A general study of the plague in England 1539-1640, with a specific reference to Loughborough / Ian Jessiman
  www.loughborough.co.uk/plague/
- Print and Censorship in Elizabethan Society
  apm.brookes.ac.uk/publishing/contexts/elizabet/contents.htm

F. Defence & Discovery
- The Spanish Armada / Dr. Simon Adams
  www.bbc.co.uk/history/state/monarchs__leaders/ adams__armada__01.shtml
- MATTINGLEY, GARRETT. *The Invincible Armada and Elizabethan England.* Ithaca: Cornell University Press, 1963.
  www.questia.com/PM.qst?a=o&d=3907257
  Subscription based.
- BIGGS, WALTER. *Drake's great armada.* New York: P.F.Collier & Son, 1910.
  historicaltextarchive.com/books.php?op=viewbook&bookid=62
- Elizabeth's Pirates
  www.channel4.com/history/microsites/H/history/pirates/index.html
  Privateers and English defence.
- Drake, Sir Francis: *El Draque* the Dragon / Jeff Howell
  historicalarchive.com/sections.php?op=viewarticle&artid=443
- RALEIGH, WALTER, SIR. *Last fight of the Revenge at Sea.* William Ponsonbie, 1591
  darkwing.uoregon.edu/%7Erbear/raleighl.html
- Elizabeth's Spy Network / Alexandra Briscoe
  www.bbc.co.uk/history/state/monarchs__leaders/spying__01.shtml

- HARRISSE, HENRY. *John Cabot, the discoverer of North America, and Sebastian his son: a chapter in the maritime history of England under the Tudors 1496-1557.* Stevens, 1896.
  www.canadiana.org/ECO/mtq?doc=05393
- Sir Francis Drake
  www.mcn.org/2/oseeler/drake.htm
  Emphasis on his round the world voyage.
- Texts of Imagination and Empire: the founding of Jamestown in its Atlantic Context
  www.folger.edu/institute/jamestown/index__main.htm
  Includes much on the English background to Virginian colonisation.

G. Writers & their Works

Ascham, Roger
- Roger Ascham (1515-1568)
  www.luminarium.org/renlit/ascham.htm
  Includes some of his works.
- ASCHAM, ROGER. *The Scholemaster.* John Daye, 1570.
  darkwing.uoregon.edu/%7Erbear/ascham1.htm

Bacon, Sir Francis
- Sir Francis Bacon: new advancement of learning
  www.sirbacon.org/toc.html
  Biographical site, including some texts; Elizabethan philosopher

Dee, John
- John Dee and the English calendar: Science, Religion and Empire / Dr. Robert Poole
  www.history.ac.uk/projects/elec/sem2.html

Elizabeth I
- Elizabeth I (1533-1603)
  www.luminarium.org/renlit/eliza.htm
  Includes her letters, speeches, poetry, *etc.*
- Queen Elizabeth I of England (b.1533, r.1558-1603): Selected Writings and Speeches
  www.fordham.edu/halsall/mod/elizabeth1.html
- The Works of Elizabeth I (1533-1603)
  www.luminarium.org/renlit/elizabib.htm
  Speeches, letters, poetry, *etc.*

Elyot, Thomas
- ELYOT, THOMAS. *The boke named the governour.*
  darkwing.uoregon.edu/%7Erbear/gov/gov1.htm
  On Henrician social graces

Foxe, John
- The British Academy John Foxe project
  www.shef.ac.uk/uni/projects/bajfp/index.html
  Project to computerise Foxe's *Acts and monuments* (1583 edition).
- Fox's *Book of Martyrs* / John Fox (ed. William Byron Forbush)
  www.reformed.org/books/fox/fox__martyrs.html
- John Foxe (1516-1587)
  www.luminarium.org/renlit/foxe.htm
  Includes links to various web editions of his *Book of martyrs.*

Hakluyt, Richard
- HAKLUYT, RICHARD. *Voyagers tales.*
  historicaltextarchive.com/books.php?op=viewbook&bookid=51
  Selections, first published late 16th c.

Hariot, Thomas
- HARIOT, THOMAS. *A brief and true report of the new found land of Virginia,* ed. Melissa S. Kennedy.
  www.people.virginia.edu/~msk5d/hariot/main.html
  Originally published London, 1588.

Harrison, William
- HARRISON, WILLIAM. *Harrison's description of England in Shakespeare's youth, 1575.*
  leehrsn.50megs.com
  Edition edited by Frederick Furnivall, 1877.
- Modern History Sourcebook: William Harrison (1534-1593): *Description of England,* 1577
  www.fordham.edu/halsall/mod/1577harrison-england.html
- HARRISON, WILLIAM. *A description of Elizabethan England.* New York: P.F.Collier, & Son, 1909-14
  www.bartleby.com/35/3/

Henry VIII
- Henry VIII (1491-1547)
  www.luminarium.org/renlit/tudor.htm
  Includes some of his writings, mainly poetry.

Hooker, Richard
- Richard Hooker (c.1554-1600) Anglican divine
  www.ccel.org/h/hooker/
  Includes a brief life.
- Richard Hooker (1554-1600)
  www.luminarium.org/renlit/hooker.htm
  Includes links with web editions of his *laws of ecclesiastical polity etc.*
- Richard Hooker's Reputation (author of *Ecclesiastical polity.*)
  Diarmaid MacCulloch
  www.findarticles.com/cf__dls/m0293/473__117/92203923/pl/article.jhtml
  From the *English historical review,* 9/2002.
- HOOKER, RICHARD. *Of the laws of ecclesiastical polity.* 1593.
  www.wwnorton.com/nael/noa/pdf/hooker__r.pdf

More, Thomas
- CHAMBERS, R.W. *Thomas More.* Ann Arbor: University of Michigan Press, 1958.
  www.questia.com/PM.qst?a=o&d=3606291
  Subscription based.
- ROPER, WILLIAM. *The mirrour of vertue in worldly greatnes, or the lyfe of Syr. T. More.*
  darkwing.uoregon.edu/%7Erebear/roper1.html
- Thomas More
  www.d-holliday.com/tmore/
- Sir Thomas More
  www.bartleby.com/people/More-T.html
  Includes full text of *Utopia.* New York: P.F.Collier & Son, 1909-14; also the *Life* by William Roper.
- The Life of Sir Thomas More / William Roper
  www.fordham.edu/halsall/mod/16Croper-more.html

Shakespeare, William
- Mr. William Shakespeare and the Internet
  shakespeare.palomar.edu/
  Portal.

Smith, Thomas
- De Republica Anglorum / Sir Thomas Smith
  www.constitution.org/eng/repang.htm
  Originally published in 1583

Tusser, Thomas
- TUSSER, THOMAS. *A hundreth good pointes of husbandrie.* 1557 (1909 edition)
  darkwing.uoregon.edu/%7Erbear/tusser1.html

Tyndale, William
- The Tyndale New Testament
  www.bl.uk/collections/treasures/tyndale.html
  Facsimile of the original printed edition.

16. The Stuart Era, 1603-1714

A. General Sites
- 17th Century Net: Gateway to the Renaissance and 17th Century on the Net
  www.17thcenturynet.net
- Time Travellers Guide to Stuart England
  www.channel4.com/history/microsites/H/history/guide17.html
- Britain 1600-1750
  www.spartacus.schoolnet.co.uk/Stuarts.htm
  Includes many biographies. For schools
- Stuart England
  www.historylearningsite.co.uk/Stuarts.htm
  Many pages; for schools
- HILL, CHRISTOPHER. *The century of revolution, 1603-1714*. New York: W.W.Norton & Co., 1966.
  www.questia.com/PM.qst?a=o&d=1362135
  Subscription based.
- 17th Century Reenacting and Living History Resources
  www.lukehistory.com/resources/index.html
  Includes a few civil war pamphlets.
- The Lampeter Corpus of Early Modern English Tracts
  **www.tu-chemnitz.de/phil/english/chairs/linguist/real/independent/
  lampeter/lamphome.htm**
  Tracts 1640-1740.
- Seventeenth Century
  pub35.bravenet.com/sitering/show.php?usernum=2940886648
  Web ring; mainly re-enactment sites.

B. Politics and Government
i. *General Works*
- GARDINER, SAMUEL RAWSON, ed. *The constitutional documents of the puritan revolution*. 3rd ed. Oxford: Clarendon Press, 1906.
  www.constitution.org/eng/conpur__.htm
  Also available by subscription at
  www.questia.com/PM.qst?a=o&d=94904867

- SCOTT, JONATHAN. *England's troubles: seventeenth-century English political instability in European context*. Cambridge: Cambridge University Press, 2000.
  www.nd.edu/~dharley/HistIdeas/texts/Scott-EnglandsTroubles-intro.PDF
  Chapter 1 only.
- RUSSELL, CONRAD. *The causes of the English Civil War: the Ford lectures delivered in the University of Oxford 1987-1988*. Oxford: Clarendon Press, 1990.
  www.questia.com/PM.qst?a=o&d=53279888
- HILL, CHRISTOPHER. *Intellectual origins of the English Revolution revisited*. Oxford: Oxford University Press, 1997.
  www.questia.com/PM.qst?a=o&d=59530844
  Subscription based.
- HILL, CHRISTOPHER. *Puritanism and revolution: studies in interpretation of the English Revolution of the 17th century*. Secker & Warburg, 1958.
  www.questia.com/PM.qst?a=o&d=33733836
  Subscription based.
- ELEY, GEOFF, ed. *Reviving the English revolution: reflections and elaborations on the work of Christopher Hill*. Verso, 1988.
  www.questia.com/PM.qst?a=o&d=97469444
  Subscription based.
- COLTMAN, IRENE. *Private men and public causes: philosophy and politics in the English civil war*. Faber & Faber, 1962.
  www.questia.com/PM.qst?a=o&d=11878134
  Subscription based.
- *House of Commons journal. vol.2. 1640-1643*. 1802.
  www.british-history.ac.uk/source.asp?pubid=33
- *House of Commons journal, volume 3. 1643-1644*.
  www.british-history.ac.uk/source.asp?pubid=9

ii. *James I*
- James VI and I
  www.luminarium.org/sevenlit/james/
  Many essays.
- His Majestie King James VI and I Page
  www.jesus-is-lord.com/Kinginde.htm
- James I (1603-25 A.D.)
  www.britannia.com/history/monarchs/mon46.html

- The English Accession of James VI: 'national' identity, gender and the personal monarchy of England
  www.findarticles.com/cf__dls/m0293/472__117/89379223/pl/article.jhtml
  From the *English historical review,* 6/2002.
- Gunpowder Plot / Guy Fawkes Electronic On-line Classroom
  www.bcpl.net/=cbladey/guy/html/main.html
- The Gunpowder Plot / David Herber
  www.britannia.com/history/gunpowder1.html
- Gunpowder Plot: High Treason in 1605
  www.innotls.co.uk/asperges/fawkes/
- The Gunpowder Plot / Alan Haynes
  www.bbc.co.uk/history/state/monarchs__leaders/
  gunpowder__haynes__01.shtml
- The Gunpowder Plot
  www.parliament.uk/documents/upload/g08.pdf
- The Guy Fawkes Gunpowder Plot Pages
  www.bcpl.net/~cbladey/guy/html/main1.html
- The Gunpowder Plot of 1605: the trial of Guy Fawkes and others
  www.armitstead.com/gunpowder/trial.html
  Transcript from *A complete collection of state-trials ...,* 1776.
- What if the Gunpowder Plot had Succeeded / Professor Ronald Hutton
  www.bbc.co.uk/history/state/monarchs__leaders/
  gunpowder__hutton__01.shtml
- The Brightnes of the Noble Leiutenants action: an intellectual ponders Buckingham's assassination / Alastair Bellany
  www.findarticles.com/cf__dls/m0293/479__118/113182796/pl/article.jhtml
  From the *English historical review,* 4/2003.

iii. *Charles I*
- **Charles I (1625-49 A.D.)**
  www.britannia.com/history/monarchs/mon47.html
- Charles I: after 1637 - not a bad king after all?
  www.historystudystop.co.uk/php/displayarticle.php?article=31&topic=emb
  For A level students.
- GREGG, PAULINE. *King Charles I.* Berkeley: University of California Press, 1981.
  ark.cdlib.org/ark:/13030/ft9vi9p2p6/
- The Personality and Political Style of Charles I / Dr. Richard Cust
  www.bbc.co.uk/history/state/monarchs__leaders/
  personality__charles__01.shtml

- Civil War, 1625-1649
  www.open2.net/civilwar/
  Open University page.
- The Chiefest Strength and Glory of this Kingdom: arming and training the 'perfect militia' in the 1630's / Henrik Langeluddecke
  www.findarticles.com/cf__dls/m0293/479__118/113182797/p1/article.jhtml
  From *English historical review,* 4/2003.
- 'Patchy and Spasmodic'?: the response of Justices of the Peace to Charles I's Book of Orders / Henrik Langeluddecke
  www.findarticles.com/cf__dls/m0293/454__113/53706852/pl/article.jhtml
  From the *English historical review,* 11/1998.
- The Petition of Right, 1628
  www.constitution.org/eng/petright.htm
  Text.

iv. *The Great Rebellion*
- British Civil Wars, Commonwealth and Protectorate 1638-60
  www.british-civil-wars.co.uk
  Includes timelines, pages on each battle, biographies, and many articles.
- FLETCHER, ANTHONY. *The outbreak of the English civil war.* New York: New York University Press, 1981.
  www.questia.com/PM.qst?a=o&d=28088250
  Subscription based.
- The English Civil War, or 'the British Civil Wars 1639-53'?
  www.historystudystop.co.uk/php/
  displayarticle.php?article=94&topic=higher
  For schools.
- KENYON, JOHN, ed. *The civil wars: military history of England, Scotland and Ireland, 1638-1600.* Oxford: Oxford University Press, 1998.
  www.questia.com/PM.qst?a=o&d=85742102
  Subscription based.
- English Civil War
  www.spartacus.schoolnet.co.uk/CivilWar.htm
  Many pages of biographies, battles, religious groups, issues, *etc.*
- Choosing Sides in the English Civil War / Dr. Mark Stoyle
  www.bbc.co.uk/history/war/englishcivilwar/choosingsides__01.shtml
- HIBBARD, CAROLINE M. *Charles I and the Popish Plot.* Chapel Hill: University of North Carolina Press, 1983
  www.questia.com/PM.qst?a=o&d=59075100
  Subscription based.

- BRUNTON, D., & PENNINGTON, D.H. *Members of the Long Parliament.* George Allen & Unwin, 1954.
  www.questia.com/PM.qst?a=o&d=3907319
  Subscription based.
- The Civil War in the West / Dr. John Wroughton
  www.bbc.co.uk/history/war/englishcivilwar/west__01.shtml
  In Somerset, Gloucestershire and Wiltshire.
- The English Civil War
  www.hillsdale.edu/academics/history/War/EMCiv.htm
  Original documents relating to the battles of Edgehill and Marston Moor, *etc.*
- Civil Supply in the Civil War: supply of victuals to the New Model Army on the Naseby Campaign, 1-14 June 1645 / Aryeh S. Nusbacher
  www.findarticles.com/cf__dls/m0293/460__115/60104298/pl/article.jhtml
  From the *English historical review,* 2/2000.
- Popular exploitation of Enemy Estates in the English Revolution / Christopher O'Riordan
  www.geocities.com/englishrevolution/popular.htm
  Originally published in *History,* **78**, 1993, pp.184-200.
- Space, Patronage, Procedure: the Court at Oxford 1642-46 / Jerome de Groot
  www.findarticles.com/cf__dls/m0293/474__117/95912939/pl/article.jhtml
  From the *English historical review,* 2/2002.
- The Trial of Charles I / Sean Kelsey
  www.findarticles.com/cf__dls/m0293/477__118/104728589/pl/article.jhtml
  From the *English historical review,* 6/2003.
- The Death Warrant of King Charles I
  www.parliament.the-stationery-office.co.uk/pa/ld199899/ldparlac/ldrpt66.htm
  Also at
  www.publications.parliament.uk/pa/ld199899/ldparlac/ldrpt66.htm
- The Execution of Charles I / Professor Ann Hughes
  www.bbc.co.uk/history/state/monarchs__leaders/charlesi__execution__01.shtml

v. *The Protectorate*

- Oliver Cromwell
  www.historystudystop.co.uk/php/displayarticle.php?article=96&topic=higher
  For schools.
- Oliver Cromwell / Professor John Morrill
  www.bbc.co.uk/history/state/monarchs__leaders/cromwell__01.shtml
- Oliver Cromwell: Constitutional Crisis in England
  mars.acnet.wnec.edu/~grempel/courses/wc2/lectures/cromwell.html
  Brief lecture.
- Oliver Cromwell (1649-1658 A.D.)
  www.britannia.com/history/monarchs/mon48.html
  The Protectorate.
- The Pamphleteers Protestant Champion: viewing Oliver Cromwell through the media of his day / Kevin A. Creed
  etext.lib.virginia.edu/journals/EH/EH34/creed34.html
- Constitutional Acts 1648-50 from Adams & Smith, *Select Documents of English Constitutional History.*
  home.freeuk.net/don-aitken/con1649.html
- The Commonwealth Instrument of Government 1653
  www.fordham.edu/halsall/mod/1653instrumentgovt.html
- United Kingdom: Flags of the Interregnum, 1649-1660
  www.crwflags.com/fotw/flags/gb-inter.html
- The Fall of Cromwell's Major Generals / Christopher Durston
  www.findarticles.com/cf__dls/M0293/n450__v113/20572945/p1/article.jhtml
  From the *English historical review,* 2/1998.
- George Monck's *Observations:* the foremost English Handbook of Generalship and Statecraft
  www.generalmonck.com/
  Brief extracts, with some details of Monck's life.
- The Battle of Dunbar (September 3, 1650) / Stephen Beck
  www.geocities.com/beckster05/Dunbar/DbMain.htm
- Richard Cromwell (1658-1659 A.D.)
  www.britannia.com/history/monarchs/mon48a.html

vi. *Radical Political Thought: Levellers & Diggers etc.*

- SCHENK, W. *The Concern for social justice in the Puritan revolution.* Longmans, Green & Co., 1948
  www.questia.com/PM.qst?a=o&d=24449570
  Subscription based.
- The Levellers: a chronology and bibliography / Roderick Moore
  www.libertarian.org/LA/levelchr.html
- The Levellers: libertarian radicalism and the English civil war / David Hoile
  www.libertarian.org/LA/leveller.html
  www.capital.demon.co.uk/LA/heritage/leveller.htm

- The Levellers and the Tradition of Dissent / Tony Benn
  www.bbc.co.uk/history/society_culture/protest_reform/
  benn_levellers_01.shtml
- Levellers
  www.levellers.org
  Includes original sources.
- PEASE, THEODORE CALVIN. *The Leveller movement: a study in the history and political theory of the English Great Civil War.* Washington: American Historical Association, 1916.
  www.questia.com/PM.qst?a=o&d=3476173
  Subscription based.
- PEASE, THEODORE CALVIN. *The leveller movement: a study in the history and political theory of the English great civil war.* Oxford University Press, 1916.
  www.constitution.org/lev/lev_mov.htm
- Selected Works of the Levellers
  www.constitution.org/lev/levellers.htm
- Street Corner Society
  www.strecorsoc.org
  Radical documents of the mid-seventeenth century; includes *An agreement of the people ...* the *Just defence of John Lilburne, etc.*
- The Land and Freedom Pages: English Civil War History
  www.bilderberg.org/land/index.htm
  The Diggers and levellers.
- The Religion of Gerard Winstanley and Digger Communism / Donald R. Sutherland
  etext.lib.virginia.edu/journals/EH/EH33/suther33.html
- The English Diggers (1649-50)
  www.diggers.org/diggers/digg_eb.html
  Includes sources.
- JORDAN, W.K. *Men of substance: a study in the thought of two revolutionaries, Henry Parker and Henry Robinson.* Chicago: University of Chicago Press, 1942.
  www.questia.com/PM.qst?a=o&d=3037861
  Subscription based.

vii. *Charles II*
- The Masquerading Monarch / Professor Ronald Hutton
  www.bbc.co.uk/history/state/monarchs_leaders/
  charlesii_masq_01.shtml
- Charles II (1660-85 A.D.)
  www.britannia.com/history/monarchs/mon49.html
- Slavery under Charles II: the Mediterranean and Tangier / G.E. Aylmer
  www.findarticles.com/cf_dls/m0293/456_114/54466587/p1/article.jhtml
  From the *English historical reivew*, 4/1999.
- A Moderate in the First Age of Party: the dilemmas of Sir John Holland, 1675-85 / John Miller
  www.findarticles.com/cf_dls/m0293/458_114/55979089/p1/article.jhtml
  From the *English historical review*, 9/1999.
- JONES, J.R. *The first Whigs: the politics of the Exclusion crisis, 1678-1683.* Oxford University Press, 1961
  www.questia.com/PM.qst?a=o&d=98156039
  Subscription based.
- Habeas Corpus Act 1679
  www.constitution.org/eng/habcorpa.htm

viii. *James II*
- James II (1685-88 A.D.)
  www.britannia.com/history/monarchs/mon50.html
- MACAULAY, THOMAS BABINGTON. *The history of England from the accession of James II.*
  www.strecorsoc.org/macaulay/tm_index.html
  Vol 1 only, covering primarily the reign of James II.
- Monmouth's Rebellion 1685
  www.regiments.org/milhist/wars/17thcent/85monmth.htm
- The Glorious Revolution 1688
  www.thegloriousrevolution.com/
- The Glorious Revolution
  www.parliament.uk/documents/upload/g04.pdf

ix. *William & Mary*
- William III and Mary II (1689-1702 A.D.)
  www.britannia.com/history/monarchs/mon51.html
- Bill of Rights, 1689
  www.constitution.org/eng/eng_bor.htm

- A Blueprint for Tyranny? Sir Edward Hales and the Catholic Jacobite Response to the Revolution of 1688 / Daniel Szechi.
  www.findarticles.com/cf__dls/m0293/466__116/74691875/pl/article.jhtml
  From the *English historical review*, 4/2001.
- Working Members of the British House of Commons, England, 1691-1693 (study number 217)
  hds.essex.ac.uk/study/browse/showabstract.php?sn=217
  Database.
- The Pattern of Distribution of the Offices of Lords Lieutenant and *Custodes Rotulorum*, 1689-1760 / Dr. David Backhouse
  www.history.ac.uk/projects/elec/sem7.html

x. *Anne*
- Anne (1702-14 A.D.)
  www.britannia.com/history/monarchs/mon52.html
- Queen Anne and the 1707 Act of Union
  www.highlanderweb.co.uk/wallace/anne.htm

B. Ecclesiastical History
- The Politics of Religious Conformity and the Accession of James I / Michael Questier
  www.nd.edu/~dharley/HistIdeas/texts/JamesI&conformity.pdf
  From *Historical research*. 71(174), 1998, pp.14-30.
- The Parochial roots of Laudianism revisited: Catholics, anti-Calvinists and 'parish Anglicans' in early Stuart England / Alexandra Walsham
  www.nd.edu/~dharley/HistIdeas/texts/Walsham-parishLaud.pdf
- William Laud and the Exercise of Caroline ecclesiastical patronage / Kenneth Fincham
  www.nd.edu/~dharley/HistIdeas/texts/Fincham-Laudpatron.pdf
  From the *Journal of ecclesiastical history*, 51(1), 2000, pp.69-93.
- Seasonable Treatises: a Godly project of the 1630's / J.T.Peacey
  www.findarticles.com/cf__dls/m0293/n452__v113/20920715/pl/article.jhtml
  From the *English historical review*, 6/1998.
  Puritan publishing project.
- HETHERINGTON, WILLIAM. *History of the Westminster Assembly of Divines.* Edinburgh: J. Johnstone, R. Groombridge, 1843.
  www.reformed.org/books/hetherington/west__assembly/
- The Confession of Faith of the Westminster Assembly of Divines
  members.aol.com/RSICHURCH/wcf1.html
  In 1646.

- An Holy and Sacramentall Paction: Federal Theology and the Solemn League and Covenant
  www.findarticles.com/cf__dls/m0293/465__116/78678852/pl/article.jhtml
  From the *English historical review*, 2/2001.
- English Dissenters
  www.exlibris.org/nonconform/engdis/index.html
  Primarily mid-17th c. Includes useful bibliography.
- Revolutionary Church Democracy 1640-1660 / Christopher O'Riordan
  www.geocities.com/englishrevolution/democrat.htm
- YULE, GEORGE. *The independents in the English civil war.* Cambridge: Cambridge University Press, 1958.
  www.questia.com/PM.qst?a=o&d=30308481
  Subscription based.
- A Quaker Page
  www.strecorsoc.org/quaker.html
  Includes some key 17-18th c. texts including works by George Fox and James Naylor, *etc.*
- REAY, BARRY. *The Quakers and the English Revolution.* Temple Smith, 1985
  www.questia.com/PM.qst?a=o&d=58674510
  Subscription based.
- Protestant Divergence in the Restoration Crisis / Martin P. Sutherland
  www.nd.edu/~dharley/HistIdeas/texts/Sutherland-Prots&Restorationcrisis.pdf
  From *Journal of religious history,* 21(3), 1997, pp.285-301.
- CRAGG, GERALD R. *Puritanism in the period of the great persecution, 1660-1688.* Cambridge: Cambridge University Press, 1957.
  www.questia.com/PM.qst?a=o&d=3694256
  Subscription based.
- The Roger Morrice Entring Book Project
  www.hist.cam.ac.uk/seminars__events/events/roger-morrice.html
  Project to edit a chronicle of public affairs, 1677-91 written by a nonconformist minister.

C. Social History
- Gender, Family, Household: 17th century norms and controversies
  www.wwnorton.com/nael/17century/topic__1/welcome.htm
- Manhood, the male body, courtship and the household in early modern England / Anthony Fletcher
  www.nd.edu/~dharley/HistIdeas/texts/Engl-manhood-courtship.pdf

- Dealing with love: the ambiguous independence of the single woman in early modern England / Pamela Sharpe
  www.nd.edu/~dharley/HistIdeas/texts/Eng-singlewomen.pdf
  From *Gender & history,* 11(2), 1999, pp.209-32.
- Love, Property and Kinship: the courtship of Philip Williams, Levant merchant, 1617-50
  www.findarticles.com/cf__dls/m0293/n451__v113/20555553/p1/article.jhtml
  From the *English historical review,* 4/1998.
- Women's Lives in the British Civil Wars
  www.earlymodernweb.org.uk/warlives/wlintro.htm
- 'My Pappa is out and my Mamma is asleep': minors, their routine activities, and interpersonal violence in an early modern town 1653-1701 / Jessica Warner & Robin Griller
  www.findarticles.com/cf__dls/m2005/3__36/99699487/p1/article.jhtml
  From the *Journal of social history,* Spring 2003. Study of Portsmouth.
- The Original Bundlers: Boaz and Ruth, and Seventeenth-Century English Courtship Practices / Yochi Fishcher-Yinon
  www.findarticles.com/cf__dls/m2005/3__35/84678617/p1/article.html
  From the *Journal of social history.* Spring 2002.
- Diaries of the Seventeenth Century
  www.bbc.co.uk/history/society__culture/society/diaries__01.shtml
- The Shakespeare Paper Trail: Documenting the Later Years
  www.bbc.co.uk/history/society__culture/art/shakespeare__later__01.shtml
- Spirits, Witches & Science: why the rise of science encouraged belief in the super-natural in 17th-century England / Richard Olson
  www.skeptic.com/01.4.olson-witches.htm
- Pioneering Glass
  www.interalpha.net/customer/cbrain/home.htm
  Drinking glasses, 1640-1702.

D. Exploration & Colonisation
- Emigrants and Settlers
  www.wwnorton.com/nael/17century/topic__4/welcome.htm
  Early 17th c. justifications for colonisation of Ireland and North America.
- Caleb Johnson's Mayflower History.com
  www.mayflowerhistory.com/
  Includes original sources.
- Thru the Looking Glass: Mayflowerfamilies.com
  www.mayflowerfamilies.com

E. Writers & their Works

Baxter, Richard
- The Richard Baxter Homepage
  members.aol.com/augusteen/Baxter.html
  Includes the writings of, and many articles on, one of the leaders of early nonconformity.
- The Reformed Pastor / Richard Baxter
  www.reformed.org/books/baxter/reformed-pastor/
  Manual for 17th c. clergymen

Boyle, Robert
- Robert Boyle (1627-91): the Robert Boyle Project, University of London
  www.bbk.ac.uk/Boyle/
- Robert Boyle
  www.groups.des.st-and.ac.uk/%7Ehistory/Mathematicians/Boyle.html
  17th c. scientist.

Bunyan, John
- John Bunyan Online
  www.johnbunyan.org
  Complete works online.
- Acacia John Bunyan Online Library
  acacia.pair.com/Acacia.John.Bunyan/
  Includes text of many works.
- John Bunyan
  www.bartleby.com/people/Bunyan-J.html
  Includes full text of *The Pilgrims Progress.* New York: P.F.Collier & Son, 1909-14.
- BUNYAN, JOHN. *The pilgrims progress.* Nath. Ponder, 1678.
  darkwing.uoregon.edu/%7Erbear/bunyan1.html

Defoe, Daniel
- A Journal of the Plague Year / Daniel Defoe
  ibiblio.org/pub/docs/books/gutenberg/etext95/jplag10.txt
  1665 study.

Evelyn, John
- Who was John Evelyn? / Guy de la Bedoyère
  www.romanbritain.freeserve.co.uk/john%20evelyn.htm
- The Diary of John Evelyn
  astext.com/history/ed-main.html
  17th c.

Filmer, Robert
- FILMER, ROBERT, SIR. *Patriarcha, or, the natural power of kings.* 1680
  www.constitution.org/eng/patriarcha.htm

Fox, George
- FOX, GEORGE. *George Fox: an Autobiography* ed. Rufus M. Jones. 1908.
  www.strecorsoc.org/gfox/
- The *Journal* of George Fox
  www.geocities.com/quakerpages/foxtoc.htm/
  From the 1924 abridged edition.
- *George Fox: an autobiography*
  www.ccel.org/f/fox/autobiography/

Graunt, John
- GRAUNT, JOHN. *Natural and political observations ... made upon the bills of mortality.* 1662.
  www.ac.wwu.edu/≈stephan/Graunt/0.html

Harrington, James
- HARRINGTON, JAMES. *The commonwealth of Oceana.* 1656
  www.constitution.org/jh/oceana.htm
- HARRINGTON, JAMES. *Oceana.* 1656.
  www.ecu.bris.ac.uk/het/harrington/oceana
- FUKUDA, ARIHIRO. *Sovereignty and the sword: Harrington, Hobbes and mixed government in the English civil wars.* Oxford: Clarendon Press, 1997.
  www.questia.com/PM.qst?a=o&d=59539192
  Subscription based.

Harvey, William
- William Harvey (1578-1657)
  www.malaspina.com/site/person__611.asp
  Medical writer.

Herbert, George
- George Herbert 1593-1633
  swc2.hccs.cc.tx.us/rowhtml/Herbert/index.htm
  Includes many articles, with some of his works.
- George Herbert (1593-1633)
  www.luminarium.org/sevenlit/herbert/index.html
  Includes works.

Heywood, Thomas
- HEYWOOD, THOMAS. *A funerall elegie upon the death of Henry, Prince of Wales, 1613.* William Welbie, 1613.
  darkwing.uoregon.edu/%7Erbear/heywood1.html

Hobbes, Thomas
- Thomas Hobbes (1588-1679)
  www.luminarium.org/sevenlit/hobbes/
  Includes links to web editions of *Leviathan, etc.*
- Thomas Hobbes / Professor John Rogers
  www.bbc.co.uk/history/state/monarchs__leaders/hobbes__01.shtml
- Thomas Hobbes
  www.bartleby.com/people/Hobbes-T.html
  Includes his *Of man, being the first part of Leviathan.* New York: P.F.Collier & Son, 1909-14.
- HOBBES, THOMAS. *Leviathan.* 1651.
  darkwing.uoregon.edu/%7Erbear/hobbes/leviathan.html
- Thomas Hobbes
  www.ecu.bris.ac.uk/het/hobbes/index.htm
  Includes full text of *Leviathan* and other works, *etc.*
- HOBBES, THOMAS. *Leviathan.* 1651.
  www.constitution.org/th/leviatha.htm

James I
- JAMES I *A counter-blaste to tobacco.* R.B., 1604
  darkwing.uoregon.edu/%7Erbear/james1.html

Locke, John
- LOCKE, JOHN. *The second treatise of civil government.* 1690
  www.constitution.org/jl/2ndtreat.htm

Milton, John
- The Milton Home Page: devoted to the life, literature and times of John Milton
  www.richmond.edu/%7Ecreamer/milton/
- John Milton
  www.bartleby.com/people/Milton-J.html
  Includes his *Areopagitica*. New York: P.F.Collier & Son, 1909-14, and other texts.
- Selected political works of John Milton
  www.constitution.org/milton/milton.htm
  Includes *Areopagitica, etc.*

North, Dudley
- NORTH, DUDLEY. *Discourses upon trade.* 1691
  www.yale.edu/lawweb/avalon/econ/tradenor.htm

Pepys, Samuel
- The Diary of Samuel Pepys
  www.pepysdiary.com/
  Full text, in progress
- Pepys Diary
  www.bibliomania.com/2/1/59/106/frameset.html
  Selections only.

Walton, Izaac
- Izaac Walton
  www.bartleby.com/people/Walton-I.html
  Includes his *The lives of John Donne and George Herbert.*

Winstanley
- SHULMAN, GEORGE M. *Radicalism and reverence: the political thought of Gerrard Winstanley.* Berkeley: University of California Press, 1989.
  ark.cdlib.org/ark:/13030/ft4669n8wx/
- WINSTANLEY, GERARD. et al. *The true levellers standard advanced.* 1649.
  darkwing.uoregon.edu/%7Erbear/digger.html

18. Hanoverian England, 1714-1815

A. Gateways, *etc.*
- Eighteenth Century Resources
  andromeda.rutgers.edu/~jlynch/18th/
  Gateway, international in scope but with much British information.
- C18-L: resources for 18th-century studies across the disciplines
  www.personal.psu.edu/special/C18/
  Includes a variety of bibliographies *etc.*
- Eighteenth Century E-Texts
  andromeda.rutgers.edu/~jlynch/18th/etext.html
  Gateway to published books on the web

B. George I & II
- George I (1714-27 A.D.)
  www.britannia.com/history/monarchs/mon53.html
- Tory Tergiversation in the House of Lords, 1714-1760
  www.history.ac.uk/projects/elec/sem17.html
- FEILING, KEITH GRAHAME. *The Second Tory Party, 1714-1832.* Macmillan & Co., 1938.
  www.questia.com/PM.qst?a=o&d=58567794
  Subscription based.
- George II (1727-60 A.D.)
  www.britannia.com/history/monarchs/mon54.html

C. George III
- The Age of George III / Marjie Bloy
  dspace.dial.pipex.com/town/terrace/adw03/e-eight/18chome.htm
  Many pages on 18th c. politics.
- George III (1760-1820 A.D.)
  www.britannia.com/history/monarchs/mon55.html
- HARRIS, ROBERT. *A patriot press: national politics and the London press in the 1740's.* Oxford: Oxford University Press, 1913.
  www.questia.com/PM.qst?a=o&d=23164787
  Subscription based.

- War and National Identity in the Mid-Eighteenth Century British Isles / Stephen Conway
  www.findarticles.com/cf__dls/m0293/468__116/79334669/pl/article.jhtml
  From the *English historical review*, 9/2001.
- Language of Loyalism: Patriotism, Nationhood and the State in the 1790's
  www.findarticles.com/cf__dls/m0293/475__118/98413764/pl/article.jhtml
  From the *English historical review*, 2/2003.

D. Church History
- Religion in Eighteenth-Century England: Reason or Revelation
  www.coursework.info/i/289.html
- Wesley Bibliography / Kenneth J. Collins
  www.ats.wilmore.ky.us/news/publications/wesley__bib/
- The Wesleys and their Times
  gbgm-umc.org/umhistory/wesley/index.html
  Includes many Wesley texts.
- John Wesley: an online exhibition
  rylibweb.man.ac.uk/data1/dg/methodist/jwol1.html
- John Wesley: holiness of heart and life
  gbgm-umc.org/UMW/Wesley/

E. Social History
- HAMMOND, J.L. & HAMMOND, BARBARA. *The village labourer, 1760-1832: a study in the government of England before the Reform Bill.* New ed, 1920.
  socserv2.socsci.mcmaster.ca/~econ/ugcm/3ll3/hammond/village.html
- The Foundling Hospital / Rhian Harris
  www.bbc.co.uk/history/society__culture/society/foundling__01.shtml
  In London, 18-20th c.
- Homosexuality in Eighteenth-Century England: a sourcebook / Rictor Norton
  www.infopt.demon.co.uk/eighteen.htm
- Making Sense of English Law Enforcement in the 18th Century / David Friedman
  www.daviddfriedman.com/Academic/England__18thc/England__18thc.html
  Originally published in *University of Chicago roundtable*.
- Georgian Underworld
  www.channel4.com/history/microsites/G/georgian__underworld/

- 'Damn you, you Informing Bitch': vox populi and the unmaking of the Gin Act of 1736 / Jessica Warner & Frank Ivis
  www.findarticles.com/cf__dls/m2005/2__33/58675448/pl/article.jhtml
  From the *Journal of social history*, Winter 1999.
- Why They State: women in the Old Bailey, 1779-1789 / Lynn Mackay
  www.findarticles.com/cf__dls/m2005/3__32/54258704/pl/article.jhtml
  From the *Journal of social history*, Spring 1999.
- *The complete Newgate Calendar.* Navarne Society, 1926.
  www.law.utexas.edu/lpop/etext/completenewgate.htm
  As published by the Navarne Society, 1926.
- Early Eighteenth-Century Newspaper Reports: a sourcebook / Rictor Norton
  www.infopt.demon.co.uk/grub/grub.htm
- Patriotic Commerce and National Revival: the Free British Fishery Society and British politics c.1749-58 / Bob Harris
  www.findarticles.com/cf__dls/m0293/456__114/54466583/pl/article.jhtml
  From the *English historical review*, 4/1999.

F. The Industrial Revolution
- Age of Industry
  history.evansville.net/industry.html
  Industrial revolution gateway
- The Industrial Revolution
  mars.acne.wnec.edu/~grempel/courses/wc2/lectures/industrialrev.html
  Brief lecture.
- The Industrial Revolution
  www.historystudystop.co.uk/php/displayarticle.php?article=18&topic=emb
  For GCSE students.
- The Industrial Revolution
  www.historylearningsite.co.uk/indrevo.htm
  For schools
- Industrial Revolution: changing landscapes, 1700-1850
  www.open2.net/lights/industrial/
- What the Industrial Revolution did for us
  www.open2.net/industrialrevolution/
- TOYNBEE, ARNOLD. *Lectures on the industrial revolution in England.* 1884
  www.ecn.bris.ac.uk/het/toynbee/indrev

- ROOT, HILTON L. *The fountain of privilege: political foundations of markets in old regime France and England*. Berkeley: University of California Press, 1994.
  ark.cdlib.org/ark:/13030/ft1779n74g/
- Textile Industry
  www.spartacus.schoolnet.co.uk/Textiles.htm
  For schools. During the industrial revolution, 18-19th c.
- Transport Revolution
  www.historystudystop.co.uk/php/displayarticle.php?article=19&topic=emb
  For GCSE students.
- The Iron Bridge: How was it Built? / David de Haan
  www.bbc.co.uk/history/society__culture/industrialisation/
  iron__bridge__01.shtml
- Britain and the Rise of Science / Lisa Jardine
  www.bbc.co.uk/history/discovery/revolutions/jardineih__01.shtml
  16-17th c.
- The Bubble Project
  is.dal.ca/~dmcneil/bubble.html
  South Sea Bubble: the financial crisis of 1720.

G. The Napoleonic Wars
- Napoleon and England / Philippe Masson
  www.napoleon.org/en/reading__room/articles/files/
  napoleon__england__partI.asp
  Continued at /napoleon__england__partII.asp
- Royal Navy During the Napoleonic Era (1793-1815)
  home.gci.net/~stall/ship1.html
- The British Navy, 1793-1802 / Peter Hicks
  www.napoleon.org/en/reading__room/articles/files/
  british__navy__17921802.asp
- The Arming of the Nation: speeches by William Pitt the Younger, July 1803
  www.napoleon.org/en/reading__room/articles/files/
  pitt__speeches__1803.asp
- Napoleon, Nelson, and the French Threat / Dan Cruickshank
  www.bbc.co.uk/history/war/french__threat__01.shtml
- SOUTHEY, ROBERT. *The life of Horatio, Lord Nelson.* 1813
  historicaltextarchive.com/books.php?op=viewbook&bookid=3
- Letters and Despatches of Horatio Nelson
  www.wtj.com/archives/nelson/

- POPE, DUDLEY. *Decision at Trafalgar.* Philadelphia: J.B.Lippincott, 1960.
  www.questia.com/PM.qst?a=o&d=1216353
  Subscription based.
- The Battle of Trafalgar (October 21, 1805) / Stephen Beck
  www.geocities.com/beckster05/Trafalgar/TrMain.html
- The Iron Duke: Arthur Wellesley, First Duke of Wellington
  www.angelfire.com/wy/dukeofwellington/
- Wellington's Despatches: Peninsula and Waterloo 1808-1815
  www.wtj.com/archives/wellington/
- Waterloo: Bias, Assumptions and Perspectives / Douglas Allan
  www.napoleon.org/en/reading__room/articles/files/allen__waterloo.asp
- A Sympathetic Ear: Napoleon, Elba, and the British / Katharine McDonagh
  www.napoleon.org/en/reading__room/articles/files/
  sympathetic__ear__elba__british.asp

G. Exploration and Empire
- Travel, Trade and the Expansion of Empire
  www.wwnorton.com/nael/18century/topic__4/welcome.htm
  In the 18th c.
- Life at Sea in the Royal Navy of the 18th Century / Professor Andrew Lambert
  www.bbc.co.uk/history/discovery/exploration/life__at__sea__01.shtml
- MASEFIELD, JOHN. *Sea life in Nelson's time.* Freeport, N.Y.: Books for Libraries Press, 1969
  www.questia.com/PM.qst?a=o&d=94909978
  Subscription based.
- Captain Cook and the Scourge of Scurvy / Jonathan Lamb
  www.bbc.co.uk/history/discovery/exploration/
  captaincook__scurvy__01.shtml
- Captain Cook: Explorer, Navigator and Maritime Pioneer / Professor Glyn Williams
  www.bbc.co.uk/history/discovery/exploration/captaincook__01.shtml
- A Vision of Empire: Thomas Whately and the 'Regulations lately made concerning the colonies' / Ian R. Christie
  www.findarticles.com/cf__dls/m0293/n451__v113/20555551/pl/
  article.jhtml
  From the *English historical review,* 4/1998. The British view of relations with the American colonies in the 1760's.

- Slavery and the Slave Trade in Britain
  www.wwnorton/nael/18century/topic__2/welcome.html
  18th c.
- The Slave Trade
  www.spartacus.schoolnet.co.uk/slavery.htm
  18-19th c., with special reference ot Britain and North America. Many pages; for schools
- English Slave Trade 1791-1799: House of Lords survey (study number 1385)
  hds.essex.ac.uk/studybrowse/showabstract.php?sn=1385
  Database.
- Was the American Revolution Inevitable? / Francis D. Cogliano
  www.bbc.co.uk/history/state/empire/american__revolution__01.shtml
- The American War of Independence: the Rebels and the Redcoats
  www.bbc.co.uk/history/state/empire/rebels__redcoats.shtml
- British-American Diplomacy 1782-1863
  www.yale.edu/lawweb/avalon/diplomacy/britian/brtreaty.htm
  Texts of various treaties *etc.*
- The History Detective: the Story of George Burdett / Dr. John Arnold
  **www.bbc.co.uk/history/lj/how__to__do__historylj/
  detective__01.shtml?site=history__howtodolj__detective**
  Emigrant from Yarmouth to New England, 17th c.
- The British Presence in India in the 18th Century
  www.bbc.co.uk/history/state/empire/east__india__01.shtml
- The Age of George III: British India / Marjie Bloy
  dspace.dial.pipex.com/town/terrace/adw03/e-eight/indiatop
- HOWSE, DEREK. *Background to discovery: Pacific exploration from Dampier to Cook.* Berkeley: University of California Press, 1990.
  ark.cdlib.org/ark:/13030/ft3489n8kn/
- South Seas: Voyaging and cross-cultural encounters in the Pacific (1760-1800)
  southseas.nla.gov.au/index.html
  Captain Cook's voyages, including his journal and other contemporary accounts.
- Australian Explorers
  www.davidreilly.com/australian__explorers/
- James Cook
  www.win.tue.nl/~engels/discovery/cook.html
  Gateway to numerous sites.

- Captain James Cook
  pages.quicksilver.net.nz/jcr/~cooky.html
  Includes bibliography.
- Captain James Cook: the world's explorer
  members.tripod.com/cuculus/cook.html
- Mutiny on the H.M.S. Bounty, Pacific, 1789
  www.lareau.org/bounty.html

H. Authors and their Writings

Bentham, Jeremy
- Jeremy's Labyrinth: a Bentham Hypertext
  www.la.utexas.edu/research/poltheory/bentham/
  Extracts from the works of Jeremy Bentham

Burke, Edmund
- Edmund Burke
  www.bartleby.com/people/Burke-Ed.html
  Includes full text of his *Reflections on the revolution in France.* New York: P. F. Collier & Son, 1909-14, and other texts.
- BURKE, EDMUND. *Reflections on the revolution in France.* 1790
  eserver.org/18th/burke.txt
- BURKE, EDMUND. *Reflections on the Revolution in France ...*
  art-bin.com/art/oreffra1.html
  Published 1790; extracts only.

Defoe, Daniel
- DEFOE, DANIEL. *An essay on the regulation of the press.__* 1704.
  darkwing.uoregon.edu/%7Erbear/defoe2.html

Law, William
- William Law, 1686-1761: On-Line Manuscripts
  www.passtheword.org/William-Law/index.html

Malthus, Thomas
- Malthus
  www.ecn.bris.ac.uk/het/malthus/index.htm
  Includes text of *An essay on the principle of population.* J. Johnson, 1798, and other writings.

Newton, Isaac
- The Newton Project
  www.newtonproject.ic.ac.uk/
- Isaac Newton Resources
  www.newton.cam.ac.uk/newton.html
  Links page.
- Newtoniana
  library.ups.edu/instruct/knight/STS/newtoniana/newtoniana.htm
  Links page and bibliography concerning Isaac Newton.
- Sir Isaac Newton (1642-1727)
  www.luminarium.org/sevenlit/newton/
  Includes some of his scientific works.

Paine, Thomas
- Thomas Paine
  www.ecn.bris.ac.uk/het/paine/index.htm
  Includes text of WHEELER, DANIEL EDWIN, ed. *Life and writings of Thomas Paine*.
- PAINE, THOMAS. *The age of reason*. 1794
  darkwing.uoregon.edu/%7Erbear/reason1.html
- Thomas Paine: Citizen of the World / Professor John Belchem
  www.bbc.co.uk/history/society__culture/protest__reform/paine__01.shtml
- Rights of Man / Thomas Paine
  www.bibliomania.com/2/1/59/106/frameset.html
  Selections only.

Ricardo, David
- Ricardo
  www.ecn.bris.ac.uk/het/ricardo/index.htm
  Includes text of *Principles of political economy*. 3rd ed. 1821.

Smith, Adam
- Adam Smith
  www.ecn.bris.ac.uk/het/smith/index.htm
  Includes text of *An inquiry into the nature and causes of the wealth of nations*. 1776, *etc.*
- The Wealth of Nations / Adam Smith
  www.bibliomania.com/2/1/59/106/frameset.html
- SMITH, ADAM. *The wealth of nations*. 1776.
  darkwing.uoregon.edu/%7erbear/wealth/wealth.html

- Adam Smith
  www.bartleby.com/people/Smith-Ad.html
  Includes full text of *Wealth of nations*. New York: P.F.Collier & Son, 1909-14, *etc.*

Wollstonecraft, Mary
- Mary Wollstonecraft: a 'speculative and dissenting spirit' / Professor Janet Todd
  www.bbc.co.uk/history/society__culture/protest__reform/
  wollstonecraft__01.shtml
  Late 18th c.
- WOLLSTONECRAFT, MARY. *Vindication of the rights of woman*.
  J. Johnson, 1792
  darkwing.uoregon.edu/%7Ebear/wollstonecraft2.html

19. The Victorian Era 1815-1914

A. Gateways & Bibliographies

- A word of Advice for Persons Relying on the Internet to Research Victorian Topics
  victorianresearch.org/advice.html
- Victoria Research Web
  victorianresearch.org/
  Gateway
- A Regency Repository of Arts, Literature, Fashion, Personalities, Inventions, Learning, the Domestic Arts, and matters Military & Political
  www.regencylady.com/repository/
  Gateway.
- Victorian Database Online
  www.victoriandatabase.com/default.cfm
  Bibliographic database, listing publications since 1945.
- The Nineteenth Century
  c19.chadwyck.co.uk/
  Catalogue of 25,000 19th c. works available on fiche.
- FORD, P., & FORD, G. *Select list of British Parliamentary papers 1833-1899*. Oxford: Basil Blackwell, 1953.
  www.questia.com/
  Search title. Subscription based.
- Victorian Periodicals: aids to research: a selected bibliography / Rosemary T. Van Arsdel
  victorianresearch.org/periodicals.html
- 19th century Pamphlets Project: a CURL project to provide enhanced access to nineteenth-century pamphlet collections (1801-1914)
  www.is.bham.ac.uk/rslp/pamphlets.htm

B. General History

- Victorian Britain
  www.learningcurve.gov.uk/victorianbritain/default.htm
  Includes facsimiles of orginal sources.
- The Victorians
  www.victorianweb.org/
  Extensive collection of pages.

- Victorian Times, 1837-1901
  www.victoriantimes.org
  For schools.
- History in Focus: the Victorian Era
  www.history.ac.uk/ihr/Focus/Victorians/index.html
  Introduction to Victorian history.
- Time Travellers Guide to Victorian Britain
  www.channel4.com/history/microsites/H/history/guide19/
- Victorian Britain
  www.bbc.co.uk/history/lj/victorian__britainlj/preview.shtml
  Includes, amongst much else:
  - Industry and Invention / Dr. Christine Macleod
  - Earning a Living in the 19th century / Geoff Timmins
  - Earning a Living: the Census as a Primary Source / Geoff Timmins
  - London's Great Stink: the Sour Smell of Success / Professor Martin Daunton
  - The Sour Smell of Success: *Bleak House* as a primary source / Professor Martin Daunton
  - Laissez Faire and the Victorians / Professor Eric Evans
  - Laissez Faire and the Victorians: H.M.I. school reports as a primary source / Professor Eric Evans
  - Ideals of Womanhood in Victorian Britain / Dr. Lynn Abrams
  - Ideals of Womanhood: Cookery Books as a Primary Source / Dr. Lynn Abrams
  - Women and Urban Life / Professor Lynda Nead
  - Women and Urban Life: private letters as a primary source / Dr. Lynda Nead
- Virtual Victorians
  www.victorians.org.uk/
  For schools.
- CLARK, G. KITSON. *The making of Victorian England*. Cambridge: Harvard University Press, 1962.
  www.questia.com/PM.qst?a=o&d=97553702
  Subscription based.
- EVANS, R.J. *The Victorian age 1815-1914*. Edward Arnold, 1958
  www.questia.com/PM.qst?a=o&d=34228603
  Subscription based.

- TREVELYAN, GEORGE MACAULAY. *British history in the nineteenth century (1782-1901).* Longmans, Green & Co., 1922.
  www.questia.com/PM.qst?a=o&d=4636223
  Subscription based.
- YOUNG, G.M. *Early Victorian England, 1820-1865.* Oxford University Press, 1934.
  www.questia.com/PM.qst?a=o&d=5527815
  Subscription based.
- HOPPER, K. THEODORE. *The mid-Victorian generation, 1846-1886.* Oxford: Clarendon Press, 1998.
  www.questia.com/PM.qst?a=o&d=35631622
- WALLER, P.J. *Town, city and nation: England, 1850-1914.* Oxford: Oxford University Press, 1983.
  www.questia.com/PM.qst?a=o&d=26335032
  Subscription based.

C. Politics & Government
- Power, Politics and Protest: The National Archives Learning Curve
  www.learningcurve.gov.uk/politics/default.htm
  In the 19th c.; includes facsimiles of sources.
- COLE, G.D.H., & FILSON, A.W. *British working class movements: select documents 1789-1875.* Macmillan & Co., 1951
  www.questia.com/PM.qst?a=o&d=7901622
  Subscription based.
- British Revolution in the Early 19th Century: How Close? / Professor Eric Evans
  www.bbc.co.uk/history/society__culture/protest__reform/
  revolution__01.shtml
- Republicanism, Socialism and Democracy in Britain: the origins of the Radical Left / Mark Bevir
  www.findarticles.com/cf__dls/m2005/2__34/68660111/pl/article.jhtml
  From the *Journal of social history,* Winter 2000.
- The Luddites: the mystery of Luddism
  www.historystudystop.co.uk/php/
  displayarticle.php?article=54&topic=mbr
- WHITE, R.J. *Waterloo to Peterloo.* New York: Russell & Russell, 1973.
  www.questia.com/PM.qst?a=o&d=9387481
  Subscription based.

- Lord Liverpool and the Alternatives to Repression in Regency England
  www.historystudystop.co.uk/php/
  displayarticle.php?article=117&topic=advanced
  For schools
- Peterloo Massacre
  www.apartacus.schoolnet.co.uk/peterloo.html
  Many pages, for schools
- Parliamentary Reform
  www.spartacus.schoolnet.co.uk/PRparliament.htm
  Many pages, especially brief biographies. For schools.
- The 1st Duke of Wellington Exhibition
  archive.lib.soton.ac.uk/wellington/
- The Duke of Wellington: Soldiering to Glory / Andrew Roberts
  www.bbc.co.uk/history/state/monarchs__leaders/wellington__01.shtml
- George IV (1820-30 A.D.)
  www.britannia.com/history/monarchs/mon56.html
- George IV: the Royal Joke? / Dr. Steven Parissien
  www.bbc.co.uk/history/state/monarchs__leaders/
  george__fourth__01.shtml
- Patronage, the Lansdowne Whigs and the Problem of the Liberal Centre, 1827/8 / Joe Bord
  www.findarticles.com/cf__dls/m0293/470__117/84302835/pl/article.jhtml
  From the *English historical review.*
- William IV (1830-37 A.D.)
  www.britannia.com/history/monarchs/mon57.html
- Members of Parliament, 1820-1880
  www.spartacus.schoolnet.co.uk/Parliament.htm
- SEYMOUR, CHARLES M.A. *Electoral reform in England and Wales: the development and operation of the Parliamentary franchise, 1832-1885.* New Haven: Yale University Press, 1915.
  www.questia.com/PM.qst?a=o&d=446340
  Subscription based.
- The 1832 Reform Act and the Chartists
  www.historystudystop.co.uk/php/
  displayarticle.php?article=63&topic=emb
- PHILLIPS, JOHN A. *The Great reform bill in the boroughs: English electoral behaviour 1818-1841.* Oxford: Clarendon Press, 1992.
  www.questia.com/PM.qst?a=o&d=14375582
  Subscription based.

- STRACHEY, LYTTON. *Queen Victoria.* H.T.A. Press, 2001. [reprint]
  historicaltextarchive.com/books.php?op=viewbook&bookid=10
- Victoria (1837-1901 A.D.)
  www.britannia.com/history/monarchs/mon58.html
- Victoria as a Girl: the Patient Rebel
  www.bbc.co.uk/history/state/monarchs__leaders/
  queen__victoria__01.shtml
- Queen Victoria and Her Prime Ministers / Christopher Hibbert
  www.bbc.co.uk/history/state/monarchs__leaders/
  victoria__ministers__01.shtml
- THOLFSEN, TRYGVE. *Working class radicalism in mid-Victorian England.* New York: Columbia University Press, 1977.
  www.questia.com/PM.qst?a=o&d=94889669
  Subscription based.
- The Peel Web / Marjie Bloy
  dspace.dial.pipex.com/town/terrace/adw03/peel/peelhome.htm
  Many pages on 19th c. history.
- Rethinking the Politics of Protection: Conservatism and the Corn Laws, 1830-52 / Anna Gambles
  www.findarticles.com/cf__dls/m0293/n453__v113/21226619/pl/
  article.jhtml
  From the *English historical review,* 9/1998.
- British Anti-Slavery / Dr. John Oldfield
  www.bbc.co.uk/history/society__culture/protest__reform/
  antislavery__01.shtml
- Bibliography of Chartism / Ursula Stange
  chartism.com/primary.html
- Chartism
  www.spartacus.schoolnet.co.uk/chartism.htm
  For schools.
- The Chartist Movement 1838-1848 / Stephen Roberts
  www.bbc.co.uk/history/society__culture/protest__reform/
  chartist__01.shtml
- 'And Your Petitioners &c': Chartist petitioning in popular politics 1838-48 / Paul A. Pickering
  www.findarticles.com/cf__dls/m0293/466__116/74691876/pl/
  article.jhtml
  From the *English historical review,* 4/2001.

- Wholesome Object Lessons: the Chartist Land Plan in Retrospect / Malcolm Chase
  www.findarticles.com/cf__dls/m0293/475__118/98413765/pl/
  article.jhtml
  From the *English historical review,* 2/2003.
- Liberal Speed, Palmerstonian Delay, and the Passage of the Second Reform Act / Kristin Zimmerman
  www.findarticles.com/cf__dls/m0293/479__118/113182794/pl/
  article.jhtml
  From the *English historical review,* 11/2003.
- Palmerston
  www.historystudystop.co.uk/php/
  displayarticle.php?article=59&topic=mbr
  For A level students
- Palmerston Papers
  archive.lib.soton.ac.uk/palmerston.shtml
  Description of the collection, with calendar.
- Disraeli and Gladstone: opposing forces in action / Robert Blake
  www.bbc.co.uk/history/state/monarchs__leaders/
  disraeli__gladstone__01.shtml
- The Disraeli Project
  qsilver.queensu.ca/english/dismen.html
  Project to edit Disraeli's letters.
- Liberalism, Socialism, and the Progressive Alliance in Britain, c.1880-1914: Bibliography
  www.dur.ac.uk/a.j.olechnowicz/libbib.htm
- Members of Parliament 1880-1920
  www.spartacus.schoolnet.co.uk/Parliament2.htm
  Many brief biographies. For schools
- PELLING, HENRY. *The origins of the Labour Party, 1880-1900.* Macmillan & Co., 1954.
  www.questia.com/PM.qst?a=o&d=11977474
  Subscription based.
- Edward VII: the First Constitutional Monarch / Lucy Moore
  www.bbc.co.uk/history/state/monarchs__leaders/edward__vii__01.shtml
- Britain 1906-1918: Contrast, Contradiction and Change
  www.learningcurve.gov.uk/britain1906-18/default.htm
  Includes facsimiles of original sources.

- COETZEE, FRANS. *For party or country: nationalism and the dilemma of popular Conservatism in Edwardian England.* New York: Oxford University Press, 1990.
  www.questia.com/PM.qst?a=o&d=57243120
  Subscription based.
- Radical Conservatism and the Working Classes in Edwardian England: the case of the Workers Defence Union / Alan Sykes
  www.findarticles.com/cf_dls/m0293/454_113/53706850/pl/article.jhtml
  From the *English historical review,* 11/1998.

D. The Church

- Revelation: Unlocking Research Resources for 19th and 20th Century Church History and Christian Theology
  www.bham.ac.uk/rslp/revelation.htm
- Mundus: Gateway to Missionary Collections in the United Kingdom
  www.mundus.ac.uk/
- CARPENTER, S.C. *Church and people, 1789-1889. A history of the Church of England from William Wilberforce to 'Lux mundi'.* Society for Promoting Christian Knowledge, 1933.
  www.questia.com/PM.qst?a=o&d=10527371
  Subscription based.
- Church Plans Online
  www.churchplansonline.org/
  Plans of 700 churches prepared for the Incorporated Church Building Society 1818-1982, and held by the Society of Antiquaries.
- INGLIS, K.S. *Churches and the working classes in Victorian England.* Routledge & Kegan Paul, 1963.
  www.questia.com/PM.qst?a=o&d=9243165
  Subscription based.
- The Oxford Movement and its leaders
  oregon.uoregon.edu/~lcrumb/oxford.html
  Discussion of a major bibliographical project.
- Tracts for the times
  justus.anglican.org/resources/pc/tracts/
  Basic texts of the Oxford Movement.
- CHADWICK, OWEN, ed. *The mind of the Oxford Movement.* Adam & Charles Black, 1960.
  www.questia.com/PM.qst?a=o&d=7822399
  Subscription based.

- MAGILL, GERARD. ed. *Discourse and context: an interdisciplinary study of John Henry Newman.* Carbondale: Southern Illinois University Press, 1993.
  www.questia.com/PM.qst?a=o&d=23025077
  Subscription based.
- HEIMANN, MARY. *Catholic devotion in Victorian England.* Oxford: Clarendon Press, 1995.
  www.questia.com/PM.qst?a=o&d=76764215
  Subscription based.

E. Social History

i. *General*

- Victoriana.com
  www.victoriana.com
  Includes many articles and links on social history, especially the middle classes.
- MITCHELL, SALLY. *Daily life in Victorian England.* Westport: Greenwood Press, 1996.
  www.questia.com/PM.qst?a=o&d=57191534
  Subscription based.
- Edwardians Online
  www.qualidata.essex.ac.uk/edwardians/about/introduction.asp
  Oral history project.

ii. *The Census*

- Focus on the Census
  www.learningcurve.gov.uk/focuson/census/census.htm
  For schools.
- Victorian Census Project
  www.staffs.ac.uk/schools/humanities_and_soc_sciences/census/vichome.htm
  Includes abstracts from the 1831 and 1861 censuses, *etc.*
- British History and the Census
  chcc.gla.ac.uk/ie_index.php
  19th century census for schools.
- 1901: Living at the Time of the Census
  www.nationalarchives.gov.uk/pathways/census/

iii. *Social Customs*

- Victorians Uncovered
  www.channel4.com/history/microsites/V/victorians/
  Victorian sexual mores.
- Sex, Drugs and Music Hall / Matthew Sweet
  www.bbc.co.uk/history/society__culture/society/pleasure__01.shtml
  Victorian leisure.
- More Sinful Pleasures? Leisure, Respectability, and the Male Middle
  Classes in Victorian England / Mike J. Huggins
  www.findarticles.com/cf__dls/m2005/3__33/61372235/pl/article.jhtml
  From the *Journal of social history,* Spring 2000.
- Opium and Empire in Victorian Britain
  www.qub.ac.uk/en/imperial/india/opium.htm
  Opium in Victorian society.

iv. *Women*

- Women and Urban Life / Professor Lynda Neal
  www.bbc.co.uk/history/lj/victorian__britainlj/women__urban1.shtml
  19th c.
- The Woman Question
  www.wwnorton.com/nael/victorian/topic__2/welcome.html
  Women's rights, 19th c. (including the franchise).
- REYNOLDS, K.D. *Aristocratic women and political society in Victorian
  Britain.* Oxford: Clarendon Press, 1988.
  www.questia.com/PM.qst?a=o&d=49023764
  Subscription based.
- Women and Parliament 1884-1945
  **www.parliament.uk/parliamentary__publications__and__archives/
  parliamentary__archives/archives__the__suffragettes.cfm**
- LOEB, LORI ANNE. *Consuming angels: advertising and Victorian
  women.* New York: Oxford University Press, U.S., 1994.
  www.questia.com/PM.qst?a=o&d=65804632
  Subscription based.

v. *Children*

- Victorian Children: what was it like for children living in Victorian
  Britain
  www.channel4.com/learning/microsites/Q/qca/victorians/
- Hidden Lives Revealed
  www.hiddenlives.org.uk/
  Lives of children in the care of the Childrens' Society, 19th c.

vi. *Work and the Working Class*

- Earning a Living in the 19th century / Geoff Timmins
  www.bbc.co.uk/history/lj/victorian__britainlj/earning__a__living__1.shtml
- The Life of the Industrial Worker in Nineteenth-Century England /
  Laura Del Col
  65.107.211.206/history/workers1.html
  Also at **www.geocities.com/couple__colour/Worker/**
  Excerpts from primary sources.
- Trade Union Movement
  www.spartacus.schoolnet.co.uk/TU.htm
  19-20th c. For schools.
- The Black Lamb of the Black Sheep: illegitimacy in the English
  working class, 1850-1939 / Ginger Frost
  www.findarticles.com/cf__dls/m2005/2__37/111897834/pl/article.jhtml
  From the *Journal of social history,* winter, 2003.

vii. *The Middle Class*

- The Rise of the Victorian Middle Class
  **www.bbc.co.uk/history/society__culture/society/
  middle__classes__01.shtml**
- LESTER, V. MARKHAM. *Victorian insolvency, bankruptcy,
  imprisonment for debt, and company winding up in nineteenth-century
  England.* Oxford: Oxford University Press, 1995.
  www.questia.com/PM.qst?a=o&d=49013783
  Subscription based.

viii. *Immigrants & Minorities*

- Images of the Black Victorians
  www.mckenziehpa.com/bv/index.html
- The Poor Jews Temporary Shelter: the development of a database on
  Jewish migration 1896-1914 / Aubrey Newman & John Graham Smith
  www.le.ac.uk/hi/teaching/papers/jewspap.html
  Description of a database listing 40,000+ Jewish migrants passing
  through London.
- CATLIN, GEORGE. *Adventures of the Ojibbeway Indians in England,
  France and Belgium: being notes of eight years travels and residence in
  Europe with his North American Indian collection.* G. Catlin, 1852.
  www.canadiana.org/ECO/
  Search author or title. Facsimile.

ix. *Poverty & the Poor Law*

- Beneath the Surface: a country of two nations / Joanne de Pennington
  www.bbc.co.uk/history/society__culture/welfare/bsurface__01.shtml
  Victorian poverty.
- Poverty, Health and Housing
  www.spartacus.schoolnet.co.uk/poverty.htm
- Beneath the Surface: Social Reports as Primary Sources
  www.bbc.co.uk/history/society__culture/welfare/
  source__bsurface__02.shtml
- The Poor Law 1834
  www.historystudystop.co.uk/php/displayarticle.php?article=2&topic=emb
  For GCSE students
- The New Poor Law and the Breadwinner Wage: contrasting assumptions / Anna Clark
  www.findarticles.com/cf__dls/m2005/2__34/68660107/pl/article.jhtml
  From the *Journal of social history,* Winter 2000.
- The Workhouse
  users.ox.ac.uk/~peter/workhouse/index.html
- The Union Workhouse
  www.judandk.force9.co.uk/workhouse.html

x. *Crime & Policing*

- Crime and the Victorians / Professor Clive Emsley
  www.bbc.co.uk/history/society__culture/society/crime__01.shtml
- Henry Brougham and Law Reform / Michael Lobban
  www.findarticles.com/cf__dls/m0293/464__115/69064674/pl/article.jhtml
  From the *English historical review,* 11/2000. Early 19th c.
- Capital Punishment U.K.
  www.richard.clark32.btinternet.co.uk/
  History, 19-20th c.
- The History of the Metropolitan Police Service
  www.met.police.uk/history/
- Casebook: Jack the Ripper / Stephen P. Ryder and John A. Piper
  www.casebook.org/

xi. *Leisure*

- The Victorian Seaside / Professor John Walton
  www.bbc.co.uk/history/society__culture/society/seaside__01.shtml
- Victorian Sport: Playing by the Rules / Alex Perry
  www.bbc.co.uk/history/society__culture/society/sport__01.shtml

- The Pubs & Taverns Index for England 1801-1900
  www.pubsindex.freeserve.co.uk

F. Economic, Industrial & Technological History

- CHAMBERS, J.D. *The Workshop of the World: British economic history from 1820 to 1880.* Oxford University Press, 1961.
  www.questia.com/PM.qst?a=o&d=61649235
  Subscription based.
- CLAPHAM, JOHN H. *An economic history of Britain: the early railway age 1820-1850.* Cambridge: Cambridge University Press, 1926.
  www.questia.com/PM.qst?a=o&d=83597736
  Subscription based.
- [Rinderpest]
  post.queensu.ca/~forsdyke/rindpst1.htm
  Government reports on a major outbreak of cattle disease in the 19th c.
- Industrialism: Progress or Decline?
  www.wwnorton.com/nael/victorian/topic__1/welcome.htm
  19th c.
- Victorian Technology / Paul Atterbury
  www.bbc.co.uk/history/society__culture/industrialisation/victorian__technology__01.shtml
- The Workshop of the World / Pat Hudson
  www.bbc.co.uk/history/society__culture/industrialisation/workshop__of__the__world.shtml
  19th c. industry.
- Workshop of the World: Advertisements as Sources of History / Pat Hudson
  www.bbc.co.uk/history/society__culture/industrialisation/source__workshop__01.shtml
- Industry and Invention / Dr. Christine MacLeod
  www.bbc.co.uk/history/lj/victorian__britain/lj/industry__invention__1.shtml
  In the Victorian era.
- 1851 Project: the Great Exhibition
  www.nal.vam.ac.uk/projects/1851.html
- All Change in the Victorian World / Bruce Robinson
  www.bbc.co.uk/history/society__culture/industrialisation/speed__01.shtml
  Speed in the Victorian era.

- Railways in the Nineteenth Century
  www.spartacus.schoolnet.co.uk/railways.htm
  For schools.
- The Brunel Collection
  www.bris.ac.uk/is/services/specialcollections/brunel.html
  Description of the papers of the great railway engineer.
- The Airy Transit Circle / Emily Winterburn
  www.bbc.co.uk/history/discovery/revolutions/airy__george__01.shtml
  Airy was astronomer royal, 1835-81.

G. Health & Medicine
- Victorian Medicine: from Fluke to Theory / Bruce Robinson
  www.bbc.co.uk/history/discovery/medicine/victorian__medicine__01.shtml
- Index of English and Welsh Lunatic Asylums and Mental Hospitals
  www.mdx.ac.uk/www/study/4__13__TA.htm
  Based on an 1844 report.
- Florence Nightingale: the Lady with the Lamp / Mark Bostridge
  www.bbc.co.uk/history/discovery/medicine/nightingale__01.shtml
- HAMLIN, CHRISTOPHER. *A science of impurity: water analysis in nineteenth century Britain.* Berkeley: University of California Press, 1990.
  ark.cdlib.org/ark:/13030/ft667nb43t

H. Defence, Empire & Discovery
i. *Defence*
- BARTLETT, C.J. *Great Britain and sea power, 1815-1853.* Oxford: Clarendon Press, 1963.
  www.questia.com/PM.qst?a=o&d=1063736
  Subscription based.
- Palmerston's Follies: a reply to the French 'threat' / Peter Hicks
  www.napoleon.org/en/reading__room/articles/files/
  hicks__portsdown__forts.asp
  Defences against the French, mid-19th c.
- The Crimean War 1854-1856
  www.geocities.com/Broadway/Alley/5443/crimopen.htm
- A New Enemy / Dan Cruickshank
  www.bbc.co.uk/history/war/wwone/invasion__ww1__01.shtml
  The German threat to England c.1900.

ii. *The British Empire*
- Queen Victoria's Empire
  www.pbs.org/empires/victoria/index.html
- Victorian Imperialism
  www.wwnorton.com/nael/victorian/topic__4/welcome.htm
- Britain's Empire in 1815 / Professor Andrew Porter
  www.bbc.co.uk/history/state/empire/britain__01.shtml
- British India before and after the Great Rebellion of 1857 / Professor Peter Marshall
  www.bbc.co.uk/history/state/empire/indian__rebellion__01.shtml
- The Epic of the Race: India 1857
  www.geocities.com/Broadway/Alley/5443/indmut.htm
  The Indian Mutiny.
- ROBINSON, RONALD, & GALLAGHER, JOHN. *Africa and the Victorians: the climax of Imperialism in the Dark Continent.* New York: St. Martin's Press, 1961.
  www.questia.com/PM.qst?a=o&d=10963083
  Subscription based.
- Perspectives: the South African War: Original and Contemporary Sources
  www.pinetreeweb.com/perspectives.htm
  Boer War, 1899-1902.
- The Boer War
  www.historystudystop.co.uk/php/
  displayarticle.php?article=29&page=2&topic=mbr

iii. *Discovery & Exploration*
- The Fate of Franklin
  www.ric.edu/rpotter/SJFranklin.html
  19th c. explorer of the Arctic.
- Sir Richard F. Burton on the Web
  www.isidore-of-seville.com/burton/
  Gateway to pages on a Victorian explorer of Africa.

I. Ideas, Authors & their Works
- *Ideas and beliefs of the Victorians: an historical revaluation of the Victorian age.* Sylvan Press, 1949.
  www.questia.com/PM.qst?a=o&d=26114770
  Subscription based.

- SEMMEL, BERNARD. *Imperialism and social reform: English social thought, 1895-1914.* Garden City, N.Y.: Doubleday, 1968.
  www.questia.com/PM.qst?a=o&d=80959038
  Subscription based.
- OTTER, SANDRA M. DEN. *British idealism and social explanation: a study in late Victorian thought.* Oxford: Oxford University Press, 1996.
  www.questia.com/PM.qst?a=o&d=59313988
  Subscription based.
- Literature of the Victorian Period / Roger Blackwell Bailey
  www.accd.edu/sac/english/bailey/victoria.htm
  Pages on 40+ prominent authors.
- A Guide to Archives of 19th c. British Publishers / Alexis Weedon
  victorianresearch.org/pubarc.html

Bagehot, Walter
- Walter Bagehot
  www.ecn.bris.ac.uk/het/bagehot/index.htm
  Includes his *The English constitution* 2nd ed. 1873, and other texts.
- The English Constitution / Walter Bagehot
  www.bibliomania.com/2/1/59/106/frameset.html
  Selections only.

Cobden, Richard
- The Letters of Richard Cobden
  www.lse.ac.uk/collections/cobdenLetters/
  On-going project.

Darwin, Charles
- The Darwin Correspondence Online Database
  darwin.lib.cam.ac.uk/
  Charles Darwin's correspondence.

Mill, James
- James Mill
  www.ecn.bris.ac.uk/het/millj/index.htm
  Includes text of *Elements of political economy.* 3rd ed. 1844, *etc.*

Mill, John Stuart
- John Stuart Mill
  www.bartleby.com/people/Mill-JS.html
  Includes his *On liberty.* Longmans Roberts & Green, 1869, with other writings.

- John Stuart Mill
  www.ecn.bris.ac.uk/het/mill/index.htm
  Includes texts of *Principles of political economy, Utilitarianism,* and *On liberty, etc.*
- John Stuart Mill
  socserv2.socsci.mcmaster.ca/~econ/ugcm/3113/mill/index.html
  Includes his works.
- MILL, JOHN STUART. *On liberty.* 1859
  art-bin.com/art/omilib.html

Ruskin, John
- The Ruskin Programme
  www.lancs.ac.uk/users/ruskin/
  Studies of the work of John Ruskin, 1819-1900.

20. The Twentieth Century, 1914-2000

A. Reference Sources
* FORD, P., & FORD, G. *A breviate of Parliamentary papers 1917-1939.*
  Oxford: Basil Blackwell, 1951.
  www.questia.com/PM.qst?a=o&d=55431824
  Subscription based.
* British Universities Film & Video Council: Researcher's Guide Online
  www.bufvc.ac.uk/databases/rgo.html
  Database of 550 film, television and radio documentation collections in
  the British Isles
* BUND: British Universities Newsreel Database
  www.bufvc.ac.uk/databases/newsreels/
  Lists 160,000 records, 1910-79
* www.britishpathe.com: 75 years of ...
  www.britishpathe.com
  British 20th c. news films
* Moving History: a guide to film and television archives in the public
  sector
  www.movinghistory.ac.uk/
* Sources for the History of Film, Television, and the Performing Arts
  www.hmc.gov.uk/7__PERFRM.htm

B. General
* HAVIGHURST, ALFRED F. *Twentieth century Britain.* New York: Harper
  & Row, 1960.
  www.questia.com/PM.qst?a=o&d=3754254
  Subscription based.
* Britain Between the Wars
  www.historystudystop.co.uk/php/
  displayarticle.php?article=64&topic=mbr
  For A level students

C. Government & Politics
* Andrew Bonar Law and the Fall of the Asquith Coalition: the
  December 1916 Cabinet Crisis / R.J.Q. Adams
  www.usask.ca/history/cjh/adam__897.htm
  From the *Canadian journal of history* 32, 1997, pp.185-200.
* Documents of the Interwar Period
  www.mtholyoke.edu/acad/intrel/interwar.htm
  International in scope, but much of British interest
* Members of Parliament, 1920-1960
  www.spartacus.schoolnet.co.uk/parliament3.htm
  Many brief biographies. For schools
* Labour History Index: a guide to labour history archives, websites,
  on-line research sources, and poster collections
  www.qbradley.freeserve.co.uk/
  Twentieth century
* PELLING, HENRY A. *A short history of the Labour Party.* Macmillan,
  1961.
  www.questia.com/PM.qst?a=o&d=59402159
  Subscription based.
* Rise of the Labour Party
  www.historystudystop.co.uk/php/
  displayarticle.php?article=57&topic=mbr
  For A level students
* History of the Labour party
  www.labour.org.uk/historyofthelabour party/
* HINTON, JAMES. *Labour and socialism: a history of the British Labour
  movement, 1867-1974.* Amherst: University of Massachusetts Press, 1983.
  www.questia.com/PM.qst?a=o&d=59325635
  Subscription based.
* Socialism
  www.spartacus.schoolnet.co.uk/socialism.htm
  Includes many brief biographies, 19-20th c. For schools
* Class Traitors: Conservative recruits to Labour, 1900-30 / Martin Pugh
  www.findarticles.com/cf__dls/m0293/n450__v113/20572946/pl/
  article.jhtml
  From the *English historical review,* 2/1998.
* David Lloyd George Exhibition 1863-1945
  www.llgc.org.uk/ardd/dlgeorge/dlg0002.htm
  Based on the collections of the National Library of Wales.

- Fighting on All Fronts: Leo Amery and the First World War
  etext/EH/EH35/ferg1.html
  From *Essays in History,* 35, 1993.
- John Maynard Keynes
  www.marxists.org/reference/subject/economics/keynes/index.htm
  Includes *The general theory of employment interest and money.* 1936
  etc.
- Comintern 'control' of the Communist Party of Great Britain 1920-43 /
  Andrew Thorpe
  www.findarticles.com/cf__dls/m0293/n452__v113/20920713/pl/
  article.jhtml
  From the *English historical review.*
- Ramsay Macdonald and the Rise of Labour / Kenneth O. Morgan
  www.globalnet.co.uk/~semp/ramsay.htm
  From *New perspective,* 1(3), 1996.
- LYMAN, RICHARD W. *The first Labour government, 1924.* Chapman &
  Hall, 1957.
  www.questia.com/PM.qst?a=o&d=9506953
  Subscription based.
- EDEN, ANTHONY. *Facing the dictators: the memoirs of Anthony Eden,
  Earl of Avon.* Boston: Houghton Mifflin, 1962.
  www.questia.com/PM.qst?a=o&d=1286645
  Subscription based. Covers 1923-38.
- Lord D'Abernon, Austen Chamberlain, and the origin of the Treaty of
  Locarno
  www.history.ac.uk/ejournal/art2.html
- The Romance of Decline: the Historiography of Appeasement and the
  British National Identity
  www.history.ac.uk/ejournal/art1.html
- Churchill: the Gathering Storm
  www.bbc.co.uk/history/war/wwtwo/
  churchill__gathering__storm__01.shtml
- Christian Conservatives and the Totalitarian Challenge 1933-40 / Philip
  Williamson
  www.findarticles.com/cf__dls/m0293/462__115/62980104/pl/article.jhtml
  From the *English historical review,* 6/2000.
- George Orwell: Voice of a Long Generation / Sir Bernard Crick
  www.bbc.co.uk/history/society__culture/art/orwell__01.shtml
- The Defence Requirements Sub-Committee, British Strategic Policy,
  Neville Chamberlain, and the Path to Appeasement / Keith Neilson
  www.findarticles.com/cf__dls/m0293/477__118/104728591/pl/article.jhtml
  From the *English historical review,* 6/2003.
- Chamberlain, the Liberals, and the Outbreak of War, 1939 / John
  Vincent
  www.findarticles.com/cf__dls/m0293/n451__v113/20555555/pl/
  article.jhtml
  From the *English historical review,* 4/1998.
- Power Brokers or just 'Glamour Boys'? The Eden Group September
  1939-May 1940 / D.J. Dutton
  www.findarticles.com/cf__dls/m0293/476__118/102139253/pl/article.jhtml
  From the *English historical review.*
- Lord Salisbury 'Watching Committee' and the Fall of Neville
  Chamberlain May 1940 / Larry L. Witherell
  www.findarticles.com/cf__dls/m0293/469__116/82469637/pl/article.jhtml
  From the *English historical review,* 11/2001.
- Churchill: the Evidence
  www.churchill.nls.ac.uk/
- Winston Churchill: Defender of Democracy / Dr. Geoffrey Best
  www.bbc.co.uk/history/war/wwtwo/churchill__defender__01.shtml
- Clement Attlee and the Post-War Labour Government, 1945-51
  www.historystudystop.co.uk/php/
  displayarticle.php?article=58&topic=mbr
  For A level students
- ROLLINGS, H. MERCER N., & TOMLINSON, J.D. *Labour governments
  and private industry: the experience of 1945-1951.*
  www.questia.com/PM.qst?a=o&d=59687914
  Subscription based.
- YOUNG, JOHN W. *Winston Churchill's last campaign: Britain and the
  cold war 1951-5.* Oxford: Clarendon Press, 1996.
  www.questia.com/PM.qst?a=o&d=9663209
  Subscription based.
- HODDER-WILLIAMS, RICHARD, ed. *Churchill to Major: the British
  Prime Ministership since 1945.* Armonk, N.Y.: M.E.Sharpe, 1995.
  www.questia.com/PM.qst?a=o&d=91973114
  Subscription based.
- Macmillan Cabinet Papers 1957-1963 Online
  www.ampltd.co.uk/collect/macdata.HTM
  Subscription based.

- Margaret Thatcher Foundation
  www.margaretthatcher.org/
  Many papers online.
- General Election Results, 9 June 1983
  www.parliament.uk/documents/upload/m09.pdf
  Later results include:
  1987, see /m11.pdf
  1992, see /m13.pdf/
  1997, see /m15.pdf/

D. Church History
- The Church of England and Religious Divisions during the Second World War: church-state relations and the Anglo-Soviet Alliance / Dianne Kirby
  www.history.ac.uk/ejournal/art4.html
- Christian Brethren Collection
  rylibweb.man.ac.uk/data2/spcoll/cba/
  At John Rylands University Library of Manchester. Includes 'The Brethren: a bibliography of secondary sources' / David Brady.

E. Social & Economic History
- Presenting Britian: posters, sewers, Bloomsbury
  www-hoover.stanford.edu/hila/exhibits__prev/Stansky/posters.htm
  Exhibition of inter-war posters
- The Role of Women in Great Britain, 1900 to 1945
  www.historylearningsite.co.uk/women%201900__1945.htm
  For schools
- Farm Lads / Stephen Caunce
  www.bbc.co.uk/history/lj/how__to__do__historylj/farm__lads__01.shtml
  Study of oral history, late 19th-early 20th c.
- The Jarrow Crusade / Christine Collette
  www.bbc.co.uk/history/society__culture/protest__reform/
  jarrow__01.shtml
- The Welfare State: Never Ending Reform / Frank Field, M.P.
  www.bbc.co.uk/history/society__culture/welfare/field__01.shtml
  19-20th c.
- Family Patterns of Social Mobility through Higher Education in the 1930's / Carol Dyhouse
  www.findarticles.com/cf__dls/m2005/4__34/76713031/pl/article.jhtml
  From the *Journal of social history*, Summer 2001.

- The State, Internal Migration, and the Growth of New Industrial Communities in Inter-War Britain / Peter Scott
  www.findarticles.com/cf__dls/m0293/461__115/62257419/pl/article.jhtml
  From the *English historical review*, 4/2000.
- The Union Makes us Strong: T.U.C. History Online
  www.unionhistory.info/
- N.H.S. History / Geoffrey Rivett
  www.nhshistory.net/
- The N.H.S. Explained: the history of the N.H.S.
  www.nhs.uk/thenhsexplained/history__of__the__nhs.asp
- Did Manual Workers Want Industrial Welfare? Canteens, latrines, and masculinity on British building sites, 1918-1970 / Nick Hayes
  www.findarticles.com/cf__dls/m2005/3__35/84678615/pl/article.jhtml
  From the *Journal of social history*, Spring 2002.
- Windrush Arrivals
  www.bbc.co.uk/history/society__culture/multicultural/arrival__01.shtml
  Emigration from Jamaica in the late 1940's.
- Gender and Working Class Identity in Britain during the 1950's / Stephen Brooke
  www.findarticles.com/cf__dls/m2005/4__34/76713029/pl/article.jhtml
  From the *Journal of social history*, Summer 2001.
- Sainsbury's Archives Virtual Museum
  www.j-sainsbury.co.uk/museum/museum.htm
  Food retailing, 19-20th c. For schools.

F. Empire & Commonwealth
- KNAPLUND, PAUL. *Britain: Commonwealth and Empire 1901-1955.* Hamish Hamilton, 1956.
  www.questia.com/PM.qst?a=o&d=1464717
  Subscription based.
- British Documents at the End of Empire Project
  www.sas.ac.uk/commonwealthstudies/british.htm
- Imperialism to Postcolonialism: perspectives on the British Empire
  www.wwnorton.com/nael/20century/topic__1/welcome.htm
  20th c.
- TSIANG, TINGFU F. *Labor and empire: a study of the reaction of British Labor, mainly as represented in Parliament, to British Imperialism since 1880.* New York: Columbia University, 1923.
  www.questia.com/PM.qst?a=o&d=3785628
  Subscription based.

- MURPHY, PHILIP. *Party politics and decolonization: the Conservative Party and British colonial policy in tropical Africa, 1951-1964.* Oxford: Clarendon Press, 1995.
  www.questia.com/PM.qst?a=oxd=59532880
  Subscription basis
- Gertrude Bell, 1868-1926
  www.gerty.ncl.ac.uk/home/index.htm
  c.1600 letters, and c.700 photographs of an early 20th c. British Arabist.
- LOUIS, WM. ROGER. *The British Empire in the Middle East, 1945-1951: Arab nationalism, the United States, and postwar imperialism.* Oxford: Clarendon Press, 1984.
  www.questia.com/PM.qst?a=o&d=22913874
  Subscription based.

G. Defence
- Technology and Warfare
  www.wwnorton.com/nael/20century/topic__2/welcome.htm
  20th c.
- Naval-History.net
  www.naval-history.net/
  20th c. naval history.
- The Defence of Britain
  www.britarch.ac.uk/projects/dob/
  Database listing c.20,000 military sites, 20th c.
- Mountbatten Papers Database
  archive.lib.soton.ac.uk/mountbatten.shtml
  Papers of a leading soldier and last Viceroy of India.
- The Peace Time Conscripts: National Service in the Post-War Years
  www.bbc.co.uk/history/war/wwtwo/peacetime__conscripts__01.shtml
- DORMAN, ANDREW, et al. *The Nott review.* 2002.
  www.british-history.ac.uk/source.asp?pubid=32
  Defence review of 1980-82.

H. World War I
- First World War.Com
  www.firstworldwar.com
- Encyclopedia of the First World War
  www.spartacus.schoolnet.co.uk/FWW.htm
  Many pages; for schools
- The First World War
  www.channel4.com/history/microsites/F/firstworldwar/
- World War One
  www.historylearningsite.co.uk/ww1.htm
  Many pages; for schools
- The First World War: Sources for History
  www.nationalarchives.gov.uk/pathways/firstworldwar/
  At the National Archives and the Imperial War Museum
- The Great War 1914-1918
  www.learningcurve.gov.uk/greatwar/default.htm
  Includes facsimiles of original sources.
- World War I Document Archives
  www.lib.byu.edu/~rdh/wwi/
  www.lib.byu.edu/estu/wwi/
  International in scope.
- Documents of World War I
  www.mtholyoke.edu/acad/intrel/ww1.htm
- First World War Who's Who
  www.firstworldwar.com/bio/
- Cousins at War / Theo Aronson
  www.bbc.co.uk/history/state/monarchs__leaders/
  cousins__at__war__01.shtml
  Royalty in the First World War.
- Lions led by Donkeys? The British Army in World War One / Dr. Gary Sheffield
  www.bbc.co.uk/history/war/wwone/kions__donkeys__01.shtml
- Researching Military Records / Peter Francis
  www.bbc.co.uk/history/war/wwone/archives__01.shtml
- World War I: Trenches on the Web
  www.worldwarl.com
- Hellfire Corner / Tom Morgan
  www.fylde.demon.co.uk/welcome.htm
  World War I battles; many biographies.
- The Western Front, 1914-18
  www.geocities.com/Broadway/Alley/5443/wfront.htm
- The Somme: World War
  www.historystudystop.co.uk/php/
  isplayarticle.php?article=76&topic=standard
  For schools
- Shot at Dawn: Cowards, Traitors or Victims? / Peter Taylor-Whiffen
  www.bbc.co.uk/history/war/wwone/shot__at__dawn__01.shtml
  In World War I

- Regimental Warpath 1914-1918
  www.warpath.orbat.com/
  Lists composition and disposition of British and Empire armies.
- The Pals Battalions in World War One / Bruce Robinson
  www.bbc.co.uk/history/war/wwone/pals__01.shtml
- The Home Front / Peter Caddick-Adams
  www.bbc.co.uk/history/lj/warslj/home__01.shtml
  In World War I
- Mass Politics and the Western Front / Dr. Stephen Badsey
  www.bbc.co.uk/history/war/wwone/war__media__01.shtml
  How the newspapers reported the war.

I. World War II

- World War II Resources: Primary Source Materials on the Web: Original Documents Regarding All Aspects of the War
  www.ibiblio.org/pha/
  International in scope; includes the *British war blue book* of 1939.
- World War Two
  www.bbc.co.uk/history/war/wwtwo/index.shtml
  Many pages, some separately listed here.
- Second World War Encyclopaedia
  www.spartacus.schoolnet.co.uk/2WW.htm
- World War II: Documents
  www.yale.edu/lawweb/avalon/wwii/wwii.htm
  Original sources for the history of the war (some also listed separately here).
- Documents of World War II
  www.mtholyoke.edu/acad/ww2.htm
  International in scope, but with much British material
- The British War Blue Book
  www.yale.edu/lawweb/avalon/wwii/bluebook/blbkmenu.htm
  Originally published as: *Documents concerning German-Polish relations and the outbreak of hostilities between Great Britain and Germany on September 3, 1939.* H.M.S.O., 1939.
- The Special Relationship: Churchill, Roosevelt, and the Emergence of the Anglo-American Alliance, 1939-1945: the British Diplomatic Files
  www.fdrlibrary.marist.edu/anglo.html
- The Atlantic Conference August 9-12, 1941
  www.yale.edu/lawweb/avalon/wwii/atlantic/atmenu.htm
  Originally published as: *Foreign relations of the United States: diplomatic papers.* Vol.1. Washington: Government Printing Office, 1958.

- The Yalta Conference
  www.yale.edu/lawweb/avalon/wwii/yalta.htm
  Text of the agreement, 1945.
- Potsdam Conference
  www.yale.edu/lawweb/avalon/decade/decade17.htm
  Text of the agreement, 1945.
- The German Threat to Britain in World War Two / Dan Cruickshank
  www.bbc.co.uk/history/war/wwtwo/invasion__ww2__01.shtml
- The Second World War Experience Centre
  www.war-experience.org
- Britain in the Early Years of World War II
  www.bbc.co.uk/history/war/wwtwo/early__years__01.shtml
- Churchill and the Holocaust / Sir Martin Gilbert
  www.bbc.co.uk/history/war/wwtwo/churchill__holocaust__01.shtml
- World War II: How the Allies Won / Professor Richard Overy
  www.bbc.co.uk/history/war/wwtwo/how__the__allies__won__01.shtml
- RICHARDS, DENIS. *Royal Air Force 1939-1945.* 2 vols. H.M.S.O., 1953.
  www.questia.com/PM.qst?a=o&d=64821947
  Continued at =54046342. Subscription based.
- The Air War and British Bomber Crews in World War Two
  www.bbc.co.uk/history/war/wwtwo/air__war__bombers__01.shtml
- WILSON, EUNICE. *Dangerous sky: a resource guide to the Battle of Britain.* Westpoint: Greenwood Press, 1995.
  www.questia.com/PM.qst?a=o&d=9596108
  Subscription based. Bibliography.
- WOOD, DEREK. *The Narrow margin: the Battle of Britain and the rise of air power, 1930-40.* Hutchinson, 1961.
  www.questia.com/PM.qst?a=o&d=85739790
  Subscription based.
- The Battle of Britain / Dr. Chris Bellamy
  www.bbc.co.uk/history/war/wwtwo/battle__of__britain__01.shtml
- Battle of Britain.com
  www.battle-of-britain.com
- The Battle of Britain
  www.raf.mod.uk/bob1940/bobhome.html
  Includes official daily reports.
- Battle of Britain
  www.geocities.com/Broadway/Alley/5443/bofb1.htm
- British Bombing Strategy in World War Two / Detlef Siebert
  www.bbc.co.uk/history/war/wwtwo/area__bombing__01.shtml

- Winston Churchill and Dresden
  www.learningcurve.gov.uk/heroesvillains/churchill/
- The Singapore Strategy and the Deterrence of Japan: Winston Churchill, the Admiralty, and the Dispatch of Force Z / Christopher M. Bell
  www.findarticles.com/cf__dls/m0293/467__116/76650909/pl/article.jhtml
  From the *English historical review,* 6/2001.
- Codes and Ciphers in the Second World War / Tony Sales
  www.codesandciphers.org.uk
- Home Front 1939-1945
  learningcurve.pro.gov.uk/homefront/default.htm
  Includes facsimiles of original sources.
- W.W.2: People's War
  www.bbc.co.uk/dna/ww2/
  Many pages, including much oral history.
- Evacuees in World War II: the true story / David Prest
  www.bbc.co.uk/history/war/wwtwo/evacuees__01.shtml
- Surviving World War Two: the Bristol Evacuees / David Garmston
  www.bbc.co.uk/history/war/wwtwo/bristol__evacuees__01.shtml
- Women Under Fire in World War II / Carol Harris
  www.bbc.co.uk/history/war/wwtwo/women__at__war__01.shtml
- War Diary of Nella Last
  www.bbc.co.uk/history/war/wwtwo/nell__last__01.shtml
  From the *Mass Observation Archive;* diary of a British housewife in World War II
- Life in Britain for German Prisoners of War
  www.bbc.co.uk/history/war/wwtwo/german__pows__01.shtml
- The Home Guard and Dad's Army / Graham McCann
  www.bbc.co.uk/history/war/wwtwo/dads__army__01.shtml
- Home Guard: Was the Home Guard an effective fighting force?
  www.learningcurve.gov.uk/homefront/preparations/homeguard/
                                                    default.htm
- The Home Guard
  www.home__guard.org.uk/
  In World War II
- The Blitz: sorting the Myth from the Reality
  www.bbc.co.uk/history/war/wwtwo/blitz__01.shtml
- Westall's War: Air Raid Disaster, North Shields, May 3rd 1941
  www.westallswar.org.uk
  Based on a novelist's personal experience.

- Island Farm: Prisoner of War Camp 198 / Special Camp XI: Bridgend, South Wales
  www.islandfarm.fsnet.co.uk/

J. *Recent Wars*
- Britain's Small Wars 1945-2001: the History of British Military Conflicts since 1945
  www.britains-smallwars.com
- The Falklands Conflict
  www.iwm.org.uk/online/falklands/falkintro.htm
- When Britain went to War
  www.channel4.com/history/microsites/F/falklands/
  Falklands War, 1982

21. County and Local History and Archaeology

A. General
- Legacies: U.K. History Local to You
  www.bbc.co.uk/legacies/
  The B.B.C.'s local history site.
- National Grid for Learning Local History Trail
  www.ngfl.gov.uk/localhistory/
- History Trail: Local History
  www.bbc.co.uk/history/lj/locallj/preview.shtml
  Includes:
  - Getting started / Alan Crosby
  - Industrial Local History / Dr. Alan Crosby & Cliff Howe
  - Landscape and Local History / Dr. Alan Crosby & Shirley Wittering
  - Village & Local History / Dr. Alan Crosby & Peter Shakeshaft
  - Urban Local History / Dr. Charles Insley
- Irish and British Villages Webring
  j.webring.com/hub?ring=biv
- Local History
  www.pro.gov.uk/pathways/localhistory/
  Illustrates the type of material in the National Archives for local history post-1700
- Victoria County History
  www.englandpast.net/
- Victoria County History: Place Index
  www.medievalgenealogy.org.uk/vch/

B. Local Histories & Archaeology
Places in this section are listed under the counties which existed prior to 1974.

Bedfordshire
Sandy
- Roman Sandy Information Resource
  www.roman-sandy.com/
  For schools.

Turvey
- The Turvey Page
  www.turvey.homestead.com/

Berkshire
- The Royal County of Berkshire
  www.britannia.com/history/berks/
  General history; many pages.

Abingdon
- A Bibliography of Local History for Abingdon
  www.mjfh1.demon.co.uk/bib.htm
- CASE, H.J., & WHITTLE, A.W.R., eds. *Settlement patterns at the Abingdon causewayed enclosure and other sites.* C.B.A. research report, **44**. 1982.
  ads.ahds.ac.uk/catalogue/library/cba/rr44.cfm
  Prehistoric sites in Abingdon and various places in Oxfordshire.
- MILES, DAVID, ed. *Archaeology at Barton Court Farm, Abingdon, Oxon.* C.B.A. research report, **50**. 1984.
  ads.ahds.ac.uk/catalogue/library/cba/rr50.cfm
  Prehistoric and Roman.
- PARRINGTON, MICHAEL. *The excavation of an iron age settlement, bronze age ring-ditches and Roman features at Ashville Trading Estate, Abingdon (Oxfordshire) 1974-76.* C.B.A. reseach report, **28**. 1978.
  ads.ahds.ac.uk/catalogue/library/cba/rr28.cfm

Cumnor
- Cumnor / John Hanson
  www.bodley.ox.ac.uk/external/cumnor/

Reading
- Reading Besieged / W.M. Childs
  www.britannia.com/history/berks/siegerdg.html
  In 1642-3.
- The Huntley & Palmer's Collection: Reading: Biscuit Town
  www.huntleyandpalmers.org.uk/
  19-20th c. history.

Ridgeway
- Hillforts of the Ridgeway
  athens.arch.ox.ac.uk/~glock/fieldwork/ridgeway/

Wallingford
- Wallingford: a brief history
  www.triangle.co.uk/about/wallhist.htm

Buckinghamshire
See Northamptonshire. Whittlewood

Cambridgeshire
- Cambridgeshire History
  www.cambridgeshire.com/
- The Cambridgeshire Ragman Rolls / Leonard E. Scales
  www.findarticles.com/cf__dls/m0293/n452__v113/20920710/pl/
  article.jhtml
  From the *English historical review*, 6/1998. The royal inquest of 1274/5.
- The William Dowsing Site
  www.williamdowsing.org/
  The journal of a puritan iconoclast active in Cambridgeshire and Suffolk, 1643-4.

Cambridge
- Cambridge: past, present and future
  www.iankitching.me.uk/history/cam/history.html
- Cambridge Heritage
  www.stirbitch.com/cantab/
- University of Cambridge: a brief history
  www.cam.ac.uk/cambuniv/pubs/history/
- *Vox Piscis,* or, the Book-Fish: Providence and the uses of the Reformation past in Caroline Cambridge
  www.findarticles.com/cf__dls/m0293/457__114/55249871/pl/article.jhtml
  From the *English historical review*, 6/1999.

Ely
- Excavating Ely's Past
  www.internet.ge.ms/elydig/

Fulbourn
- The Story of a Mental Hospital: Fulbourn, 1858-1983 / David H. Clark
  www.human.nature.com/free-associations/clark/

Wandlebury
- Wandlebury Hill Fort
  www.arch.cam.ac.uk/projects/wandlebury.html

Cheshire *see also* Cumberland & Staffordshire

Chester
- The Defences of Chester
  www.julianbaum.co.uk/ChesterDefences/Main.html
  Roman reconstruction.
- The Roman Elliptical Building at Chester: the Flavian Capital of Britannia(?)
  www.julianbaum.co.uk/Chester-Project/EB/EB.html

Congleton
- Congleton Borough Charters / David Roffe
  www.roffe.freeserve.co.uk/charters.htm

Kelsall
- Home Page Kelsall 19th Century Social History
  www.the-dicksons.org/kelsall/Kelsall%20Home%20Page.htm

Knutsford
- Virtual Knutsford
  www.virtual-knutsford.co.uk/
  Click on 'History'.

Neston
- Neston U.D.C. Building Plans Online
  www.cheshire.gov.uk/recoff/LACNestonUDCBuildingPlans/home.asp

Cornwall
- Cornish History
  www.webmesh.co.uk/cornish.htm
  Predominantly prehistoric and pre-Anglo-Saxon.
- Victoria County History of Cornwall
  www.cornwallpast.net
  Includes many drafts on religious houses; also useful bibliography.
- The Cornish: a Neglected Nation?
  www.bbc.co.uk/history/state/nations/cornish__nation__01.shtml
- Cornish Mining: World Heritage Site Bid
  www.cornish-mining.org.uk/
- Past, Present and Future: a review of Cornish historical studies / Bob Keys & Garry Tregidga
  www.marjon.ac.uk/cornish-history/review/index.html
  From *Cornish history;* includes some full text articles.

- Cornwall, Earl Richard, and the Barons War / Mark Page
  www.findarticles.com/cf__dls/m0293/460__115/60104282/pl/article.jhtml
  From the *English historical review*, 2/2000. Mid-13th c.

Crift Farm
- The Crift Farm Project
  www.brad.ac.uk/acad/archsci/field__proj/crift/crift.html
  Archaeology of medieval tin smelting.

Leskernick
- The Leskernick Project
  www.ucl.ac.uk/leskernick/home.html/
  Bronze Age settlement on Bodmin Moor.

Lynher
- Lynher Parishes History Site
  www.lynherparishes.co.uk/
  Covers St. Ive, Linkinhorne, and South Hill.

West Penwith
- West Penwith Resources
  www.west-penwith.org.uk/

Cumberland
- N.W.W.S.: North-West Wetlands Survey
  www.lancs.ac.uk/depts/archaeo/pages/services/nwws1.htm
  Archaeological survey covering Cumberland, Westmorland, Lancashire, Cheshire and Staffordshire.

Cleator Moor
- Cleator Moor
  www.themoor.ukf.net/

Whitehaven
- Whitehaven: then and now
  www.whitehaven.ukf.net/

Derbyshire
- Thomas Bateman's Ten Years Diggings
  www.nottingham.ac.uk/~aczkde/tenyrs/bindex.html
  In 19th c. Derbyshire and Staffordshire

- Alastair's Derbyshire Stone Circles Page
  www.geocities.com/athens/parthenon/6197/
- Anglo-Saxon Derbyshire
  www.nott.ac.uk/~aczkde/asd/database.html
  Database of archaeological sites, with bibliography.
- Peakland Heritage
  www.peaklandheritage.org.uk/index.asp
- North East Derbyshire Web Pages
  www.geocities.com/others/1992/ned.html
- Census Enumerators Books: Four Rural Areas 1851-1881 (study number 2708)
  hds.essex.ac.uk/studybrowse/showabstract.php?sn=2708
  Database of returns from various parishes in Derbyshire, Norfolk, Shropshire and the North Riding of Yorkshire.
- Victoria County History of Derbyshire
  www.derbyshirepast.net
  Includes draft text for Scarsdale Hundred.

Bonsall
- The Bonsall History Project
  www.bonsallhistory.org.uk/

Fox Hole Cave
- Early Neolithic Dates on Human Bone from Fox Hole Cave, Derbyshire / A.T. Chamberlain
  www.shef.ac.uk/~capra/3/foxholedates.html

Willington
- Archaeological Recording at Willington Gravel Quarry, Derbyshire
  www.eng-h.gov.uk/archcom/projects/summarys/html98__9/cc2517.htm

Devon
- General History of the County of Devon
  www.devonwebpages.co.uk/history.htm
  Gateway.
- The History of Devon
  www.britannia.com/history/devon/
  Many pages.

- Community Landscapes Project
  www.ex.ac.uk/projects/devonclp/
  Devon project to involve the public in archaeology.
- Devon Library and Information Services: Local Studies Service: Maps
  www.devon.gov.uk/library/locstudy/home8.html
  Includes historic maps of Devon and Exeter.

Dartmoor
- Prehistoric Archaeology: Dartmoor Factsheet
  www.dartmoor-npa.gov.uk/dnp/factfile/archaeo.pdf

Dartmouth
- Dartmouth History
  www.dartmouth.org.uk/history.htm
- Gallants Bower, Dartmouth: a Civil War fort revealed / Shirley Blaylock, *et al.*
  **www.nationaltrust.org.uk/environment/html/archeaol/__fspapers/
  fs__arch2.htm**

Exeter
- Exeter Cathedral Keystones & Carvings: a catalogue raisonne of the medieval interior sculpture and its polychromy / Avril K. Henry & Anna C. Hulbert
  hds.essex.ac.uk/exetercath/
- The Medieval Jews of Exeter / Rev. Michael Adler
  www.eclipse.co.uk/exeshul/history/medievaljew.htm
  From *Devonshire Association ... transactions* **63,** 1931, pp.221-40.
- Exeter Synagogue Archive
  www.jewishgen.org/jcr-uk/community/exe/history.htm
  Exeter Jewish history.
- Thomas Shapter: the history of cholera in Exeter 1832
  www.ex.ac.uk/Affiliate/stloyes/graeme/shaptint.htm

Exeter Diocese
- Bishops of Exeter
  www.exeter-cathedral.org.uk/Clergy/bishops.html
  Brief biographies from George Oliver's *Lives of the bishops of Exeter.*

Hallsands
- Old Hallsands
  www.hallsands.org.uk/
  Late 19th c. - early 20th c.

Lydford
- Lydford, Devonshire: the Dartmoor Village of National Historical Importance
  www.lydford.co.uk/
  Primarily historical, including 'The Anglo-Saxon history of Lydford'.

Plymouth
- Brian Moseley's Plymouth Data Website
  www.plymouthdata.info/

Yealmpton
- Archaeological Research at Kitley Caves, Yealmpton, Devon / Dr. Andrew Chamberlain
  www.shef.ac.uk/~ap/research/yeal.html

Dorset
- Enclosures in the Southern Counties 1700-1900 (study number 3278)
  hds.essex.ac.uk/studybrowse/showabstract.php?sn=3278
  Includes enclosure agreements from Dorset, Hampshire, Sussex and Wiltshire.

Holton Lee
- Early History of the English Channel Project
  csweb.bournemouth.ac.uk/consci/ehec/
  Includes details of excavation at Holton Lee, Dorset.

Kimmeridge
- Prehistoric and Romano-British Kimmeridge Shale / G. T. Denford
  ads.ahds.ac.uk/catalogue/projArch/denford__na__2000/

Kingston Lacy
- A 'fare maner place': the medieval manor house at Kingston Lacy
  **www.nationaltrust.org.uk/environment/html/archeaol/__fspapers/
  fs__arch3.htm**

Knowlton
- Research at the Knowlton Henge complex
  csweb.bournemouth.ac.uk/consci/text__kn/knhome.htm
  Neolithic.

Portland

- The Bioarchaeology of the Culverwell Shell Midden / K. D. Thomas
  ads.ahds.ac.uk/catalogue/projArch/culverwell__ba__2000/
  Mesolithic site on the Isle of Portland, Dorset.

Purbeck

- Purbeck papers / David A. Hinton
  ads.ahds.ac.uk/catalogue/library/purbeck__papers__1991.cfm
  Archaeological reports.
- Research on Roman Purbeck / John Palmer
  www.stx69.demon.co.uk/archaeology.html
  Includes database of the Roman Purbeck limestone industry.

Durham *see also* Northumberland and Yorkshire

- Past Perfect: the virtual archaeology of Durham and Northumberland
  www.pastperfect.info/
- Keys to the Past
  www.keystothepast.info/
  Details of many thousand archaeological sites in Co. Durham and Northumberland.
- Victoria County History of Durham
  www.durhampast.net
  Includes text for Darlington.
- Settlement and Waste in the Palatinate of Durham: a research project funded by E.S.R.C.
  www.dur.ac.uk/r.h.britnell/Settlement%20and%20Waste.htm
- Medieval Charters and the Landscape: between Durham and the Sea, 1100-1500 / Richard Britnell
  www.dur.ac.uk/r.h.britnell/haswell/
  Between__Durham__and__the__Sea.htm
  Includes facsimiles of charters.
- Durham Miner
  www.durham-miner.org.uk
- Both Praying and Playing: Muscular Christianity and the Y.M.C.A. in north-east County Durham
  www.findarticles.com/cf__dls/m2005/2__35/82066736/pl/article.jhtml
  From the *Journal of social history,* Winter 2001.

Durham

- The Employees of Durham Priory, 1494-1519
  www.dur.ac.uk/r.h.britnell/Priory__employees.htm

Gateshead

- A Short History of Gateshead / I. C. Carlton
  www.genuki.org.uk/big/eng/DUR/GatesheadHistory/

Norton

- SHERLOCK, STEPHEN J., & WELCH, MARTIN G. *An Anglo-Saxon cemetery at Norton, Cleveland.* C.B.A. research report **82.** 1992.
  ads.ahds.ac.uk/catalogue/library/cba/rr82.cfm

Seaham

- Story of Seaham
  www.seaham.i12.com/sos/sos/html

Thorpe Thewles

- HESLOP, D. H. *The excavation of an iron age settlement at Thorpe Thewles, Cleveland 1980-1982.* C.B.A. research report **65.** 1987.
  ads.ahds.ac.uk/catalogue/library/cba/rr65.cfm

Essex

- BUCKLEY, D.G. ed. *Archaeology in Essex to A.D.1500.* C.B.A. research report **34.** 1980.
  ads.ahds.ac.uk/catalogue/library/cba/rr34.cfm
- A Statistical Survey of Given Names in Essex Co., England, 1182-1272 / Nicola de Bracton
  www.florilegium.org/files/NICOLAA/names__essex__art.txt
- Biographical Database based on Morant's *History of Essex* 1768 (study number 3037)
  hds.essex.ac.uk/studybrowse/showbastract.php?sn=3037

Chelmsford

- GOING, C.J. *The mansio and other sites in the south eastern sector of Caesaromagus: the Roman pottery.* C.B.A. research report **62.** 1987.
  ads.ahds.ac.uk/catalogue/library/cba/rr62.cfm
  At Chelmsford.
- DRURY, P.J. *The mansio and other sites in the south eastern sector of Caesaromagus.* C.B.A. research report **66.** 1988.
  ads.ahds.ac.uk/catalogue/library/cba/rr66.cfm
- WICKENDEN, N.P. *The temple and other sites in the north eastern sector of Caesaromagus.* C.B.A. research report **75.** 1991.
  ads.ahds.ac.uk/catalogue/library/cba/rr75.cfm

- CUNNINGHAM, C.M., & DRURY, P.J. *Post medieval sites and their pottery: Moulsham Street, Chelmsford.* C.B.A. research report **54**. 1985. ads.ahds.ac.uk/catalogue/library/cba/rr54.cfm

Chelmsford Diocese
- RODWELL, WARWICK, & RODWELL, KIRSTY. *Historic churches: a wasting asset.* C.B.A. research report **19**. 1977. ads.ahds.ac.uk/catalogue/library/cba/rr19.cfm
  Survey of churches in the Diocese of Chelmsford, especially the Archdeaconry of Colchester.

Colchester
- Colchester's Roman Water Feature / Jess Jephcott thearchof.topcities.com/Roman/colchester.htm
- CRUMMY, PHILIP. *Aspects of Anglo-Saxon and Norman Colchester.* C.B.A. research report **39**. 1981. ads.ahds.ac.uk/catalogue/library/cba/rr39.cfm
- Medieval Colchester www.dur.ac.uk/r.h.britnell/
  Medieval%20Colchester%20home%20page.htm
  Includes an edition of the Colchester chronicle, 1372-9, calendar of deeds 14-15th c., list of bailiffs and M.P.'s, *etc.*

Earls Colne
- Earls Colne, Essex: Records of an English Village 1375-1854 linux02.lib.cam.ac.uk/earlscolne/
  Includes transcripts of virtually all surviving documents for the village's history.

Grays Thurrock
- Bygone Grays Thurrock www.pavitt4.fsnet.co.uk/
  Mainly photographs.

Great Chesterford
- EVISON, VERA, *et al.* *An Anglo-Saxon cemetery at Great Chesterford, Essex.* C.B.A. research report **91**. 1994. ads.ahds.ac.uk/catalogue/library/cba/rr91.cfm

Harwich
- Ship Tax for Harwich Area, 1636 hds.essex.ac.uk/studybrowse/showabstract.php?sn=1341

Heybridge
- Elms Farm Project, Heybridge, Essex / M. Atkinson & S. Preston www.eng-h.gov.uk/archcom/projects/summarys/html97__8/4514.htm
  Iron Age, Roman and Saxon site.

Kelvedon
- RODWELL, K.A., ed. *The prehistoric and Roman settlement at Kelvedon, Essex.* C.B.A. research report **63**. 1988. ads.ahds.ac.uk/catalogue/library/cba/rr63.cfm

Kelvedon Hatch
- The History of Kelvedon Hatch www.historyhouse.co.uk/

Little Waltham
- DRURY, P.J. *Excavations at Little Waltham, 1970-71.* C.B.A. research report **26**. 1978. ads.ahds.ac.uk/catalogue/library.cba/rr26.cfm

Maldon
- Maldon Archaeological Reports www.maldonsx.freeserve.co.uk/

Rivenhall
- RODWELL, W.J., & RODWELL, K.A. *Rivenhall: investigations of a villa, church and village, 1950-1977.* C.B.A. research report **55 & 80**. 1986-93. ads.ahds.ac.uk/catalogue/library/cba/rr55.cfm
  Continued at /rr80.cfm
  History of the settlement.

Romford
- Romford Now & Then: Glimpses of the Past in the Present www.romford.org/

Saffron Walden
- BASSETT, S.R. *Saffron Walden: excavations and research 1972-80.* C.B.A. research report **45**. 1982. ads.ahds.ac.uk/catalogue/library/cba/rr45.cfm
  Prehistoric, Roman and medieval periods.

Sheepen
- NIBLETT, ROSALIND. *Sheepen: an early Roman industrial site at Camulodunum.* C.B.A. research report 57. 1985.
ads.ahds.ac.uk/catalogue/library/cba/rr57.cfm

Sutton Hoo
- A Select Bibliography on Sutton Hoo, 1939-1993
www.the-orb.net/bibliographies/sut__hoo.html

Gloucestershire & Bristol
- Gloucestershire County Council: Heritage and History: Useful National and Local Websites
www.gloucestershire.gov.uk/index.cfm?articleid=175
Includes links to local societies.
- Gloucestershire Miscellany
www.mindmagi.demon.co.uk/glos/
Original sources; brief.
- The Medieval Ceramic Industry of the Severn Valley / Alan George Vince
www.postex.demon.co.uk/thesis/thesis.htm
Ph.D. thesis, University of Southampton 1984. Covers Gloucestershire, Herefordshire, Monmouthshire and Worcestershire.

Bristol see also London & Middlesex
- Bristol Information: Aspects of Bristol History and Genealogy
www.bristolinformation.co.uk
- Bristol: a historical perspective
members.lycos.co.uk/brisray/bristol/bperspct.htm
- The Widening Gate: Bristol and the Atlantic economy 1450-1700 / David Harris Sacks
ark.cdlib.org/ark:/13030/ft3f59n8d1/

Chedworth
- Excavations in the 'Garden Court' at Chedworth Roman Villa, Gloucestershire / Dr. Maureen Carroll
www.shef.ac.uk/uni/academic/A-C/ap/research/chedworth/chedworth.html

Cotswold Edge
- Cotswold Edge
www.cotswoldedge.org.uk/
Covers Charfield, Dursley, North Nibley, and Wotton under Edge.

Deerhurst
- RAHTZ, PHILIP. *Excavations at St. Mary's church, Deerhurst.* C.B.A. research report 15. 1976
ads.ahds.ac.uk/catalogue/library/cba/rr15.cfm

Gloucester
- A History of the City of Gloucester
www.softdata.co.uk/gloucester/history.htm
- The History of Gloucester
www.glos.city.gov.uk/libraries/templates/page.asp?FolderID=74
For schools.
- Gloucester Asylums
www.gloucesterasylums.co.uk/

Selsley
See Woodchester

Nailsworth
- URDANK, ALBION MERE. *Religion and society in a Cotswold Vale: Nailsworth, Gloucestershire, 1780-1865.* Berkeley: University of California Press, 1990.
ark.cdlib.org/ark:/13030/ft2d5nb1fm/

Stonehouse
- Residence and Kinship in Stonehouse, Gloucestershire, 1558-1804
hds.essex.ac.uk/studybrowse/showabstract.php?sn=3896
Database.

Woodchester
- A History of Woodchester and Selsley / Graham Thomas
www.grahamthomas.com/history1.html
Includes a page on the Roman villa.

Hampshire *see also* Dorset
- The Peasant Land Market in Southern England, 1260-1350
www.dur.ac.uk/r.h.britnell/winchester%20before%201350.htm
Based on estate accounts of the Bishop of Winchester.
- Peasant Land Market in Southern England 1260-1350 (Study number 4086)
hds.essex.ac.uk/studybrowse/showabstract.php?sn=4086
Database of entry and marriage fines recorded in the pipe rolls of the Bishop of Winchester.

- The Transfer of Customary Land on the Estate of the Bishopric of Winchester 1350-1415: a project funded by the Leverhulme Trust
  www.dur.ac.uk/r.h.britnell/Winchester__1350.htm
- The English Civil War in Hampshire
  www.soton.ac.uk/~hi248/group2website0203/

Alice Holt
- LYNE, M.A.B., & JEFFERIES, S.R. *The Alice Holt / Farnham Roman pottery industry.* C.B.A. research report **30**. 1979.
  ads.ahds.ac.uk/catalogue/library/cba/rr30.cfm

Basingstoke
- Basingstoke History
  www.maxlove.co.uk/basingstoke.htm

Chalton
See Sussex. Torberry

Danebury
- CUNLIFFE, BARRY. *Danebury: an iron age hill fort in Hampshire.* C.B.A. research report **52 & 73**. 1984-91
  ads.ahds.ac.uk/catalogue/library/cba/rr52a.cfm
  Continued at **/rr52b.cfm** **/rr73a.cfm** & **/rr73b.cfm**
- The Danebury Excavations Digital Archive / Danebury Trust
  ads.ahds.ac.uk/catalogue/projArch/danebury__var__2003/

Farnham
See Alice Holt

Hayling Island
- Internal Organisation and Deposition at the Iron Age temple on Hayling Island (Hampshire) / Anthony King & Graham Soffe
  www.barnarch.u-net.com/Hayling.htm

Isle of Wight
- Isle of Wight History Centre
  freespace.virgin.net/roger.hewitt/iwias/
  Hosted by the Isle of Wight Archaeology Society

Lymington
- Buckland Rings, Lymington, Hampshire: report on geophysical survey, April 1993
  robin.eng-h.gov.uk/reports/buckland/
  Iron age hill-fort.

New Forest
- New Forest History
  www.hants.gov.uk/newforesthistory/

Old Basing
- The History of the Siege of Basing House, Old Basing, Hampshire: Civil War stronghold holds out for three years / David Nash Ford
  www.britannia.com/history/hants/siegebsg.html

Rowner
- Information Available for the Parish of Rowner, near Portsmouth, Southern England in 1642
  www.portsdown.demon.co.uk/

Silchester
- Silchester: the Roman Town of Calleva
  www.readingmuseum.org.uk/collections/silchester.htm

Southampton
- Great Sites: Hamwic / Helena Hamerow
  www.britarch.ac.uk/ba/ba66/feat3.shtml
  From *British archaeology* **66**. 2002.
- MORTON, A.D. *Excavations at Hamwic: Vol. 1: excavations 1946-83, excluding Six Dials and Melbourne Street.* C.B.A. research report **84**. 1992.
  ads.ahds.ac.uk/catalogue/library/cba/rr84.cfm
- HODGES, RICHARD, *et al. The Hamwih pottery: the local and imported wares from 30 years excavations at Middle Saxon Southampton and their European context.* C.B.A. research report **37**. 1981.
  ads.ahds.ac.uk/catalogue/library/cba/rr37.cfm
- HOLDSWORTH, PHILIP. *Excavations at Melbourne Street, Southampton, 1971-76.* C.B.A. research report **33**. 1980.
  ads.ahds.ac.uk/catalogue/library/cba/rr33.cfm
  Anglo-Saxon town.

- Medieval Southampton
  ishi.lib.berkeley.edu/history155/slides/southampton/
  Archaeology and maps.

Winchester
- The Council, Siege, and Rout of Winchester
  www.britannia.com/history/siegewinch.html
  In Stephen's reign, 1141.

Herefordshire *see also* Gloucestershire
- Historic Herefordshire Online
  www.smr.herefordshire.gov.uk/
- Herefordshire Field Names Database
  www.smr.herefordshire.gov.uk/hfn/db.php

Hereford
- Hereford.uk.com: History
  www.hereford.uk.com/history/
- SHOESMITH, R. *Hereford city excavations, volume 1. Excavations at Castle Green.* C.B.A. research report **36**. 1980.
  ads.ahds.ac.uk/catalogue/library/cba/rr36.cfm
  Medieval site.
- SHOESMITH, R. *Hereford city excavations, volume 2: excavations on and close to the defences.* C.B.A. research report **46**. 1982.
  ads.ahds.ac.uk/catalogue/library/cba/rr46.cfm
- SHOESMITH, R. *Hereford city excavations, volume 3: the finds.* C.B.A. research report **56**. 1985.
  ads.ahds.ac.uk/catalogue.library/cba/rr56.cfm

Hertfordshire

Brickendon
- A History of Brickendon: What a Liberty
  www.cityscapebooks.co.uk/brickendon

Letchworth
- Letchworth Garden City: a Bibliography
  www.angelfire.com/nb/letchworth/

St. Albans
- St. Albans History and Archaeology / Chris Saunders
  www.salbani.co.uk/

- Reformation and Reaction at St. Albans Abbey, 1530-58 / James G. Clark
  www.findarticles.com/cf__dls/m0293/461__115/62257418/pl/article.jhtml
  From the *English historical review,* 4/2000

Huntingdonshire

St. Ives
- The Law Merchant and the Fair Court of St. Ives, 1270-1324 / Stephen Edward Sachs
  www.stevesachs.com/papers/paper__thesis.html

Somersham
- Somersham.info
  www.somersham.info/

Kent
- Kent-History.Com
  www.kent-history.com/
- LEACH, PETER E., eds. *Archaeology in Kent to A.D. 1500.* C.B.A. research report **48**. 1982.
  ads.ahds.ac.uk/catalogue/library/cba/rr48.cfm
- The History of Health and Medicine in Kent / Ian Coulson
  www.kented.org.uk/ngfl/medhist/

Canterbury
- Archaeology at St. George's Clocktower
  www.hillside.co.uk/arch/clocktower/
  In Canterbury; 1st-18th c; includes report on human bones.
- Human Bone Studies in Canterbury Cathedral / Trevor Anderson
  www.hillside.co.uk/arch/cathedral/bones.html

Dartford
- Local History
  easyweb.easynet.co.uk/~mchatwin/localhst.htm
  Of Dartford.
- Dartford from Prehistory to the Modern Age
  www.dartfordarchive.org.uk/

Dover
- The History of Dover
  www.dover.gov.uk/museum/history/history.htm

- The Dover Bronze Age Boat: the world's oldest known seagoing boat
  www.dover.gov.uk/museum/boat/home.htm
- Buckland Anglo-Saxon Cemetery Excavations, Castle View, Mayfield Avenue, Dover / Keith Parfitt
  www.canterburytrust.co.uk/schools/keysites/buckland.htm

Faversham
- Faversham History
  www.faversham.org/history/

Greenwich
- The History of Greenwich Palace / John Timbs
  www.britannia.com/history/londonhistory/grw-pal2.html

Sandwich
- Studies of Sandwich
  sandwich.usersnetlink.co.uk/studies/studies.html

Lancashire see also Cumberland
- About Lancs: Lancashire Link List
  www.aboutlancs.com/
  Includes many links to local history sites.
- Cotton Times: Understanding the Industrial Revolution
  www.cottontimes.co.uk/
  Primarily concerned with Lancashire, 18-19th c.
- Spinning the Web: the Story of the Cotton Industry
  www.spinningtheweb.org.uk/
  In Lancashire.

Ashton under Lyne
- Ashton under Lyne.com
  www.ashton-under-lyne.com/

Blackburn
- Blackburn, Cotton, and the Industrial Revolution
  www.aboutlancs.com/cotton.htm

Cartmel
  See Furness

Eccles
- Eccles, Manchester: Canals and Revolution
  www.angelfire.com/hi5/canals/

Furness
- The Wilkinson Family, Iron Masters: a series of historical essays
  www.iron.oakengates.com/
  Industrial revolution in Furness and Cartmel.

Knowsley
- Knowsley Local History: its people and heritage
  history.knowsley.gov.uk/

Liverpool
- Liverpool: an online history
  www.liverpool2007.org.uk
- Mike Royden's Local History Page: Local History of Liverpool
  www.btinternet.com/~m.royden/mrlhp/index.html
- Liverpool Trade and Shipping 1744-1786 (study number 2923)
  hds.essex.ac.uk/studybrowse/showabstract.php?sn=2923
  Database.
- Liverpool Community 1649-1750
  hds.essex.ac.uk/studybrowse/showabstract.php?sn=3882
  Database.

Manchester
- Our Manchester
  manchesterhistory.net/
- Charity, Status, and Leadership: charitable image and the Manchester man / Peter Shapely
  www.findarticles.com/cf_dls/m2005/n1_v32/21186981/p1/article.jhtml
  From the *Journal of social history,* Fall 1998.
- Youth Gangs, Masculinity and Violence in Late Victorian Manchester and Salford / Andrew Davies
  www.findarticles.com/cf_dls/m2005/2_32/53449343/p1/article.jhtml
  From the *Journal of social history,* Winter 1998.

Merseyside
- National Museums, Liverpool: excavation archive
  ads.ahds.ac.uk/catalogue/projArch/nmgm_none_2002/
  Sites on Merseyside.

Newton le Willows
- Newton le Willows
  www.n-le-w.co.uk

Pendle
- The Pendle Witches
  www.lancs.ac.uk/users/history/studpages/lanchistory/pendle.htm

Ribchester
- BUXTON, K., & HOWARD-DAVIS, C., *et al. Bremetenacum: excavations at Roman Ribchester, 1980, 1989-1990.* Lancaster: Lancaster University Archaeological Unit, [199-]
  ads.ahds.ac.uk/catalogue/library/rib__eh__2001.cfm
  Full text not on-line; only the files originally published on a CD issued with the book.

Warrington
- Warrington Past and Present
  www.warrington-past-present.cwc.net/main2.htm

Widnes
- Widnes Old and Widnes New
  freespace.virgin.net/barry.miller1/

Leicestershire
- Urban Heirarchy and Functions in the East Midlands in the Late Middle Ages, 1300-1550 (study number 3822)
  hds.essex.ac.uk/studybrowse.showabstract.php?sn=3822
  Covers Leicestershire, Lincolnshire, Northamptonshire and Rutland.

Appleby
- The Tudor Inventories from Appleby, 1530-1601
  www.the-orb.net/atherstone/inventory.html

Birstall
- A Bronze Age Burnt Mound at Watermead Country Park, Birstall / Susan Ripper
  www.le.ac.uk/archaeology/ulas/birstall.html

Hinckley
- The Buildings of Hinckley: an online architectural resource for this historic market town and industrial centre in the English Midlands
  www.hinckley.netfirms.com/

Leicester
- Leicester: the dignity of a city 655-1926 / Daniel Williams
  www.le.ac.uk/hi/teaching/papers/will1.html
- Leicester Research
  www.leicesterreseach.co.uk/
- Leicester Archdeaconry Court Proceedings: case of Winter vs. Petcher, 1597-98
  www.the-orb.net/atherstone/leicester.html
- Lay Religious Beliefs: the spiritual testimonies of early eighteenth-century Presbyterian communicants / David L. Wykes
  www.le.ac.uk/hi/teaching/papers/wykes1.html
  In Leicester.
- MELLOR, JEAN E., & PEARCE, T. *The Austin Friars, Leicester.* C.B.A. research report 35. 1981
  ads.ahds.ac.uk/catalogue/library/cba/rr35.cfm
  Excavation of a medieval friary.

Wymeswold
- Wymeswold Local History
  www.wymeswold.org/localhis.htm

Lincolnshire *see also* Leicestershire
- Heritage Trust of Lincolnshire
  www.lincsheritage.org/
- Lincolnshire History Project
  www.magicjon.fsnet.co.uk/
- Medieval Earthworks of South Lincolnshire / David Roffe
  www.roffe.freeserve.co.uk/earthworksframe.htm

Ancaster
- Ancaster in Roman Times / Jenny Stevens & Henny Shotter
  www.lincsheritage.org/vt/ancaster/life.html

Barton upon Humber
- Barton through the Ages
  www.barton-net.org/history/history__intr.html
  Barton upon Humber
- St. Peters Church Project, Barton-upon-Humber
  www.stpetersbarton.org.uk/
  Building archaeology.

Boston
- Boston in Medieval Times
  www.lincsheritage.org/vt/boston/life.html

Fillingham
- The Fillingham Project: a late Anglo-Saxon Cemetery in Lincolnshire
  www.shef.ac.uk/~ap/research/Fillingham/Fillpjct.html

Flixborough
- Flixborough Anglo-Saxon Settlement, North Lincolnshire
  www.hullcc.gov.uk/archaeology/flixboro.htm

Lincoln
- The Survey of Lincoln
  www.postex.demon.co.uk/index.html

North Kesteven
- Archaeology in North Kesteven: an introduction
  www.lincsheritage.org/ca/nkdc/nkdc.html

London & Middlesex
- Local London Timeline
  www.mdx.ac.uk/www/study/localtim.htm
- HARBEN, HENRY H. *A dictionary of London.* 1918
  www.british-history.ac.uk/source.asp?pubid=3
- Greenwood's Map of London, 1827
  users.bathspa.ac.uk/greenwood/
- Victorian London A-Z Street Index
  www.gendocs.demon.co.uk/Lon-str.html
- EKWALL, EILERT. *Street-names of the City of London.* 1954.
  www.british-history.ac.uk/source.asp?pubid=4
- Victoria County History of Middlesex and the City of London
  www.middlesexpast.net
- SHELLEY, HENRY C. *Inns and Taverns of Old London.* Boston:
  L.C.Page & Co., 1909.
  www.building-history.pwp.blueyonder.co.uk/Primary/Inns.htm
- Epidemic Disease in London / J.A.I. Champion (ed.)
  www.history.ac.uk/cmh/epipre.html
  Collection of working papers.
- London's Past Online: a bibliography of London history
  www.history.ac.uk/cmh/lpol/

- The Bolles Collection on the History of London
  perseus.mpiwg-berlin.mpg.de/cache/perscoll-Bolles.html
  Includes many original texts
- PERRING, DOMINIC, & RUSKAMS, STEVE, et al. *Early development of
  Roman London West of the Wolbrook.* C.B.A. research report **70**. 1991.
  ads.ahds.ac.uk/catalogue/library/cba/rr70.cfm
  1st & 2nd centuries.
- MALONEY, CATHERINE, & MOULINS, DOMINIQUE DE. *The Upper
  Wolbrook in the Roman period.* C.B.A. research report **69**. 1990.
  ads.ahds.ac.uk/catalogue/library/cba/rr69.cfm
- WILLIAMS, TIM. *The archaeology of Roman London, volume 3: Public
  buildings in the south west quarter of Roman London.* C.B.A. research
  report **88**. 1993.
- KEENE, D.J. *Historical gazetteer of London before the Great Fire.* 1987.
  www.british-history.ac.uk/source.asp?pubid=8
  Detailed property histories of 5 central parishes.
- Medieval London's Military History
  www.deremilitari.org/RESOURCES/SOURCES/medievallondon.htm
  Brief original sources.
- Bedlam: custody, cure and care, 1247-1997
  www.museumoflondon.org.uk/MOLsite/exhibits/bedlam/f__bed.htm
  Exhibition at the Museum of London.
- WILLIAMS, GWYN A. *Medieval London: from commune to capital.* 1963.
  www.british-history.ac.uk/source.asp?pubid=5
  Biographical information on London aldermen, 1300-1500.
- Metropolitan Market Networks c.1300-1600: London, its region and the
  economy of England (study number 4245)
  hds.essex.ac.uk/studybrowse/showabstract.php?sn=4245
  Database.
- THRUPP, SYLVIA L. *The merchant class of medieval London.* 1948.
  www.british-history.ac.uk/source.asp?pubid=6
  Biographical information on 31 London aldermen, 1300-1500
- Family Strategies in Medieval London: financial planning and the urban
  widow, 1123-1473 / Susan M. B. Steuer
  www.luc.edu/publications/medieval/vol12/12ch6.html
  From *Essays in medieval studies* 12, 1995.
- EKWALL, EILERT. *Two early London subsidy rolls.* 1951.
  www.british-history.ac.uk/source.asp?pubid=11
  Lay subsidies of 1292 and 1319.

- Pre-Reformation Churchwardens Accounts and Parish Government: lessons from London and Bristol / Clive Burgess
  www.findarticles.com/cf__dls/m0293/471__117/86230454/pl/article.jhtml
  From the *English historical review*, 4/2002.
- Violent & Sudden Death in c.14 London: cases from the London coroners rolls
  www.keele.ac.uk/depts/hi/resources/Indexes/medieval.htm
  Click on 'London coroners'.
- Burial of the Plague Dead in Early Modern London / Vanessa Harding
  www.history.ac.uk/cmh/epiharding.html
- A London Provisioners Daybook 1550-1563: online demonstration
  www.umich.edu/%7Emachyn/demo.html
- The Stuart London Project
  www.shef.ac.uk/hri/stuartlondon.htm
  Electronic edition of John Stow's *Survey of London and Westminster*. 1720. In progress.
- EARLE, PETER. *The Making of the English middle class: business, society and family life in London, 1660-1730*. Berkeley: University of California Press, 1989.
  ark.cdlib.org/ark:/13030/ft8489p27k/
- WOODHEAD, J.R. *The rulers of London 1660-1689: a biographical record of the aldermen and common councilmen of the City of London*. 1966
  www.british-history.ac.uk/source.asp?pubid=7
  In preparation.
- Red Sky at Night / Bruce Robinson
  www.bbc.co.uk/history/society__culture/society/great__fire__01.shtml
  The Fire of London 1666
- London after the Great Fire / Dr. John Schofield
  www.bbc.co.uk/history/society__culture/society/after__fire__01.shtml
- SPENCE, CRAIG. *London in the 1690's: a social atlas*. 2000.
  www.british-history.ac.uk/source.asp?pubid=27
  In progress.
- KEENE, DEREK, *et al*, eds. *Metropolitan London in the 1690's: four shillings in the pound aid 1693/4 for the City of London, the City of Westminster and metropolitan Middlesex*. 1992
  www.british-history.ac.uk/source.asp?pubid=26
  In progress.
- GLASS, D.V. ed. *London inhabitants within the walls, 1695*. London Record Society, 1966.
  www.british-history.ac.uk/source.asp?pubid=31
  Tax assessments.
- Ten Generations: London Life since 1700
  www.tengenerations.org.uk/10Gen/index.jsp
- The Victorian Dictionary; a guide to the social history of Victorian London
  www.victorianlondon.org
- Monuments and Dust: the Culture of Victorian London
  www.iath.virginia.edu/mhc/
  jefferson.village.virginia.edu/london/
  Extensive visual, textual and statistical representation of the city
- Charles Booth Online Archive: Charles Booth and the Survey into Life and Labour in London (1886-1903)
  booth.lse.ac.uk
  Catalogue of materials relating to Booth's survey.
- Charles Booth's 1889 Descriptive Map of London Poverty
  www.umich.edu/%7Erisotto/home.html
- MAYHEW, HENRY. *London labour and the London poor*. Volume 1
  etext.lib.virginia.edu/toc/modeng/public/MayLond.html
- The City as Hero: Victorian London in Life and Literature
  www.gober.net/victorian/
  Course from the English Dept. of the University of Massachusetts; many research projects.
- Monuments and Dust: the Culture of Victorian London
  www.iath.virginia.edu/london/
- Victorian London
  mars.acnet.wnec.edu/~grempel/courses/wc2/lectures/victoria.html
  Brief lecture.
- London's Great Stink: the Sour Smell of Success / Professor Martin Daunton
  www.bbc.co.uk/history/lj/victorian__britainlj/
  smell__of__success__1.shtml
  Health in 19th c. London.
- The Lunacy Commission: a study of its origin, emergence and character / Andrew Roberts
  www.mdx.ac.uk/www/study/01.htm
  For the metropolis

- BARRET-DUCROCQ, FRANCOISE. *Love in the time of Victoria: sexuality, class and gender in nineteenth-century London.* Verso, 1991.
  www.questia.com/PM.qst?a=o&d=28597306
  Subscription based.
- Jack the Ripper as the Threat of Outcast London
  etext.lib.virginia.edu/journals/EH/EH35/haggard1.html
  From *Essays in history* 35, 1993.
- Voices Online
  www.museumoflondon.org.uk/MOLsite/londonsvoices/web/mainmenu.asp
  Oral history of London, 20th c.
- A History of the County of Middlesex: online draft / Patricia Crott (ed.)
  www.british-history.ac.uk/source.asp?pubid=13
  Victoria County History volume.

Brockley Hill
- Brockley Hill / Sulloniacae / David Beesley
  thearchof.topcities.com/Roman/brockley.htm

Cheapside
- Hearth tax returns 1662-3 (14 Chas II)
  www.british-history.ac.uk/source.asp?pubid=16
  For Cheapside. In progress.
- Hearth tax returns 1666
  www.british-history.ac.uk/source.asp?pubid=15
  For Cheapside. In progress.

Covent Garden
- MoLAS: Royal Opera House 1996: digital archive
  ads.ahds.ac.uk/catalogue/projArch/rop95__molas/
  Museum of London dig on a Middle Saxon site in Covent Garden.

East End
- Dicken's London: the East End
  www.mars.acnet.wnec.edu/~grempel/courses/wc2/lectures/dickens.html

Hackney
- Brickfield
  www.brickfields.org.uk/
  History of Hackney
- Tudor Hackney
  www.learningcurve.gov.uk/tudorhackney/default.asp

Islington
- BAKER, T.F.T. ed. *A history of the County of Middlesex.* vol.8. 1985.
  www.british-history.ac.uk/source.asp?pubid=30
  Covers Islington and Stoke Newington.

Knightsbridge
- *Survey of London, volume 45: Knightsbridge.*
  www.british-history.ac.uk/source.asp?pubid=25
  In progress.

St. Bartholomews
- MOORE, NORMAN BART. ed. *The book of the foundation of Dr. Bartholomew's Church in London.* Early English Text Society, original series 163. 1923.
  www.questia.com/PM.qst?a=o&d=100131053
  Subscription based.

St. Giles in the Field
- *Survey of London: volume 3: St. Giles-in-the-Fields.* 1912
  www.british-history.ac.uk/source.asp?pubid=24
  In progress.

St. Paul's
- LANG, JANE. *Rebuilding St. Paul's after the Great Fire of London.* Oxford University Press, 1956.
  www.questia.com/PM.qst?a=o&d=5953481
  Subscription based.

Shoreditch
- Quakers Around Shoreditch / Andrew Roberts
  www.mdx.ac.uk/www/study/quasho.htm

Soper Lane
- Soper Lane
  www.et-tu.com/soper-lane/
  Study of medieval silk-women in London

Spitalfields
- COX, MARGARET. *Life and death in Spitalfields, 1700 to 1850.* C.B.A. occasional paper. 1996.
  ads.ahds.ac.uk/catalogue/library/cba/op21.cfm

- *The Spitalfields project.* C.B.A. research report **85-6**. 1993
  ads.ahds.ac.uk/catalogue/library/cba/rr85.cfm
  vol.2. is at /rr86.cfm
  Excavation of an 18th c. burial vault.
- Christ Church, Spitalfields: investigation of the burial crypt 1984-1986
  ads.ahds.ac.uk/catalogue/projArch/spitalfields__var__2001/

Stoke Newington
See Islington

Norfolk *see also* Derbyshire
- Virtual Norfolk: Norfolk History Online
  virtualnorfolk.uea.ac.uk/
- BROWNE, THOMAS, SIR. *Hydriotaphia: urn-burial, or, a discourse of the sepulchral urns lately found in Norfolk.* 1869
  darkwing.uoregon.edu/%7Erbear/browne/hydriotaphia.html
- Aspects of Burial: four inhumation cemeteries in East Anglia
  www.eng-h.gov.uk/archcom/projects/summarys/html97__8/2130.htm
  At Morning Thorpe, Bergh Apton, Spong Hill and Westgarth.
- Little Domesday, Norfolk / David Roffe
  www.roffe.freeserve.co.uk/norfolk.htm
- Norfolk 1382: a sequel to the Peasants Revolt / Herbert Eiden
  www.findarticles.com/cf__dls/m0293/456__114/54466586/pl/article.jhtml
  From the *English historical review,* 4/1999.
- [Land and Labour in Norfolk 1440-1580] / Jan Whittle
  www.oup.co.uk/pdf/0-19-820842-1.pdf

Cromer
- The History of Cromer and its People
  www.geocities.com/Heartland/Park/3496/page1.html

Great Yarmouth
- Great Yarmouth's History
  web.ukonline.co.uk/members/g.woodcock/gyarm/history/history.htm

Norwich
- Norwich 800
  www.iats.norfolk.gov.uk/NES/Curriculum/Norwich800/Norwich800.html
  For schools.

- The Norfolk and Norwich Millenium Project
  www.esinet.norfolk.gov.uk/millenium/
  Excavation on the site of the new library in Norwich.
- The Foundation of Norwich Cathedral
  web.archive.org/web/19981201233835/www.iats.norfolk.gov.uk/
  Cathnet/Cathedral/Foundation/Foundation.html

Sedgeford
- Sedgeford Historical and Archaeological Research Project
  www.sharp.org.uk/

Thetford
- Thetford Forest Archaeology
  www.harnser.net/

Northamptonshire *see also* Leicestershire

Brigstock
- BENNETT, JUDITH M. *Women in the medieval English countryside: gender and household in Brigstock before the plague.* New York: Oxford University Press, 1989.
  www.questia.com/PM.qst?a=o&d=24352707
  Subscription based.

Cosgrove
- Victoria County History of Northamptonshire
  www.northamptonshirepast.net
  Includes draft text for Cosgrove.

Northamptonshire *see also* Leicestershire

Cottingham
- Cottingham History.co.uk: a history of the village of Cottingham, Northamptonshire
  www.cottinghamhistory.co.uk/

Easton Maudit
- The Romano-British Villa at Easton Maudit
  www.eastonvi.freeserve.co.uk/

Nether Heyford
- Whitehall Farm Roman Villa and Landscape Project
  www.whitehallvilla.co.uk/
  At Nether Heyford, Northamptonshire.

Peterborough
- BIDDICK, KATHLEEN. *The other economy: pastoral husbandry on a medieval estate.* Berkeley: University of California Press, 1989.
  ark.cdlib.org/ark:13030/ft8199p22b/
  Peterborough Abbey estates
- REILLY, LISA A. *An architectural history of Peterborough Cathedral.* Oxford: Clarendon Press, 1997.
  www.questia.com/PM.qst?a=o&d=13920125
  Subscription based.

Raunds
- Raunds Prehistoric / Stephane Rault & Jan Harding
  museums.ncl.ac.uk/raunds/

Whittlewood
- Whittlewood Project
  www.le.ac.uk/elh/whittlewood/index.htm
  Project to study medieval settlements on the boundary of Buckinghamshire and Northamptonshire.

Woodnewton
- Woodnewton Home Page
  www.family.history.dial.pipex.com/w/Windex.htm

Northumberland *see also* Durham & Yorkshire
- The History of Northumberland
  www.britannia.com/history/northumberland/
  Extensive.
- Tomorrow's History: made in the North East
  www.tomorrows-history.com/index.htm
  Regional local studies site for Northumberland and Durham; extensive site.

Alnwick
- Patronage, Politics and the Modernization of Leisure in Northern England: the case of Alnwick's Shrove Tuesday Football Match / Neal Garham
  www.findarticles.com/cf_dls/m0293/474_117/95912940/p1/article.jhtml
  From the *English historical review,* 11/2002. 19th c. study.

Bamburgh
- The Bamburgh Research Project
  www.bamburghresearchproject.co.uk/

Benwell
- Benwell: Centre of the Universe
  museums.ncl.ac.uk/archive/frameset/1frame.htm
  Archaeology for schools.

Carrawburgh
- Museum of Antiquities Virtual Mithraem
  museums.ncl.ac.uk/archive/mithras/intro.htm
  Virtual reconstruction of a 3rd century temple to Mithras at Carrawburgh.

Hadrian's Wall
- Hadrian's Wall
  www.aboutscotland.com/hadrian/

Howick
- Britain's Oldest House? A journey into the Stone Age / Julian Richards
  www.bbc.co.uk/history/archaeology/oldest_house_01.shtml
  Mesolithic site in Howick, Northumberland.
- The Howick Project: a Mesolithic Hut and Bronze Age Cist Cemetery on the Northumberland Coast
  www.ncl.ac.uk/howick/

Newcastle upon Tyne
- Tour of the Medieval Newcastle Quayside
  www.medieval-quayside.de.vu/
- A History of the Mayors and Lord Mayors of Newcastle upon Tyne
  www.newcastle.gov.uk/lordmayor.nsf/a/history/
  Includes list since 1216.

Yeavering
- Yeavering Saxon Royal Palace
  www.pastperfect.info/sites/yeavering/
- Great Sites: Yeavering / David A. Hinton
  www.britarch.ac.uk/ba/ba58/feat3.shtml

Nottinghamshire

- Nottinghamshire History and Archaeology
  www.nottshistory.org.uk/default.htm
- Nottinghamshire Heritage Gateway
  www.thorotonsociety.org.uk/gateway.htm
- Village Survey in Nottinghamshire / Keith Challis & Mike Bishop
  www.nottingham.ac.uk/tpau/projects/ves/
- BROWN, CORNELIUS. *A history of Nottinghamshire.* 1896.
  www.nottshistory.org.uk/Brown1896/brown.htm
- Nottinghamshire and the North: a Domesday Study
  www.roffe.freeserve.co.uk/phd/title.htm

Greasley

- HUBE, RUDOLPH BARON VON. *Griseleia in Snotinghscire: an illustrated history from the earliest times, and from reliable sources, of the parish and parish church of Greasley and Priory of Beauvale ...* Nottingham: Murrays Nottingham Book Co., 1901
  www.nottshistory.org.uk/vonhube1910/titlepage.htm

Nottingham

- Pre-Conquest Nottingham / David Roffe
  www.roffe.freeserve.co.uk/nottingham.htm

Retford

- PIERCY, JOHN SHADRACH. *The history of Retford in the County of Nottingham.* 1828
  www.nottshistory.org.uk/piercy1828/piercy.htm

Woodborough

- Woodborough Heritage: Woodborough Photographic Recording Group, & Woodborough Local History Group
  www.woodborough-heritage.org.uk

Oxfordshire

- Continuity and Change in English Rural Society: the formation of Poor Law Unions in Oxfordshire / Byung Khun Song
  www.findarticles.com/cf_dls/m0293/456_114/54466584/pl/article.jhtml
  From the *English historical review*, 4/1999.
- Victoria County History of Oxfordshire
  www.oxfordshirepast.net/
  Includes drafts of a number of chapters.

Deddington

- Deddington Online: History
  www.deddington.org.uk/history/

Eynsham

- O.A.U.: Excavations at Eynsham Abbey, 1989-92: digital archive
  ads.ahds.ac.uk/catalogue/projArch/eynsham_OAU/

Farmoor

- LAMBRICK, GEORGE, & ROBINSON, MARK. *Iron age and Roman riverside settlements at Farmoor, Oxfordshire.* C.B.A. research report 32. 1979.
  ads.ahds.ac.uk/catalogue/library/cba/rr32.cfm

Great Tew

- A History of the County of Oxford, volume XI / Alan Crossley
  www.british-history.ac.uk/source.asp?pubid=1
  Victoria County History volume published 1983, covering Great Tew.

Oxford

- CROSSLEY, ALAN, ed. *A history of the County of Oxford.* Volume IV. 1979.
  www.british-history.ac.uk/source/asp?pubid=10
  Victoria County History volume for the City of Oxford.
- The Story of Oxford
  www.oxfordshire.gov.uk/index/libraries_heritage_countryside/ oxfordshire_museums_service/virtualexhibitions/storyofoxford.htm
- DENT, C.M. *Protestant reformers in Elizabethan Oxford.* Oxford: Oxford University Press, 1983.
  www.questia.com/PM.qst?a=o&d=23162945
  Subscription based.
- BROCK, M.G. *Nineteenth-century Oxford.* The history of the University of Oxford, vol. VI. Oxford: Oxford University Press, 1997.
  www.questia.com/PM.qst?a=o&d=96997307
  Subscription based.
- Prosopography of Corpus Christi College, Oxford, 1517-1603 (study number 3789)
  hds.essex.ac.uk/studybrowse/showabstract.php?sn=3789
  Database.

Thame
- Thame Local History
  www.thamehistory.net/

Wootton Hundred
- *A History of the County of Oxford,* volume XII
  www.british-history.ac.uk/source.asp?pubid=2
  Victoria county history volume covering Wootton Hundred, including Woodstock.

Rutland
See Leicestershire

Shropshire *see also* Derbyshire

Bridgnorth
- The Bridgnorth Caves Project
  www.arch-ant.bham.ac.uk/bufau/bridgnorth_caves/

Cleobury Mortimer
- Trial Excavations on the Site of a Seventeenth-Century Clay Tobacco Pipe Kiln near Cleobury Mortimer, Shropshire, 2001
  ads.ahds.ac.uk/catalogue/projArch/cleobury_higgins_2001/

Oakengates
- Oakengates: History
  www.oakengates.com/history/history_frame.htm

Wroxeter
- The Wroxeter Hinterland Project
  www.arch-ant.bham.ac.uk/bufau/research/wh/base.html

Somerset
- The History of Somerset
  www.britannia.com/history/somerset/
  Extensive.
- Aspects of Somerset History
  www.somerset.gov.uk/archives/ASH/
- North Somerset Archaeological Coastal Survey
  www.hildich.co.uk/

- Archaeology Research: the archaeology of South West British landscapes
  www.bris.ac.uk/Depts/Archaeology/research/swlandscapes.html
  Research at Bristol University including studies of Exmoor, South Cadbury environs, and Stanton Drew.

Bath
- Bath Past: the history of Bath, United Kingdom
  www.building-history.pwp.blueyonder.co.uk/Bath/

Lopen
- Lopen Roman Mosaic
  www.lopenmosaic.co.uk/

Meare
- Reconstructing a Medieval Landscape
  www.ex.ac.uk/archaeology/rmeare.html
  Study of Meare, Somerset.

Shapwick
- The Shapwick Project
  www.wkac.ac.uk/shapwick/
  Archaeological study of a medieval village.

Shepton Mallet
- Shepton Mallet Online
  www.shepton-mallet.org.uk/history/overview.htm

South Cadbury
- South Cadbury Environs Project
  members.aol.com/RTabor8387/project.htm
- South Cadbury Environs Project
  members.aol.comRTabor8387/scephome.htm/

Stanton Drew
- Stanton Drew Stone Circles
  www.eng-h.gov.uk/archaeometry/StantonDrew/

Staffordshire *see also* Cumberland & Derbyshire
- Staffordshire History
  www.staffshistory.org.uk/

- Victoria County History of Staffordshire
  www.staffordshirepast.net/
  Includes sample text for Burton and Tutbury.
- Staffordshire Past Track
  www.staffspasttrack.org.uk/
- The Romans in Staffordshire
  www2002.stoke.gov.uk/museums/pmag/archaeology/romans/
  romanindex.htm
- Staffordshire & South Cheshire Poor Law Unions
  www.staffs.ac.uk/schools/humanities__and__soc__sciences/
  tours/plustart.htm

Acton Trussell
- Acton Trussell Roman Villa
  website.lineone.net/~pvag

Handsworth
- Digital Handsworth: A History of the ancient parish of Handsworth
  www.digitalhandsworth.org.uk/

Sedgley
- The Ancient Manor of Sedgley
  members.iinet.net.au/~inphase/public__html/sedgley/

Smethwick
- Smethwick Heritage
  www.smethwick-heritage.co.uk/

Stoke on Trent
- The Local History of Stoke on Trent
  www.thepotteries.org/
- Exploring the Potteries
  www.exploringthepotteries.org.uk/

Tamworth
- RAHTZ, PHILIP, & MEESON, ROBERT, eds. *An Anglo-Saxon watermill at Tamworth: excavations in the Bolebridge Street area of Tamworth, Staffordshire in 1971 and 1978.* C.B.A. research report 83. 1992
  ads.ahds.ac.uk/catalogue/library/cba/rr83.cfm

Tutbury
- Tutbury: Local History and Information about this Staffordshire Village
  www.tutbury.cjb.net/

West Bromwich
- West Bromwich Town Hall Research Project
  www.sandwellsilversurfers.net/westbromtownhallresearch/

Wolverhampton
- The History of Wolverhampton
  www.localhistory.scit.wlv.ac.uk/history/history.htm
- A Brief History of Victorian Wolverhampton: a study of the urban development of Wolverhampton during the Victorian Era / John Wallis
  www.scit.wlv.ac.uk/local/victorian.wton.html
- Black and Ethnic Minority Experience
  www.be-me.org/
  In Wolverhampton, post-1945.

Suffolk *see also* Cambridgeshire
- The Suffolk Churches Site
  www.suffolkchurches.com/

Brandon
- Brandon Heritage Project
  www.brandon-heritage.co.uk/

Bury St. Edmunds
- St. Edmundsbury: our historic past
  www.stedmundsbury.gov.uk/sebe/visit/History.cfm
- Chronicle of the Abbey of St. Edmund's / Jocelin of Brakelond (1173-1202)
  www.fordham.edu/halsell/basis/jocelin.html

Clare
- A Short History of Clare, Suffolk / Gladys A. Thornton
  www.clare-uk.com/about/short__history/

Lakenheath
- Two Anglo-Saxon Buildings discovered at Lakenheath
  www.suffolkcc.gov.uk/e-and-t/archaeology/eriswell/buildings.html

Mildenhall
- The Mildenhall Treasure
  www.mildenhallmuseum.co.uk/mildenhall__treasure.htm
  Roman silver.

Redgrave Park
- Redgrave Park: a historical tour
  www.holt-wilson.freeserve.co.uk/redgrave1.htm

Surrey
- Surrey Choice Net: History
  www.surreychoicenet.co.uk/
  Click on 'History'. Many pages.
- Ideal Homes. Suburbia in Focus
  www.ideal-homes.org.uk/
  History of the suburbs of S.E.London (including Bexley, Bromley, Greenwich, Lambeth, Lewisham and Southwark), 19-20th c.

Southwark
- Wrong Side of the River: London's disreputable South Bank in the sixteenth and seventeenth century / Jessica A. Browner
  etext.lib.virginia.edu/journals/EH/EH36/browner1.html
  History of Southwark.

Sussex *see also* Dorset
- DREWETT, P.L., ed. *Archaeology in Sussex to A.D. 1500*. C.B.A. research report **29**. 1978.
  ads.ahds.ac.uk/catalogue/library/cba/rr29.cfm
- Sussex Hill Forts
  www2.prestel.co.uk/aspen/sussex/hillfort.html
- Romans in Sussex
  www.romansinsussex.co.uk/
  Partly for schools.

Battle
- A Soldiers View of Battle through the Ages / Tony Pollard and Neil Oliver
  www.bbc.co.uk/history/archaeology/soldiers__view__01.shtml

Belle Tout
- Belle Tout Neolithic and Beaker Enclosures
  csweb.bournemouth.ac.uk/consci/belletout/

Bognor Regis
- Bognor Regis: Local History Information
  www.bognor-local-history.co.uk

Boxgrove
- Boxgrove Projects
  www.ucl.ac.uk/boxgrove/
  Middle pleistocene site.

Cowfold
- Cowfold District
  www.cowfold.info/

Crowlink
- A Project Design for the Excavation of a Round Barrow near Crowlink, East Sussex / Christopher Greatorex
  www.eng-h.gov.uk/archcom/projects/summarys/html98__9/cc2105.htm

Torberry
- CUNLIFFE, B.W. *Iron Age sites in central southern England*. C.B.A. research reports **16**. 1976.
  ads.ahds.ac.uk/catalogue/library/cba/rr16.cfm
  Reports from excavations at Torberry, Sussex, and Chalton, Hampshire.

Wolstonbury
- Wolstonbury Prehistoric Enclosures
  csweb.bournemouth.ac.uk/consci/wolstonbury/

Warwickshire
- Windows on Warwickshire
  www.windowsonwarwickshire.org.uk/

Alcester
- MAHANY, CHRISTINE, ed. *Roman Alcester: southern extramurual area 1964-1966 excavations, part 1: stratigraphy and structure*. C.B.A. research report **96**. 1994.
  ads.ahds.ac.uk/catalogue/library/cba/rr96.cfm

Aston
- Astonbrook through Astonmanor: dedicated to preserving the history of Aston
  www.astonhistory.co.uk/

Bidford on Avon
  See Chesterton

Birmingham
- The Millenibrum Project: Bringing Birminghams History to Life
  www.millenibrum.org/
  History from 1945.
- On the Beat in Birmingham / David Cross
  www.bbc.co.uk/history/society__culture/society/beat__01
  19th c.

Chesterton
- Warwickshire Archaeology Research Team
  www.adamsz.fnsnet.co.uk/
  Reports on various projects around Chesterton and Bidford-on-Avon, *etc.*

Coventry
- Coventry History
  www.exponet.co.uk/historic-cov/

Kenilworth
- Kenilworth Castle and the History of Kenilworth
  www.cv81pl.freeserve.co.uk/kenilworth.htm

Solihull
- Solihull Local History
  www.solihull-online.com/history.htm

Spon End
- Spon-Line Coventry
  www.sponend.org.uk/hist/index.htm
  History of Spon End, Coventry.

Westmorland *see also* Cumberland

Ambleside
- Ambleside Museum and Armitt Library: Ambleside Roman Fort bibliography and Finds Database
  ads.ahds.ac.uk/catalogue/projArch/AmblesideRomanFort/

Wiltshire *see also* Dorset
- Victoria County History of Wiltshire
  www.wiltshirepast.net/
- Timescape Wiltshire
  www.wiltshire.gov.uk/timescape/twopener.htm
- Barrows, Ritual, Landscape, and Land-Use in the Early Bronze Age of Central-Southern England
  www.arch-ant.bham.ac.uk/bufau/research/sb/barhtml.htm
  Covers the Stonehenge, Avebury, and Dorset Ridgeway areas.

Amesbury
- The Amesbury Archer: the King of Stonehenge? / Andrew Fitzpatrick
  www.bbc.co.uk/history/archaeology/king-stonehenge__01.shtml
  Bronze age burial site.

Avebury
- Negotiating Avebury Project / Mark Gillings, *et al.*
  www.arch.soton.ac.uk/Research/Avebury/
  Megalithic.

Bradford on Avon
- St. Laurence's Chapel, Bradford-on-Avon
  www.arch.soton.ac.uk/research/bradford/
  Building archaeology.

Clarendon
- Clarendon Palace, nr. Salisbury, Wiltshire
  www.wkac.ac.uk/archaeology/curent%20research/Clarendon/
  Archaeological investigation of a medieval palace.

Cranborne Chase
- Survey and Excavations on Enclosures in Cranborne Chase
  csweb.bournemouth.ac.uk/consci/proj__cran/titles.htm
  Neolithic and Romano-British.

Durrington
- The Stonehenge Riverside Project: new approaches to Durrington Walls / Mike Parker Pearson
  www.shef.ac.uk/uni/academic/A-C/ap/research/Stonehenge.html

Fyfield
- Fyfield and Overton Project 1959-1988 / P.J. Fowler
  ads.ahds.ac.uk/catalogue/projArch/fyfod/
  Landscape archaeology.

Overton
See Fyfield

Roundway Down
- Excavation on Roundway Down, North Wiltshire / Sarah Semple and Howard Williams
  www.ex.ac.uk/archaeology/rroundway.html

Stonehenge
- Construction of Stonehenge: a process of blood, sweat and tears / Sandra Dimitrakapoulus
  www.exn.ca/mysticplaces/construction.asp

Worcestershire *see also* Gloucestershire
- Worcestershire Past
  home.freeuk.com/whe/
  Many articles.
- Unpublished Excavation Reports
  ads.ahds.ac.uk/catalogue/library/greylit/
  From Worcestershire County Archaeological Service.
- Welcome to the Worcestershire On-line Fabric Type Series
  www.worcestershireceramics.org/
  Pottery database.
- Worcestershire Domesday Database, 1066-1086 (study number 3039)
  hds.essex.ac.uk/studybrowse/showabstract.php?sn=3039
- Introduction to the Civil War in Worcestershire
  www.worcestershire.gov.uk/home/index.cs-index/cs-archeo/
  cs-archeo-surv-civil-intro.htm

Badsey
- Badsey
  www.badsey.net/

Bordesley
- The Bordesley Abbey Project
  www.rdg.ac.uk/bordesley/
  Monastic archaeology.
- ASTILL, G.G. *A medieval industrial complex and its landscape: the metal working watermills and workshops of Bordesley Abbey.* C.B.A. research report **92.** 1993.
  ads.ahds.ac.uk/catalogue/library/cba/rr92.cfm

Droitwich
- WOODIWISS, SIMON. *Iron age and Roman salt production and the medieval town of Droitwich: excavations at the Old Bowling Green and Friar Street.* C.B.A. research report **81.** 1992.
  ads.ahds.ac.uk/catalogue/library/cba/rr81.cfm

Holt
- Local History: Holt and Little Witley, Worcestershire
  www.phancocks.pwp.blueyonder.co.uk/localhistory/localhis.htm

Kempsey
- The History of Kempsey
  www.geocities.com/Athens/Academy/5386/

Little Witley
See Holt

Yorkshire *see also* Derbyshire
- North East England History Pages
  www.thenortheast.fsnet.co.uk/
  Covers Yorkshire, Durham and Northumberland.
- The History of Yorkshire
  www.britannia.com/history/yorkshire/
  Extensive.
- Some Yorkshire History
  yorksforts.netfirms.com/
- Yorkshire Rock Art: exploring Yorkshire's Neolithic & Bronze Age rock carvings
  www.alkelda.f9.co.uk/

- SPRATT, D.A., ed. *Prehistoric and Roman archaeology of north-east Yorkshire.* C.B.A. research report 87.
  ads.ahds.ac.uk/catalogue/library/cba/rr87.cfm
- *Victoria County History* of Yorkshire East Riding
  www.yorkshirepast.net
  Includes draft text for Driffield.
- West Yorkshire Archaeology Service Geophysical Surveys: digital archive.
  ads.ahds.ac.uk/catalogue/projArch/wyas/WYAS__intro.cfm
  13 surveys.
- The West Yorkshire Mesolithic Project
  www.eng-h.gov.uk/arch.com/projects/summarys/html96__7/1486rec.htm
- Towards a Social Archaeology of Later Prehistoric and Romano-British Field Systems in South Yorkshire, West Yorkshire and Nottinghamshire / Adrian Chadwick
  www.shef.ac.uk/assem/2/2chad.html
- Gazetteer of the Religious Gilds and Services of late Medieval Yorkshire
  www.york.ac.uk/inst/cms/resources/gilds
- Monasteries of the Yorkshire Dales & Moors / David Nash Ford
  www.britannia.com/history/yorksmon/
  Pages on 24 monasteries.
- 'Intended as a Terror to the Idle and Profligate': embezzlement and the origins of policing in the Yorkshire worsted industry, c.1750-1777 / Richard J. Soderlund
  www.findarticles.com/cf__dls/m2055/n3__v31/20574143/pl/article.jhtml
  From the *Journal of social history,* Spring 1998.
- Lead Mining in the Yorkshire Dales
  www.mroe.freeserve.co.uk/
- The Cistercians in Yorkshire
  cistercians.shef.ac.uk/
- Yorkshire Quaker Heritage Project
  www.hull.ac.uk/oldlib/archives/quaker/
- From History to Her Story: Yorkshire Women's Lives Online, 1100 to the Present
  www.archives.wyjs.org.uk/nof.htm

Calderdale
- From Weaver to Web: Online Visual Archive of Calderdale History
  www.calderdale.gov.uk/wtw/
- Living with History: Industrial Heritage of Calderdale / Martin Roe
  www2.halifaxtoday.co.uk/calderheritage/calderhome.htm

Catterick
- WILSON, P.R., *et al. Cataractonium: Roman Catterick and its hinterland, excavations and research, 1958-1997.* C.B.A. research report 128. 2002.
  ads.ahds.ac.uk/catalogue/library/cba/rr128fiche.cfm
  Selections from the original report.

Cottam
- Anglo-Saxon and Viking Yorkshire
  www.york.ac.uk/depts/arch/staff/sites/york-environs/menu.htm
  Archaeological study of Cottam.
- Burrow House Farm, Cottam: an Anglian and Anglo-Scandinavian settlement in East Yorkshire / J.D. Richards
  ads.ahds.ac.uk/catalogue/projArch/cottam__ba/

Dewsbury
- Now Then Dewsbury
  www.nowthen.org/

Driffield
- The Driffield Navigation
  www.driffieldnavigation.co.uk

Elmet
- The Elmet Heritage Site
  www.oldtykes.co.uk/Elmet.htm
  An ancient British Kingdom, and the area's later history.

Halifax
- The Halifax Gibbet
  www.metaphor.dk/guillotine/Pages/gibbet.html
  Includes list of persons executed, mainly 16-17th c.

Hayton
- The Landscape Archaeology of Hayton, East Yorkshire
  www.arch.soton.ac.uk/Research/Hayton/
  Roman fort.

Leeds
- Leeds History from the Seventh Century to the Present Day
  www.leeds-uk.com/history.htm
  Chronology.
- Leodis: Leeds
  www.leodis.info/
- The Urban Geography of Leeds: an historical analysis of urban development / Mike Lewis
  www.brixworth.demon.co.uk/leeds/

Nidderdale
- Nidderdale: Landscape and history
  www.nidderdale.org/

Sheffield
- 1 Dig Sheffield
  www.idigsheffield.org.uk/
  Archaeology in Sheffield and the Peak District.

Stainforth
- Stainforth 2001: from 632 to the 21st Century
  homepage.ntlworld.com/adge.covell/

Star Carr
- Star Carr
  www.arch.cam.ac.uk/projects/starcarr.html
  Mesolithic site.

Studley Royal
- Garden Archaeology at Studley Royal Water Gardens
  www.nationaltrust.org.uk/environment/html/archeool/papers/studley1.htm

Sutton Common
- Sutton Common: the excavation of an Iron Age enigma
  www.ex.ac.uk/suttoncommon/

Terrington
- Terrington: a North Yorkshire Virtual Village
  www.terrington-village.com/

Thornborough
- The Neolithic Monument Complex of Thornborough, North Yorkshire
  museums.ncl.ac.uk/thornborough/

Towton
- The Battle of Towton Landscape Project
  www.brad.ac.uk/acad/archsci/depart/resgrp/archpros/
  Towton__Landscape/
  Includes details of the mass grave project. The Battle of Towton took place in 1461.
- The Towton Battlefield Archaeological Survey
  mysite.freeserve.com/TowtonBattlefield

Vale of York
- Alluvial Archaeology in the Vale of York
  www.yorkarchaeology.co.uk/valeofyork/

Wakefield
- BAILDON, WILLIAM PALEY, ed. *Court Rolls of the Manor of Wakefield, 1274-1297.* Yorkshire Archaeological Society record series 29. 1900.
  www.fordham.edu/halsall/source/1274wakefield-courtrolls.html

West Heslerton
- Heslerton Parish Project
  www.landscaperesearchcentre.org/Heslerton%20Projects.htm
  Archaeology of West Heslerton, North Yorkshire.

Wetwang
- Wetwang: the story of a Dig / Julian Richards
  www.bbc.co.uk/history/lj/archaeologylj/wetwang__01.shtml
  Excavation of a Yorkshire burial mound, c.100 B.C. - 30 A.D.

Wharram Percy
- Wharram Percy: the lost medieval village / Ken Tompkins
  loki.stockton.edu/~ken/wharram/wharram.htm

Whitby
- Whitby Abbey Headland Project
  www.eng-h.gov.uk/projects/whitby/wahpsae/

Wolds
- The Wolds Research Project
  www.york.ac.uk/depts/arch/Wolds/

Wrenthorpe
- Wrenthorpe History Web
  www.wrenthorpe.com/

York
- HALL, R.A., ed. *Viking age York and the North.* C.B.A. research report 27. 1978
  ads.ahds.ac.uk/catalogue/library/cba/rr27.cfm
- Jorvik (York)
  www.viking.no/e/england/york/
- Data Archive for Plant and Invertebrate Remains from Anglo-Scandinavian 16-22 Coppergate, York
  ads.ahds.ac.uk/catalogue/projArch/coppergate_2001/
- A History of York from Baine's Gazetteer
  www.genuki.org.uk/big/eng/YKS/ARY/York/YorkHistoryContents.html
- Urban Conflict in Late Fourteenth-Century England: the Case of York in 1380-1 / Christina D. Liddy
  www.findarticles.com/cf_dls/m0293/475_118/98413763/pl/article.jhtml
  From the *English historical review,* 2/2003.
- The Medieval Carmelite Priory at York: a chronology / Fr. Richard Copsey
  www.carmelite.org/chronology/york.htm
- York Bridgemasters Accounts / Philip M. Stell
  www.yorkarchaeology.co.uk/bridgemasters/

Channel Islands
- Guernsey Medieval Wrecks Project: Rescue Archaeology in St. Peter Port Harbour, Guernsey: an internet interim report
  cma.soton.ac.uk/Research/Guernsey/

Isle of Man
- Manx Archaeology
  www.manxarch.iofm.net/
  Mainly photographs.
- A Manx Note Book: An electronic compendium of matters past and present connected with the Isle of Man / Frances Coakley (ed.)
  www.isle-of-man/manxnotebook/

- Crime, Litigation and the Courts in the Isle of Man circa 1550-1704
  www.smo.uhi.ac.uk/~stephen/projfull.pdf

Bilown
- Bilown Neolithic Landscape Project
  csweb.bournemouth.ac.uk/consci/billown/index.htm

Rushen
- [Rushen Abbey]
  www.york.ac.uk/depts/arch/staff/sites/rushen/menu.htm

22. Ireland

A. Gateways

- WWW-VL: History of Ireland
  www.ukans.edu/kansas/eire/index.html
- Academic Info: Irish History Gateway: Directory of On-line Resources for the History of Ireland
  www.academicinfo.net/histirish.html
- Irish History on the Web
  larkspirit.com/history/
  Gateway; includes many sites not listed here.
- Irish Resources in the Humanities
  www.irith.org/index.jsp
  Gateway
- Historical Text Archive: Ireland
  historicaltextarchive.com/links.php?op=viewslink&sid=45
- CELT: Corpus of Electronic Texts: the online resource for Irish history, literature and politics
  www.ucc.ie/celt/
  Includes many original sources, some listed below.

B. Bibliographies

- Writings on Irish History / Sarah Ward-Perkins (ed.)
  www.tcd.ie/Modern__History/irish__bibliography/
  Major bibliography; in progress.
- Enhanced British Parliamentary Papers on Ireland 1801-1922
  www.eppi.ac.uk
- The Database of Irish Historical Statistics
  www.qub.ac.uk/cdda/iredb/dbhme.htm

C. Institutions: Libraries, Archives, Museums, *etc.*

i. *Directories*

- R.A.S.C.A.L.: Research and Special Collections Available Locally (Northern Ireland)
  www.rascal.ac.uk/
  Directory of research resources in Northern Ireland.
- Irish Archives, Manuscript Libraries and Related Resources
  www.nationalarchives.ie/othersirish.html

ii. *Institutions*

- The National Archives of Ireland
  www.nationalarchives.ie
- National Library of Ireland
  www.nli.ie/
- Public Record Office of Northern Ireland
  proni.nics.gov.uk/
- Centre for Marine Archaeology
  www.ulst.ac.uk/faculty/science/crg/cma.htm
  At the University of Ulster
- Centre for the Study of Rural Ireland
  www.ilstu.edu/~ceorsor/CSRI.htm
- Irish Centre for Migration Studies
  migration.ucc.ie/
  At University College, Cork.
- Irish Diaspora Studies
  www.brad.ac.uk/acad/diaspora/
  At the University of Bradford.
- The Linen Hall Library
  www.linenhall.com/
  In Belfast.
- The Discovery Programme
  www.discoveryprogramme.ie/
  Irish archaeological research institution.
- Irish Architectural Archive
  www.iarc.ie/
  Listing of resources for architectural history.
- Irish Manuscripts Commission
  www.irishmanuscripts.ie/
  Site under construction.
- The Irish National Heritage Park
  www.wexfordirl.com/Heritage/hpark/main.htm
  In Wexford.
- Ulster History Circle
  www.ulsterhistory.co.uk/
  Blue plaque organization.

iii. *Societies*

- National Committee for History: Irish Committee of Historical Sciences
  www.historians.ie/

- Economic and Social History Society of Ireland
  www.eh.net/eshsi/
- Eighteenth Century Ireland Society
  www.mic.ul.ie/ecis/ECIS.htm
- Institute of Archaeologists of Ireland
  www.instituteofarchaeologistsofireland.ie/
- Irish Georgian Society
  www.irish-architecture.com/igs/
  Architectural heritage.
- Irish Labour History Society
  www.ilhsonline.org/
- Society for the Study of Nineteenth-Century Ireland
  www.qub.ac.uk/en/socs/ssnci.html

iv. *County & Local Societies*
- Federation of Local History Societies
  homepage.eircom.net/~localhist/index.html

Antrim
- The Glens of Antrim Historical Society
  www.antrimhistory.net/

Armagh
- Creggan History Society
  members.tripod.com/~cregganhistory/
- Poyntzpass & District Local History Society
  www.poyntzpass.co.uk/

Cavan
  See Fermanagh

Down
- Ards Historical Society
  www.ardshistoricalsociety.org/
  Based in Newtownards.

Dublin
- Balbriggan & District Historical Society
  www.geocities.com/balbrigganhistorical/index.html

- Skerries Historical Society
  indigo.ie/~skerries/history/

Fermanagh *see also* Monaghan
- Border Counties History Collective
  homepage.eircom.net/~historycollective/
  Association of history groups in Fermanagh, Cavan and Leitrim.

Kildare
- County Kildare Archaeological Society
  kildare.ie/archaeology/

Leitrim
  See Fermanagh

Londonderry
- The Desertmartin Local History Group
  www.desertmartin.historygroup.btinternet.co.uk/
- Burrishoole Roots
  www.geocities.com/Heartland/Park/7461/
  Homepage of Newport Historical Society.

Monaghan
- Clogher Historical Society
  www.clogherhistoricalsoc.com/
  Covers Co. Monaghan, parts of Cos. Fermanagh and Tyrone, *etc.*

Offaly
- Offaly Historical & Archaeological Society
  www.offalyhistory.com/

Tipperary
- Cumann Staire Chontae Thiobraid Arann: County Tipperary Historical Society
  www.iol.ie/~tipplibs/Welcome.htm

Tyrone
  See Monaghan

Ulster
- The Federation for Ulster Local Studies
  www.ulsterlocalhistory.org/

- Ulster Historical Foundation
  www.ancestryireland.co.uk/
- The Ulster Local History Trust
  www.ulht.org/
  Provides grants for local projects.
- Ulster Place-Name Society
  www.ulsterplacenames.org/

D. Journals
- Archaeological and Historical Journals
  www.xs4all.nl/%7Etbreen/journals.html
  For Ireland.
- Table of Contents of Journals and other sources
  www.ucc.ie/locus/journals.html
  Celtic journals links page.
- Newsplan Database
  www.nls.ie/new__serve.htm
  Union list of Irish newspapers held in various repositories.
- Insight: New perspective in Irish Studies
  www.irishinsight.net
  On-line journal.
- The journal of Irish Archaeology
  www.ucg.ie/jia/
  Contents listing and some abstracts.
- Peritia: journal of the Medieval Academy of Ireland
  www.ucc.ie/peritia/
  Includes contents listing and some abstracts.
- County Tipperary Historical Society journal
  www.iol.ie/~tipplibs/Journals.htm
  Contents listing.

E. Archaeology
- Irish Archaeology
  www.xs4all.nl/~tbreen/ireland.html
  Basic directory.
- Irish Archaeology on the Internet
  www.xs4all.nl/~tbreen/links.html
- The Archaeology of Ancient Ireland
  mockingbird.creighton.edu/english/micsun/IrishResources/archaeol.htm
  Introduction.

- A Brief Guide to Irish Archaeological Sites
  www.iol.ie/~sec/sites.htm
  Guide to types of monuments.
- Irish Radiocarbon Date Database
  www.ucc.ie/archaeology/radiocarbon/
- Stones of Ireland
  www.stonepages.com/ireland/ireland.html
- Archaeoastronomy ... the astronomical significance of megalithic sites in Ireland
  www.bluehorizonlines.org/
- Fulachta Fiadh: an Irish mystery
  www.angelfire.com/fl/burntmounds/
  Study of Irish burnt mounds.
- Excavations.ie: database of Irish excavation reports
  www.excavations.ie/Pages/HomePage.php
- Environment and Heritage Service
  www.ehsni.gov.uk/
  Of Northern Ireland. Includes the 'Monuments and Buildings Record' databases.

F. Long Periods
i. *General*
- A History of the Irish Race
  www.ireland.org/irl__hist/default.htm
- Desmond's Concise History of Ireland / Jerry Desmond
  members.tripod.com/~JerryDesmond/index-2.html
- History of Ireland
  www.fortunecity.com/bally/sligo/93/past/index.htm
  Many articles.
- History of Ireland: Primary Documents
  library.byu.edu/~rdh/eurodocs/ireland.html
- A Chronology of Key Events in Irish History, 1170 to 1967
  cain.ulst.ac.uk/othelem/chron/ch67.htm

ii. *Miscellaneous Subjects*
- Ireland's History in Maps
  www.rootsweb.com/~irlkik/ihm
- The Locus Project
  www.ucc.ie/locus/
  Project to compile a historical dictionary of Irish place and tribal names.

- The Irish in Britain 1750-1922: a bibliographic essay / Donalld MacRaild
  www.brad.ac.uk/acad/diaspora/guides/brit.shtml
- The Congregational Union of Ireland
  www.proni.nics.gov.uk/records/private/cr7__1.htm
- Northern Ireland: the Search for Peace
  news.bbc.co.uk/2/hi/events/northern__ireland/history/default.stm
  Many brief articles, 1170-1998.
- Labour History of Ireland
  flag.blackened.net/revolt/ireland__history.html
- Sources for Women's History in the National Archives
  www.nationalarchives.ie/women.html
  Of Ireland.
- The Women's History Project
  www.nationalarchives.ie/wh/
  Includes two major databases: 'The directory of Sources for the History of Women in Ireland', and ' Women in 20th century Ireland: sources from the Department of the Taoiseach 1922-1966'.

G. Ancient Ireland to 1000 A.D.
- Old Irish and Early Christian Ireland: a basic bibliography / Charles D. Wright
  www.the-orb.net/bibliographies/oldirish.html
- The Archaeology of Ancient Ireland
  mockingbird.creighton.edu/english/micsun/IrishResources/archaeol.htm
- Some Spared Stones of Ireland / Anthony Weir
  www.irishmegaliths.org.uk
  Megaliths.
- THOMAS, CHARLES, .ed. *The iron age in the Irish Sea province*. C.B.A. research report 9. 1972.
  ads.ahds.ac.uk/catalogue/library/cba/rr9.cfm
  i.e. Ireland and Wales.
- *The Annals of Ulster*
  www.ucc.ie/celt/published/T10000A/
  Continued at **/T10000B/** and **/T10000C/**
- *Chronicon Scotorum*
  www.ucc.ie/celt/published/T100016/S
- On the Life of St. Patrick
  www.ucc.ie/celt/published/T201009/
- The Confession of St. Patrick
  www.ucc.ie/celt/published/L201060/

- The Confession of St. Patrick
  www.britannia.com/history/docs/patrick1.html
- Irish Monks and the Voyage of St. Brendan
  www.heritage.nf.ca/exploration/brendan.html
  5-6th c.
- The Life of Columban / Adamnan
  www.ucc.ie/celt/published/T201040/
- The Life of St. Columban, by the Monk Jonas (7th century)
  www.fordham.edu/halsall/basis/columban.html
  From the 1733 edition. Irish missionary to the continent.
- Rule of St. Columba, 6th century
  www.fordham.edu/halsall/source/columba-raile.html
  Monastic rule of an Irish missionary to Scotland.
- Brehon Law Project: the digital corpus of ancient Irish law
  ua__tuathal.tripod.com/testdefault.html
  Project to create a digital edition of old Irish laws.
- Brian Boru: the last great High King of Ireland
  www.ireland-information.com/articles/brianboru.htm
  10-11th c.

H. Medieval Ireland, 1000-1500 A.D.
- The Bull of Pope Adrian IV empowering Henry II to Conquer Ireland, A.D. 1155
  www.yale.edu/lawweb/avalon/medieval/bullad.htm
  English translation.
- Ireland and the invasions by the English and Scots c.1170-1320 / Professor Simon Schama
  www.bbc.co.uk/history/state/nations/ireland__invasion__01.shtml
- The Two Nations of Medieval Ireland / Professor Robin Frame
  www.bbc.co.uk/history/state/nations/medieval__ireland__01.shtml
- *Annales Hiberniae* / James Grace of Kilkenny
  www.ucc.ie/celt/published/L100001/
- *Annals of Loch Cé*, A.D. 1014-1590
  www.ucc.ie/celt/published/T100010A/
  Continued at T100010B/
- The Medieval Irish Plea Rolls: an introduction / Philomena Connolly
  www.nationalarchives.ie/pleas__1.html

I. Ireland, 1500-1800

- Catastrophic Dimensions: the Rupture of English and Irish Identities in Early Modern Ireland, 1534-1615 / D. W. Cunnane
  etext.lib.virginia.edu/journals/EH/EH41/Cunnane41.html
  From *Essays in history* 41, 1999.
- Turning Ireland English / Professor Steven Ellis
  www.bbc.co.uk/history/state/monarchs__leaders/
  elizabeth__ireland__01.shtml
  Under Elizabeth I.
- Sligo to the Causeway Coast
  www.spanish-armada-ireland.com/
  Account of a Spanish Armada wreck in Ireland.
- Ireland and the War of the Three Kingdoms / Micheal ó Siochrú
  www.bbc.co.uk/history/state/nations/ireland__kingdoms__01.shtml
- Battle of the Boyne
  www.bcpl.net/cbladey/orange.html
- Laws in Ireland for the Suppression of Popery, commonly known as the Penal Laws
  www.law.umn.edu/irishlaw/
  18th c.
- The Stanhope / Sunderland Ministry and the Repudiation of Irish Parliamentary Independence / D. W. Hayton
  www.findarticles.com/cf__dls/m0293/n452__v113/20920712/pl/
  article.jhtml
  From the *English historical review*, 6/1998.
  Early 18th c.
- Irish Affairs in the Age of George III / Marjie Bloy
  dspace.dial.pipex.com/town/terrace/adw03/e-eight/ireland.htm
  14 pages on 18-19th c. Irish history.
- 1798 Ireland
  www.iol.ie/~fagann/1798/
- The 1798 Irish Rebellion / Professor Thomas Bartlett
  www.bbc.co.uk/history/state/nations/irish__reb__01.shtml
- The Rebellion of 1798: document facsimile pack
  www.nationalarchives.ie/1798intro.html
- The Year of Liberty
  www.thewildgeese.com/pages/1798.html

J. The Nineteenth and Twentieth Centuries

- Ireland 1800-1921
  www.historystudystop.co.uk/php/displayarticle.php?article=60&topic=mbr
  For A level students.
- Act of Union Virtual Library
  www.actofunion.ac.uk/
  Collection of pamphlets, newspapers, and original manuscripts relating to the union of Ireland and Britain
- Ireland 1845 to 1923.
  www.historylearningsite.co.uk/ireland__1848__to__1922.htm
  For schools
- Cork Multi-Text Project in History
  www.ucc.ie/ucc/depts/history/multitext.htm
  19-20th c. Irish history for schools.
- Local Ireland: History
  www.local.ie/general/history/
  Includes pages on the Great Famine, the 1798 uprising, the Williamite war, and World War II.
- Peter Gray's Homepage
  www.soton.ac.uk/~pg2/
  Includes bibliography of his works on 19th c. Irish history.
- National Education Records
  www.nationalarchives.ie/natschs.html
  Of Ireland.
- Wellington and the Government of Ireland, 1832-46 / P. Gray
  www.archives.lib.soton.ac.uk/wellington/pdfsforall/pol__gray__ed.pdf
- The Birth of Concurrent Endowment: George Cornewall Lewis, the *London Review*, and the Irish Church Debate 1835-6 / D. A. Smith
  www.findarticles.com/cf__dls/m0293/457__114/5524987/pl/article.jhtml
  From the *English historical review*, 6/1999.
- Sources in the National Archives for Researching the Great Famine
  www.nationalarchives.ie/famine.html
- Great Hunger Collection Online
  www.quinnipiac.edu/x6779.xml
  Collection of digitized texts and sources.
- The Triumph of Dogma: the ideology of famine relief / Peter Gray
  www.historyireland.com/magazine/features/feat2.html
  Originally published in *Feature*, 3(2), 1995.

- The Irish Famine
  www.bbc.co.uk/history/state/nations/famine__01.shtml
- The Great Famine, 1845-1850
  www.nationalarchives.ie/famine.html
  Research guide from the National Archives of Ireland.
- Interpreting the Irish Famine 1846-1850
  www.people.virginia.edu/%7Eas5e/Irish/Famine.html
- Ireland's Great Famine, 1845-1849
  www.wesleyjohnston.com/users/ireland/past/famine/index.htm
- Views of the Famine
  vassun.vassar.edu/%7Esttaylor/FAMINE/
  In Ireland, 1840's.
- Visual Representation: the Irish Famine of 1845-50
  www.qub.ac.uk/en/imperial/ireland/famine.htm
- A 'perverse and ill-fated people': English Perceptions of the Irish 1845-52 / Ed. Lengel
  etext.lib.virginia.edu/journals/EH/EH38/Lengel.htm
  From *Essays in history* 38, 1996.
- Ferreting Out Evil: the Records of the Committee on Evil Literature
  www.nationalarchives.ie/evil__article__1.html
- Changing Distribution of Protestants in Ireland, 1861-1991
  www.irelandstory.com/past/protestants__1861__1991.html
- Elections: Northern Ireland Elections
  www.ark.ac.uk/elections/
  Includes pages giving results since 1885.
- The Ulster Covenant
  www.proni.gov.uk/ulstercovenant/
  List of over 500,000 signatories, 1912.
- The Great War 1914-1918 / Karl Murray
  users.tibus.com/th-great-war/
  As it affected Ulster.
- Athy Heritage Centre: World War I
  www.kildare.ie/hospitality/historyandheritage/AthyHeritage/wwI.htm
  In Co. Kildare.
- Ulster and the Great War
  www.pitt.edu/pugachev/greatwar/ulster.htm
  Gateway site.
- Roger Casement: Secrets of the Black Diaries / Paul Tilzey
  www.bbc.co.uk/history/society__culture/protest__reform/
  casement__01.shtml

- 1916: The Rising
  users.bigpond.com/kirwilli/1916/
- 1916: the Easter Rising
  home.fiac.net/marshaw/1916.htm
- Ireland, 1916, and beyond / Henry W. Massingham
  www.theatlantic.com/unbound/flashbks/ireland/massi.htm
- Michael Collins
  www2.cruzio.com/~sbarrett/mcollins.htm
- The Irish Civil War, 1922-1923: a military study of the conventional phase, 28 June - 11 August 1922 / Paul V. Walsh
  www.libraryautomation.com/nymas/irishcivilwar.html
- Parliamentary Debates: Official Report / Díospóireachtái Parlaiminte, 1919-2002
  www.oireachtas-debates.gov.ie/
  For Ireland.
- 'Operations abroad': the I.R.A. in Britain 1919-23 / Peter Hart
  www.findarticles.com/cf__dls/m0293/460__115/60104292/pl/article.jhtml
  From the *English historical review,* 2/2000.
- Reconstruction and Resettlement: the politicization of Irish migration to Australia and Canada, 1919-29 / Kent Fedorowich
  www.findarticles.com/cf__dls/m0293/459__114/58282442/pl/article.jhtml
  From the *English historical review,* 11/1999.
- The Roots of My Preoccupations / Conor Cruise O'Brien
  www.theatlantic.com/unbound/flashbks/ireland/cruis794.htm
- Twentieth Century Witness: Ireland's Fissures and my Family
  www.theatlantic.com/unbound/flashbks/ireland/cruis194.htm
- Guide to Sources Relating to Ireland and European Unity / Bernadette Chambers
  www.nationalarchives.ie/eec.html
- A History of the Department of Education in Northern Ireland 1921-2000 / Grace McGrath
  proni.nics.gov.uk/Education/history.htm
- Foreign Adoptions and the Evolution of Irish Adoption Policy, 1945-52 / Moira J. Maguire
  www.findarticles.com/cf__dls/m2005/2__36/95829287/pl/article/jhtml
  From the *Journal of social history,* Winter 2002.
- CAIN Web Service: Conflict Archive on the Internet: the Northern Ireland Conflict (1968 to the present)
  cain.ulst.ac.uk

- Bloody Sunday: Derry, January 30, 1972
  hometown.aol.com/BRuke1/Derry.html
- The Bloody Sunday Inquiry
  www.bloody-sunday-inquiry.org.uk/
- Hidden Truths: Bloody Sunday, 1972
  www.icp.org/exhibitions/hidden_truths/ht2.html
- The Diary of Bobby Sands, March 1981
  larkspirit.com/hungerstrikes/diary.html
  I.R.A. hunger striker.

K. County and Local History and Archaeology

Antrim
- Belfast Exposed Photography
  www.belfastexposed.com/
  Project to digitise 500,000 images of the city.
- The *Belfast newsletter* index, 1737-1800 / John C. Greene
  www.ucs.louisiana.edu/bnl/Main.html
- Segregation and Social Structure in early 20th Century Belfast (study number 1660)
  hds.essex.ac.uk/studybrowse/showabstract.php?sn=1660
  Database.

Cork
- Medieval Cork
  www.enfo.ie/library/bs/bs31.htm

Down
- Excavation at Ballynahatta 5, Ballynahatta Townland, County Down, 1999: a preliminary report / B. Hartwell
  www.qub.ac.uk/arcpal/ballynahatta.htm
- Carrickmines Castle Online
  carrickminescastle.org/

Dublin
- Clontarf: a history / Brendan MacRaois
  website.lineone.net/~clontarf/history.htm
- Chapters of Dublin's History
  indigo.ie/~kfinlay/
  Includes full text of several books.
- Medieval Dublin
  www.enfo.ie/library/bs/bs16.htm

- A Terrible Beauty: Dublin, Easter 1916
  www.geocities.com/Broadway/Alley/5443/eropen.htm
- The Discovery of a Viking Burial at Ship Street Great, Dublin
  www.mglarc.com/projects/ship_st.htm
- Archaeological Excavation at Smithfield 2002
  www.mglarc.com/projects/smithfield_flash/home.htm
  In Dublin; post-medieval.
- Excavation of a Bronze Age Ring Barrow near Grange Castle, Dublin 22 / Ian Doyle
  www.mglarc.com/projects/grangecastle.htm

Galway
- Hardiman's History of Galway
  www.galway.net/galwayguide/history/hardiman/
- Survey of Ballinakill Abbey, Glinsk, Co. Galway / Richard Crumlish
  homepages.iol.ie/~sec/glinsk.htm

Kerry
- Ordhreacht Chorca Dhuibhne: Dingle Peninsula Heritage: Archaeology
  www.corca-dhuibhne.com/archaeology.html

Kildare
- Excavation of Three Neolithic Houses in Corbally, Co. Kildare / Avril Purcell
  www.mglarc.com/projects/corballyfinal.htm

Laois
- Dunamase
  homepage.eircom.net/~dunamase/Dunamase.html
  Medieval castle.

Limerick
- The Limerick Main Drainage: excavations on the bed of the Abbey River / Edmund O'Donovan
  www.mglarc.com/projects/lmd.htm

Mayo
- County Mayo: an outline history / Bernard O'Hara & Nollaig O'Muraile
  www.mayo-ireland.ie/Mayo/History/HPreHist.htm
  Continued at /H4to16.htm

- The Céide Fields of North Mayo
  www.ucd.ie/ucdnews/feb96/feature.html

Meath
- Knowth.com
  www.knowth.com
  Megalithic passage tombs in Co. Meath.
- Light Years Ago: a tour of Newgrange and Cairn T, Loughcrew
  ireland.iol.ie/~tobrien/new.htm
  Prehistoric Cairns.
- Archaeological Excavations at Moynagh Lough, Nobber, Co. Meath /
  John Bradley
  www.harp.net/Nobber/NobHstry.htm
  Prehistoric - 800 A.D.

Offaly
- Archaeology in Ireland: investigations of the Celtic High Cross in
  Clonmacnois (County Offaly, Ireland)
  ww2.hawaii.edu/~mearson/clonmacnois.html

Tipperary
- Medieval Settlement in Cashel, Co. Tipperary / Edmond O'Donovan
  www.mglarc.com/projects/cashel.html

Waterford
- Dungarvan Museum
  www.dungarvanmuseum.org/
  In Co. Waterford; includes extensive pages on local history.

22. Scotland

A. Bibliographies
- Scottish Bibliographies Online
  www.nls.uk/catalogues/resources/index.html
  Includes the *Bibliography of Scotland,* the *Scottish Book Trades Index,*
  Scottish books 1505-1640, etc.
- Scottish Medieval Bibliography / Sharon L. Krossa
  www.medievalscotland.org/scotbiblio/
- Women in Scottish History: Bibliographic Resources / Prof. E. Ewan
  www.uoguelph.ca/~eewan/
- Annotated Bibliography of Scottish Premodern Women's History /
  Sharon L. Krossa (ed.)
  www.medievalscotland.org/historia-scotarum/biblio/

B. Libraries, Archives & Museums
- S.C.O.N.E.: Scottish Collections Network
  scone.strath.ac.uk
  Directory of Scottish library, archives and museum collections.
- Scottish Archives Network
  www.scan.org.uk/
  Includes a directory to archive repositories in Scotland, and a catalogue
  of their holdings, *etc.*
- S.C.R.A.N. Online
  www.scran.ac.uk/
  Scottish Cultural Research Access Network: over 300,000 images from
  museums, archives, galleries and universities.
- National Archives of Scotland
  www.nas.gov.uk/
- The National Library of Scotland
  www.nls.uk
- The Royal Commission on the Ancient and Historical Monuments of
  Scotland
  www.rcahms.gov.uk
- Accessing Scotlands Past
  www.accessingscotlandspast.org.uk/
  At the Royal Commission on Ancient and Historical Monuments of
  Scotland

- National Museums of Scotland
  www.nms.ac.uk
  Umbrella sites for 5 museums.
- Scottish Museums Council
  www.scottishmuseums.org.uk/
  Includes directory of Scottish museums.
- The Virtual Museum of Scotland
  www.museum.scotland.net/main.htm
  Museum of Scotland site.
- The Glasgow Police Museum
  gphs1800.tripod.com
- The Hunterian
  www.hunterian.gla.ac.uk
  In Glasgow.

C. Archaeology
- Scottish Archaeological Internet Reports
  www.sair.org.uk
  Online reports.
- Treasure Trove in Scotland
  www.treasuretrove.org.uk/
- CANMORE: the N.M.R.S. Database
  www.rcahms.gov.uk/canmoreintro.html
  The National Monuments Record of Scotland.

D. Societies
i. *National*
- A.H.S.S.: the Architectural Heritage Society of Scotland
  www.ahss.org.uk/
- Council for Scottish Archaeology
  www.britarch.ac.uk/csa/
- Eighteenth Century Scottish Studies Society
  www.ecsss.org/
- Scottish Archaeological Forum
  www.scottisharchaeologicalforum.org.uk/saf__home.htm
- Scottish Church History Society
  www.schs.org.uk/
- Scottish Group for the Study of the Book
  www.nls.uk/professional/sgsb/index.html

- The Scottish Labour History Society
  slhs.org.uk/
  Includes index to journal.
- Scottish Military Historical Society
  www.btinternet.com/~james.mckay/dispatch.htm
- Scottish Place-Name Society
  www.st-andrews.ac.uk/institutes/sassi/spns/
  Includes bibliography.
- The Scottish Society of the History of Medicine
  www.st-andrews.ac.uk/~~sshm/
- Scottish Studies Foundation
  www.scottishstudies.ca/
  Based in Toronto.
- Scottish Womens History Network
  www.swhn.org.uk/
- Society of Antiquaries of Scotland
  www.socantscot.org/

ii. *County and Local*
- Friends of Grampian Stones
  www.globalnet.co.uk/~stones/
- Dumfriesshire & Galloway Natural History and Antiquarian Society
  users.quista.net/dgnhas/
  Includes index to the Society's *transactions*.
- Edinburgh Archaeological Field Society
  www.eafs.org.uk/
- Glasgow Archaeological Society
  www.glasarchsoc.org.uk/
- Lanark and District Archaeological Society
  www.btinternet.com/~ian.borthwick/LADAS/
- Orkney Heritage Society
  www.orkneycommunities.co.uk/OHS/
- Renfrewshire Historical & Archaeology Web: Renfrewshire Local History Forum
  www.rlhf.info/
- Shetland Amenity Trust
  www.shetland-heritage.co.uk/amenitytrust/
- Tayside & Fife Archaeological Committee
  www.tafac.freeuk.com/

E. Journals
- *Scottish History*
  www.scottish-history.com/
  On-line journal.
- *Scottish labour history*
  slhs.org.uk/prublications.htm
  Includes contents listing.
- *Archaeologia Scotica: transactions of the Society of Antiquaries of Scotland*
  ads.ahds.ac.uk/cfm/archway/volumeSelector.cfm?rcn=2917
  Full text of vols.1-5, 1792-1890.
- *Proceedings of the Society of Antiquaries of Scotland*
  ads.ahds.ac.uk/cfm/archway/volumeSelector.cfm?rcn=1340
  Full text of vols.1-127, 1851-1997. For general indexes, see:
  ads.ahds.ac.uk/catalogue/library/psas/psasGeneralIndexes.cfm

F. University Departments, Centres & Institutions
- Archaeology at the University of Edinburgh
  www.arcl.ed.ac.uk
- Archaeology: University of Glasgow
  www.gla.ac.uk/archaeology/
- GUARD: Glasgow University Archaeological Research Division
  www.guard.arts.gla.ac.uk/
  Includes reports on a variety of projects.
- The Forth Naturalist and Historian
  www.fnh.stir.ac.uk/
  Based at Stirling University.
- Research Centre in Scottish History
  www.strath.ac.uk/Departments/History/
  At the University of Strathclyde. Click on name.
- Strathclyde Centre in Gender Studies
  www.strath.ac.uk/Departments/scigs/
- Scottish Oral History Centre
  www.strath.ac.uk/Departments/History/oral/oral.html
  At the University of Strathclyde.

G. Archaeological Units
- Archaeology Service
  www.aberdeenshire.gov.uk/web/archaeology.nsf/html/
  57ERBF?OpenDocument/
  For Aberdeenshire, Moray and Angus.

- S.U.A.T.: Scottish Urban Archaeological Trust
  www.suat__demon.co.uk/
  Based in Perth, but active throughout Scotland.
- Scottish Borders Heritage
  www.scottishbordersheritage.co.uk/
  Scottish Borders Council Archaeology and Countrywide Service website.
- The Highland Council Archaeological Unit
  www.higharch.demon.co.uk/
- Am Baile
  www.ambaile.org.uk/en/
  History and culture of the Scottish Highlands and islands; includes sites and monuments record.
- Highland Sites and Monuments Record
  www.ambaile.org.uk/smr/index.jsp
- Stewartry Archaeological Trust
  www.sat.org.uk/
  In Kirkcudbrightshire.
- Orkney Archaeological Trust
  www.orkneydigs.org.uk/
- Perth and Kinross Heritage Trust
  www.pkht.org.uk
- West of Scotland Archaeology Service
  www.wosas.org.uk/
  Covers Argyll, Ayrshire, and the Clyde Valley; includes database of the sites and monuments record.

H. Maps
- Charting the Nation: Maps of Scotland and Associated Archives, 1550-1740
  www.chartingthenation.lib.ed.ac.uk/
- Pont Maps Web Site
  www.nls.uk/pont/index.html
  Scottish maps drawn by Timothy Pont, late 16th c.
- Ordnance Survey Large Scale Scottish Town Plans 1847-1895
  www.nls.uk/digitallibrary/map/townplans/index.html

I. Long Periods
i. *General*
- Scottish History and Famous Scots
  www.siliconglen.com/Scotland/history.html
  Collection of articles.

- Scottish History Online / Robert Gunn
  members.aol.com/skyelander/main.html
  Many articles, mainly medieval.
- Scottish History Online
  www.scotshistoryonline.co.uk/
  Collection of articles.
- Scotland's Past
  www.scotlandspast.org/
  Collection of articles.
- A Brief History of Scotland
  www.britannia.com.celtic/scotland/history__scotland.html
- The History of the Scots, the Picts, and the Britons / David F. Dale
  ourworld.compuserve.com/homepages/DavidDale1/Hisco.htm
  Early Scottish history.
- DICKINSON, WILLIAM CROFT. *Scotland from the earliest times to 1603.* Thomas Nelson & Sons, 1962
  www.questia.com/PM.qst?a=o&d=58543554
  Subscription based.
- FERGUSON, WILLIAM. *The identity of the Scottish nation: an historic quest.* Edinburgh: Edinburgh University Press, 1998.
  www.questia.com/PM.qst?a=o&d=54868029
  Subscription based.
- In Search of Scotland
  www.bbc.co.uk/history/scottishhistory/index.shtml
  Outline pages on Scottish history.

ii. *Miscellaneous Sites*
- Scottish History
  www.bbc.co.uk/scotland/history/
- Scotland 1460-1960
  www.spartacus.schoolnet.co.uk/Scotland.htm
  Brief biographical sketches for schools
- The Scottish Parliament Project
  www.st-andrews.ac.uk/~scotparl/
  Aims to publish the acts of the pre-1707 parliament, *etc.*
- Scottish Labour History Collections
  www.nla.uk/catalogues/online/labour/index.html
- The Scottish Episcopal Church: a new history / Gavin White
  www.episcopalhistory.org.uk/
  1750-1950.

- Scottish Economic History Database, 1550-1780
  www.ex.ac.uk/%7Eajgibson/scotdata/scot__database__home.html
- Sapphire: Scotland's Archive of Print and Publishing History Records
  www.sapphire.ac.uk/
- Scottish Textile Heritage Online
  www.scottishtextiles.org.uk/
- Scottish Clothing Resources
  www.medievalscotland.org/clothing/
  History of clothing in Scotland.
- Drawn Evidence: Scotlands Development through its Architectural Archive from Industrialisation to the Millenium, 1780-2000
  www.drawn-evidence.dundee.ac.uk/dundee__dr/index.jsp
  Virtual archive of plans and drawings.
- G.A.S.H.E.: Gateway to Archives of Scottish Higher Education
  www.gashe.ac.uk/
  Database of archival collections.
- Scot Wars: Scottish Military History & Re-enactment
  www.scotwars.com/

J. Prehistory
- Ancient Scotland Tour
  www.stonepages.com/tour/
- Coastal archaeology and erosion in Scotland
  www.historic-scotland.gov.uk/index.wwd__whatwedo/
  wwd__archaeology/wwd__coatsal__archaeology.htm
- Historic Scotland: archaeology: carbon dating
  www.historic-scotland.gov.uk/index/wwd__whatwedo/
  wwd__archaeology/wwd__carbondatingsearch.htm
  Database of carbon-dated sites in Scotland.
- Scotland's First Settlers
  www.moray.ac.uk/ccs/settlers.htm
  Mesolithic period.
- Ancient Stones of Scotland
  www.stonepages.com/ancient__scotland/
- Scottish Crannogs / Barrie Andrian
  www.bbc.co.uk/history/lj/archaeologylj/crannog__01.shtml
  Iron age homesteads on artifical islands.

K. The Picts
- Pict Resources and References
  www.tylwythteg.com/pict1.html

- The Pictish Nation
  members.tripod.com/~Halfmoon/index.html
- The Pictish Pages
  www.scotshistoryonline.co.uk/thepicts.html
- The Picts: An Introduction
  www.holyrood.org.uk/picts/
- A Consideration of Pictish Names
  www.s-gabriel.org/names/tangwystyl/pictnames/

L. Medieval Scotland
- Medieval Scotland
  www.medievalscotland.org/
  Collection of articles, with many links, and bibliography.
- GRANT, ALEXANDER, ed. *Medieval Scotland: crown, lordship and community. Essays presented to G.W.S. Barrow.* Edinburgh: Edinburgh University Press, 1993.
  www.questia.com/PM.qst?a=o&d=89654869
  Subscription based.
- HUDSON, BENJAMIN T. *Kings of Celtic Scotland.* Westpont: Greenwood Press, 1994.
  www.questia.com/PM.qst?a=o&d=15284138
  Subscription based
- STRINGER, K.J. *Earl David of Huntingdon, 1152-1219: a study in Anglo-Scottish history.* Edinburgh: Edinburgh University Press, 1985.
  www.questia.com/PM.qst?a=o&d=55521271
  Subscription based.
- William Wallace: the Truth behind the man
  www.highlanderweb.co.uk/wallace/index.html
  13-14th c., also includes pages on later Scottish history.
- Stirling Bridge
  www.geocities.com/Broadway/Alley/5443/stirlingbrig.htm
  Battle of Stirling Bridge, 1297.
- Robert Bruce, King of Scots 1306-1329
  www.robert-the-bruce.com
- Bannockburn
  www.geocities.com/Broadway/Alley/5443/bannopen.htm
  1314
- The Declaration of Arbroath
  www.geo.ed.ac.uk/home/scotland/arbroath.html
  1320.

- Declaration of Independence 1320: Robert the Bruce and His Pledge to the Nation: the Declaration of Arbroath 1320
  www.scotshistoryonline.co.uk/arbroath.html
- The Declaration of Arbroath 1320
  www.geo.ed.ac.uk/home/scotland/arbroath.html
  Text.

M. The Early Modern Period
- MACKIE, R.L. *King James IV of Scotland: a brief survey of his life and times.* Edinburgh: Oliver & Boyd, 1958.
  www.questia.com/PM.qst?a=o&d=10454836
  Subscription based.
- GOODARE, JULIAN. *State and society in early modern Scotland.* Oxford: Oxford University Press, 1999.
  www.questia.com/PM.qst?a=o&d=22769786
  Subscription based.
- BURNS, J.H. *The true law of kingship: concepts of monarchy in early-modern Scotland.* Oxford: Clarendon Press, 1996.
  www.questia.com/PM.qst?a=o&d=13709330
  Subscription based.
- The Admission of Lairds to the Scottish Parliament / Julian Goodare
  www.findarticles.com/cf__dls/m0293/469__116/82469636/p1/article.jhtml
  From the *English historical review,* 11/2001. Late 16th c.
- ALLAN, DAVID. *Virtue, learning, and the Scottish enlightenment: ideas of scholarship in early modern history.* Edinburgh: Edinburgh University Pres, 1993.
  www.questia.com/PM.qst?a=o&d=59391096
  Subscription based.
- First Scottish Books
  www.nls.uk/digitallibrary/chepman/
  Early 16th c printed books.
- The Survey of Scottish Witchcraft, 1563-1736 / Julian Goodare, *et al.*
  www.arts.ed.ac.uk/witches/index.html
  Includes database of witchcraft trials.
- Witchcraft Trials in Scotland
  homepages.tesco.net/~eandcthomp/
- The Scottish Contribution to the Enlightenment / D. John Robertson
  www.history.ac.uk/projects/elec/sem12.html
- Scotland and the Four Nations of Britain / Fiona Watson
  www.bbc.co.uk/history/state/nations/four__nations__01.shtml
  History of nationalism.

- The World of Mary Queen of Scots
  www.marie-stuart.co.uk/
- Mary Queen of Scots
  home.earthlink.net/~zzz12/
- Mary, Queen of Scots, and the Earl of Bothwell / Dr. Saul David
  www.bbc.co.uk/history/state/monarchs__leaders/
  mary__queenscots__bothwell__01.shtml
- CROSBY, ALLAN, & BRUCE, JOHN, eds. *Accounts and papers relating to Mary Queen of Scots.* Camden Society, 1867
  www.questia.com/PM.qst?a=o&d=6468961
  Subscription based.
- The Reformation in Scotland
  www.educ.msu.edu/homepages/laurence/reformation/Scotland/
  Scotland.Htm
  Brief gateway; mostly sites related to John Knox.
- John Knox (15?? to 1572)
  www.newgenevacenter.org/biography/knox2.htm
- John Knox
  history.hanover.edu/early/knox.html
  Collection of his writings.
- The First Blast of the Trumpet against the Monstrous Regiment of Women 1558 / John Knox
  www.swrb.ab.ca.newslett/actualnls/FirBlast.htm
- The Barwis Affair: Political Allegiance and the Scots during the British Civil Wars / David Scott
  www.findarticles.com/cf__dls/m0293/463__115/66746346/pl/article.jhtml
  From the *English historical review,* 9/2000.

N. The Eighteenth Century
- Conditional Britons: the Scots Covenanting Tradition and the Eighteenth-Century British State / Colin Kidd
  www.findarticles.com/cf__dls/m0293/474__117/95912937/pl/article.jhtml
  From the *English historical review,* 11/2002.
- Management or Semi-Independence? The Government of Scotland from 1707-1832 / Dr. Alex Murdoch
  www.history.ac.uk/projects/elec/sem19.html
- Institution and Ideology: the Scottish Estates and Resistance Theory / Professor J. H. Burns
  www.history.ac.uk/projects/elec/sem14.html

- The Jacobite Heritage
  www.jacobite.ca/
  Includes many original sources
- The Jacobite Course / Louise Yeoman
  www.bbc.co.uk/history/state/nations/scotland__jacobites__01.shtml
  Primarily in Scotland.
- The Drawn Sword: Engravings and Woodcuts from the MacBean Stuart and Jacobite Collection
  george.qmlib.abdn.ac.uk/macbean.html
  Jacobite rebellions.
- Culloden: the death of the clans
  www.geocities.com/Broadway/Alley/5443/cull.htm
  1746.
- Marital Breakdown in Scotland 1684-1832 (study number 3628)
  hds.essex.ac.uk/studybrowse/showabstract.php?sn=3628
  Database of divorce records.
- Marriage Litigation in Scotland 1694-1830 (study number 3970)
  hds.essex.ac.uk/studybrowse/showabstract.php?sn=3970
  Database of litigation.
- The Darien Venture / Dr. Mike Abeji
  www.bbc.co.uk/history/state/nations/scotland__darien__01.shtml
  The attempt to found a Scottish colony in Panama, 18th c.
- No Unsuitable Match: defining rank in eighteenth and early nineteenth-century Scotland / Leah Leneman
  www.findarticles.com/cf__dls/m2005/3__33/61372239/pl/article.jhtml
  From the *Journal of social history,* Spring 2000.
- BRYSON, GLADYS. *Man and society: the Scottish inquiry of the Eighteenth Century.* Princeton: Princeton University Press, 1945.
  www.questia.com/PM.qst?a=o&d=72565966
  Subscription based. Origins of the study of social sciences.
- The Highland Clearances
  www.theclearances.org/
- The Cultural Impact of the Highland Clearances / Ross Noble
  www.bbc.co.uk/history/state/nations/scotland__clearances__01.shtml
- Ty's David Hume Homepage / D. Tycerium Lightner
  www.geocities.com/Athens/3067/hume.html
  18th c. Scottish philosopher. Includes links to his writings on the web.
- The Hume Society
  www.humesociety.org/
  For the study of David Hume's philosophy.

O. The Nineteenth Century

- Description of *Statistical accounts of Scotland*
  edina.ac.uk/stat-acc-scot/description.shtml
  Contemporary reports on Scottish parishes, c.1790-1830.
- BROWN, STEWART J., & FRY, MICHAEL, eds. *Scotland in the age of the disruption.* Edinburgh: Edinburgh University Press, 1993.
  www.questia.com/PM.qst?a=o&d=2922120
  Subscription based. The split in the Scottish church, 1843.
- Births in Scotland 1861-1911: By county and gender (study number 4146)
  hds.essex.ac.uk/studybrowse/showabstract.php?sn=4146
  Database of births; no names. For deaths, see =4147.
- Scots Abroad
  www.nls.uk/catalogues/online/scotsabroad/index.html
  Various databases relating to Scottish emigration to North America, Australia, *etc.*
- The Voice of Radicalism
  www.abdn.ac.uk/diss/historic/radicalism/index.hti/
  In N.E.Scotland, c.1800-1930.

P. The Twentieth Century

- An Index to Modern Political Manuscripts in the National Library of Scotland
  www.nls.uk/catalogues/online/political-mss/index.html
  Mainly 20th c.
- LEVITT, IAN. *Poverty and welfare in Scotland, 1890-1948.* Edinburgh: Edinburgh University Press, 1988.
  www.questia.com/PM.qst?a=o&d=59389781
  Subscription based.
- HARVIE, CHRISTOPHER. *No gods and precious few heroes: twentieth-century Scotland.* Edinburgh: Edinburgh University Press, 1993.
  www.questia.com/PM.qst?a=o&d=59688172
  Subscription based.
- JONES, DAVID T., *et al. Rural Scotland during the war.* Oxford University Press, 1926.
  www.questia.com/PM.qst?a=o&d=58977596
  Subscription based.
- PATTERSON, LINDSAY. *The autonomy of modern Scotland.* Edinburgh: Edinburgh University Press, 1994.
  www.questia.com/PM.qst?a=o&d=35885088
  Subscription based.

Q. Local History & Archaeology

Angus
- Angus Archives Virtual Serach Room
  www.angus.gov.uk/history/searchroom.htm
  Many original documents

Argyllshire
- Dunadd: an early Dalriadic capital / A. Lane & B. Campbell
  ads.ahds.ac.uk/catalogue/projArch/dunadd__var__2001/
- Rannoch Archaeological Project
  rannocharchaeology.arts.gla.ac.uk/
- Western Scotland
  www.arcl.ed.ac.uk/arch/clivebonsall/page6.htm
  Prehistoric projects at the Isle of Ulva, and Oban.

Ayrshire
- New Cumnock: History of the Parish of New Cumnock / Robert Guthrie
  members.tripod.com/bob__newcumnock/nchome/welcomex.html

Caithness
- Caithness Archaeological Project
  www.arcl.ed.ac.uk/arch/caithness/

East Lothian
- The Iron Age Hill Forts of East Lothian
  www.wgwell.plus.com/elnforts/

Kirkcudbrightshire
- Old Kirkcudbright: Glimpses of the History of an Ancient Parish and Burgh
  www.old-kirkcudbright.net

Lanarkshire
- Glasgow Digital Library
  gdl.cdlr.strath.ac.uk/index.html
- The Glasgow Network of Aligned Sties
  www.geocities.com/alignedsites/
  Prehistoric Glasgow.

- Glasgow Householders 1832-1911 (study number 2838)
  hds.essex.ac.uk/studybrowse/showabstract.php?sn=2838
  Database of valuation rolls, 1861, 1881 & 1911, and the cholera rate book 1832.
- Labour Elites and Electorates in Glasgow, 1922-1974 (study number 1007)
  hds.essex.ac.uk/studybrowse/showabstract.php?sn=1007
  Database.

Midlothian
- Defamation in the Lothians and Argyll 1750-1800 (study number 4066)
  hds.essex.ac.uk/studybrowse/showabstract.php?sn=4066
  Database of litigation in the Edinburgh and Argyll Commissary Courts.
- History of Leith
  www.leithhistory.co.uk/

Orkney
- Orknejar: the heritage of the Orkney Islands
  www.orkneyjar.com/

Perthshire
- LENEMAN, LEAH. *Living in Atholl: a social history of the estates, 1685-1785.* Edinburgh: Edinburgh University Press, 1986.
  www.questia.com/PM.qst?a=o&d=51244979
  Subscription based.
- The Roman Gask
  www.morgue.demon.co.uk/Pages/Gask/
  Roman frontier works of the Gask Ridge, Perthshire.

Renfrewshire
- Renfrewshire History & Archaeology Web: Renfrewshire Local History Forum
  www.rlhf.info/
  Includes list of journal contents.

Ross & Cromarty
- Recent Archaeological Research in Lewis
  www.arcl.ed.ac.uk/arch/lewis/

Shetland
- Old Scatness Broch & Jarlshof Environs Project
  www.brad.ac.uk/acad/archsci/field__proj/scat/mk4/
- The Iron Age and Norse Settlement at Bornish, South Uist: an interim report on the 1996 excavations / Niall Sharples
  www.cf.ac.uk/hisar/archaeology/reports/hebrides96/

23. Wales

A. Gateways & Bibliographies
- Wales on the Web
  www.walesontheweb.org/
  Gateway.
- Hanes Cymru
  webexcel.ndirect.co.uk/gwarnant/hanes/hanes.htm
  Gateway to Welsh history.
- Celtic Studies Bibliography
  www.humnet.ucla.edu/humnet/celtic/csanabib.html
- Early Modern Bibliographies: Wales
  www.earlymodernweb.org.uk/embiblios/emwalesbib.htm
- The National Gazetteer of Wales
  homepage.ntlworld.com/geodata/ngw/home.htm

B. Institutions
i. *General*
- Welsh Record Offices and Archives on the Web
  www.oz.net/~markhow/welshros.htm
- Archives Council Wales
  www.llgc.org.uk/cac/
- Council for British Archaeology Wales
  pages.britishlibrary.net/cba.wales
  Includes contents listing of *Archaeology in Wales*.
- Museum of Welsh Life, St. Fagans
  www.nmgw.ac.uk/mwl/
- The Princess Gwenllian Society
  www.ad-je-leaver.freeserve.co.uk/cydgg.htm
  The princess was the daughter of Llewellyn, the last ruling Prince of Wales.
- Royal Commission on the Ancient and Historical Monuments of Wales
  www.reahmw.org.uk/
  Includes 'Core Archaeological Record Index' (CARN) database, the 'National Monuments Record of Wales', and the Chapels database, *etc.*
- Y Ganolfan Gelraidd: University of Wales Centre for Advanced Welsh & Celtic Studies
  www.aber.ac.uk/~awcwww/

- Wales and the Marches Catholic History Society
  homepage.ntlworld.com/d.chidgey/
- Welsh Mines Society
  www.welshmines.org

ii. *Archaeological Units*
- Cambria Archaeology
  www.acadat.com/
  Covers Cardiganshire, Carmarthenshire and Pembrokeshire.
- The Clwyd-Powys Archaeological Trust
  www.cpat.org.uk/
- Archaeleg Cambria Archaeology
  www.acadat.com/Index1.htm
  Website of the Dyfed Archaeological Trust.
- The Glamorgan-Gwent Archaeological Trust
  www.ggat.org.uk/
- Gwynedd Archaeological Trust
  www.heneb.co.uk/

iii. *Journals*
- The North American journal of Welsh Studies
  spruce.flint__umich.edu/≈ellisjs/journal.htm
  Online journal.
- Welsh history review
  www.uwp.co.uk/acatalog/
                    Online__Catalog__Welsh__History__Review__31.html
  Includes contents listings.

iv. *County & Local Societies*
Anglesey
- Anglesey Antiquarian Society and Field Club
  www.hanesmon.btinternet.co.uk/

Cardiganshire
- Aberystwyth & District Archaeological Society
  www.aberarchsoc.org.uk/

Carmarthenshire
- Llanelly Historical Society
  www.rootsweb.com/~wlscfhs/llanindex.htm

Glamorganshire

- Axis Historical Society
  www.barryaxis.org.uk/
  Covers Barry.
- Cardiff Archaeological Society
  www.cardiffarchsoc.org.uk/

Monmouthshire

- Gwent County History Association
  gwent-county-history-association.newport.ac.uk/
- Abergavenny Local History Society
  irenamorgan.users.btopenworld.com/
- Chepstow Archaeological Society
  www.scruth.f9.co.uk/cas/index.html

Montgomeryshire

- Powysland Club
  powyslandclub.co.uk
  Covers Montgomeryshire.
- Llanfairfechan Historical Society
  www.llanhistsoc.freeserve.co.uk/

C. Collections

- The Architecture of Wales: Architectural Drawings in the National Library of Wales
  www.llgcc.org.uk/ardd/pensaeri/architect.htm
- The Welsh Political Archive
  www.llgc.org.uk/lc/awg__s__cynn.htm
  Housed at the National Library of Wales.
- South Wales Coalfield Collection
  www.swan.ac.uk/swcc/
  Mining archives collection at University College Swansea.

D. Introductory History Pages

- A Short History of Wales / Owen M. Edwards
  historicaltextarchive.com/books.php?op=viewbook&bookid=53
- V Wales: A Short History of Wales / Owen M. Edwards
  www.red4.co.uk/ebooks/shorthistory.htm
- The Long Struggle for Identity: the story of Wales and its people / Peter N. Williams
  www.britannia.com/history/wales/whist.html

- [Wales] History
  www.ngfl-cymru.org.uk/7-0-0-0__vtc__vymru/7-3-0-0-ks3/40357.htm
  Pages on 'Wales and Early Modern Britain' and 'Wales and Industrial Britain' for schools.
- Wales: Building a Nation: the Roots of Devolution / John Davies
  www.bbc.co.uk/wales/history/davies/
  Web-based history of Wales.
- Data Wales
  www.data-wales.co.uk/
  Collection of popular articles.
- Wales 1400-1800
  www.spartacus.schoolnet.co.uk/wales.htm
  Brief biographies of over 30 Welsh men & women. For schools
- Wales: a Culture Preserved / Professor Rees Davies
  www.bbc.co.uk/history/state/nations/culture__preserved__01.shtml
  General discussion of the survival of Wales as a nation.
- Casglu'r Tlysau / Gathering the Jewels
  www.gtj.org.uk/
  Welsh cultural history.
- WILLIAMS, GLANMOR. *Renewal and reformation: Wales c.1415-1642.* Oxford: Oxford University Press, 1993.
  www.questia.com/PM.qst?a=o&d=35524255
  Subscription based.
- BRIGGS, STEPHEN. *Welsh industrial heritage.* C.B.A. research report **79.** 1992
  ads.ahds.ac.uk/catalogue/library/cba/rr79.cfm
- Historical Aspects of the Welsh Slate Industry / D. Dylan Pritchard
  www.slateroof.co.uk/ddpint.html
- The Slate Industry of North and Mid Wales / David Sallery
  www.penmorfa.com/Slate/

E. Welsh Archaeology

- The Prehistoric Monuments of Wales: a survey / Herbert E. Roese
  web.ukonline.co.uk/heroese/
- Stones of Wales
  www.stonepages.com/wales/wales.html
  Photographs of burial chambers, cairns, stone circles, *etc.*
- Siluria
  www.cymru9.fsnet.co.uk/
  Archaeology in South Wales.

- Megalithic Wales
  www.geodrome.demon.co.uk/megalith/stone.htm
  Brief descriptions of megalithic sites.
- Offa's Dyke Initiative
  www.cpat.org.uk/offa/

F. Medieval Wales
- The Kings and Princes of Wales
  www.britannia.com/wales/fam1.html
- British or Welsh? National Identity in Twelfth-Century Wales / Huw Price
  www.findarticles.com/cf__dls/m0293/468__116/79334666/pl/article.jhtml
  From the *English historical review*, 9/2001.
- Wales: English Conquest of Wales, c.1200-1415
  www.bbc.co.uk/history/state/nations/wales__conquest__01.shtml
- A letter from Llywelyn ab Iorwerth, Prince of Wales, to Stephen de Segrave, co-regent for King Henry III of England, during the summer of 1230
  www.ukans.edu/carrie/jjcrump/intro.html
  In Latin.
- Wales at the Time of the Treaty of Montgomery in 1267: mapping medieval Wales / John Garnons Williams
  www.gwp.enta.net/walhist.html
  Includes list of place names.
- PRICE, HUW. *Native law and the church in medieval Wales.* Oxford: Clarendon Press, 1993.
  www.questia.com/PM.qst?a=o&d=49494920
  Subscription based.

G. Wales in the Early Modern Period
- Welsh Rulers of Britain: Henry VII, Henry VIII, Edward VI, and Elizabeth I
  www.britannia.com/wales/fam2.htm
  And their rule in Wales.
- Women and Gender in Early Modern Wales: a guide to sources and further reading / Simone Clark and Michael Roberts
  www.aber.ac.uk/history/bigbib.html
- Documents on Crime and the Law in Wales, c.1500-1800
  www.earlymodernweb.org.uk/waleslaw/

H. Nineteenth & Twentieth Century Wales
- Wales 1801-1919
  www.wales1801-1919.ac.uk/
  Nineteenth century short title catalogue of Welsh publications.
- Welsh Mormon History
  www.welshmormonhistory.org/
- Report of Commission of Enquiry into the State of Education in Wales, 1847
  www.genuki.org.uk/big/wal/CGN/CommsEnq.html

I. Welsh County & Local History
Cardiganshire
- Mines in Mid-Wales
  www.users.globalnet.co.uk/~lizcolin/08__minex.htm
  In Cardiganshire, Montgomeryshire and Radnorshire.

Plwyf Llangynfelyn
- Plwyf Llangynfelyn: a parish history
  www.llangynfelyn.org/hafan.html

Carmarthenshire
- The Carmarthenshire Place-Name Survey
  web.onetel.net.uk/~rapanui/place__names.htm
- CRAGOE, MATTHEW. *An Anglican aristocracy: the moral economy of the landed estate in Carmarthenshire, 1832-1895.* Oxford: Clarendon Press, 1996.
  www.questia.com/PM.qst?a=o&d=9839212
  Subscription based.

Dryslwyn
- The Dryslwyn Castle Project
  www.dur.ac.uk/Archaeology/about__staff/CC/Dryslwyn.html

Kidwelly
- Kidwelly History
  www.kidwellyhistory.co.uk

Llanegwad
- Llanegwad
  www.llanegwad-carmarthen.co.uk
  Includes many historical pages.

Carnarvonshire

Carnarvon

- CASEY, P.J., & DAVIES, J.L., *et al. Excavations at Segontium (Caernarfon) Roman fort 1975-1979.* C.B.A. research report **90.** 1993
  ads.ahds.ac.uk/catalogue/library/cba/rr90.cfm

Rhiwbach

- Rhiwbach Slate Quarry and its Tramway / David Sallery
  www.penmorfa.com/Rhiwbach/

Flintshire

Rhuddlan

- QUINNELL, HENRIETTA, & BLOCKLEY, MARION R. *et al. Excavations at Rhuddlan, Clwyd 1969-73: mesolithic to medieval.* C.B.A. research report **95.** 1994.
  ads.ahds.ac.uk/catalogue/library/cba/rr95.cfm

Shotton

- The History of Shotton, Deeside / Keith Atkinson
  www.anglefire.com/fl/shotton/

Glamorganshire

Aberfan

- The Aberfan Disaster 21 October 1966
  www.nuff.ox.ac.uk/politics/aberfan/home.html

Cardiff

- Cardiff History Web
  www.swanseahistoryweb.org.uk/subheads/cindex.htm
- Cardiff: the Building of a Capital
  www.glamro.gov.uk/
  Click on title. Database of building regulation plans.
- Bay People: an Oral History of Settlers in Cardiff's Tiger Bay
  www.bbc.co.uk/wales/about/baypeople.shtml

Gwybodaeth

- Mine of Information: Gwybodaeth am y Glofeydd
  www.mineofinfo.ac.uk/
  South Wales coalfield.

Rhondda

- My Tribute to the Rhondda
  www.therhondda.co.uk/
  Socio-economic history, 1800-1950.

Swansea

- Swansea History Web
  www.swanseahistoryweb.org.uk/

Merionethshire

Ffestiniog

- Rhosydd: a Ffestiniog Slate Quarry / David Sallery
  www.penmorfa.com/Rhosydd/

Monmouthsire

Abertillery

- Abertillery Online
  www.abertillery.net/

Caerleon

- Caerleon
  www.caerleon.net/

Cwmtillery

- Cwmtillery Online
  www.cwmtillery.com/

Monmouth

- 'Divided into Parties': Exclusion Crisis in Monmouth / Newton E. Key & Joseph P. Ward
  www.findarticles.com/cf__dls/m0293/464__115/69064673/pl/article.jhtml
  From the *English historical review,* 11/2000.

Newport

- Friends of the Newport Ship
  www.thenewportship.com/
  How a medieval ship is being saved in Newport.

Montgomeryshire

- Powys Heritage Online
  history.powys.org.uk

Breiddin

- MUSSON, C.R., *et al. The Breiddin hillfort: a late prehistoric settlement in the Welsh Marches.* C.B.A. research report **76**. 1991.
  ads.ahds.ac.uk/catalogue.library/cba/rr76.cfm

Dolforwyn

- Excavations at Dolforwyn Castle / Daniel Mersey
  www.castleswales.com/dolforn1.html
  13th c.
- [Dolforwyn Castle, Powys]
  www.york.ac.uk/depts/arch/staff/sites/dolforwyn/menu.htm
  Medieval castle excavations.

Pembrokeshire

- Collectanea Menevensea
  www.llgc.org.uk/drych/drych__s070.htm
  History of St. David's Diocese; manuscript written in 1820.
- North Pembrokeshire Historical Archaeology Project / Harold Mytum
  www.york.ac.uk/depts/arch/staff/sites/henllys/resdeshf.htm
  Medieval-20th c. excavations.

Castell Henllys

- Castell Henllys
  www.york.ac.uk/depts/arch/castellhenllys/web/
  Iron age fort with Roman and medieval buildings *etc.*

Radnorshire

Abbey Cwmhir

- Abbey Cwmhir, Radnorshire
  www.cpat.org.uk/projects/longer/abbeyc/abbeyc.htm

Subject Index

Index of Journals

Author Index

Institution Index

155

Place Name Index

Places are indexed under the names of their historic counties, except in the few instances where entries relate to other regional entities.